CW01209917

Out of the Wilderness

Best Wishes to Roger

Clive Holt

Out of the Wilderness
A DIRECTOR'S LIFE AT BURNLEY FC

CLIVE HOLT
WITH DAVE THOMAS

pitch

First published by Pitch Publishing, 2023

Pitch Publishing
9 Donnington Park,
85 Birdham Road,
Chichester,
West Sussex,
PO20 7AJ
www.pitchpublishing.co.uk
info@pitchpublishing.co.uk

© 2023, Clive Holt with Dave Thomas

Every effort has been made to trace the copyright.
Any oversight will be rectified in future editions at the
earliest opportunity by the publisher.

All rights reserved. No part of this book may be reproduced,
sold or utilised in any form or transmitted in any form or by
any means, electronic or mechanical, including photocopying,
recording or by any information storage and retrieval system,
without prior permission in writing from the Publisher.

A CIP catalogue record is available for this book
from the British Library.

ISBN 978 1 80150 385 3

Typesetting and origination by Pitch Publishing
Printed and bound in Great Britain by TJ Books, Padstow

Contents

Acknowledgements .9
and Thanks. 9
Foreword by Sean Dyche. 11
Introduction 13
1. 1986/87 Nearly the End 25
2. 1987/88 Into a Final 37
3. 1988/89 Miller Resigns 46
4. 1989/90 Just What Am I Doing Here? 55
5. 1990/91 A Bit of a Spat 65
6. 1991/92 Light at the End of the Tunnel 73
7. 1992/93 and 1993/94 Back to Wembley 81
8. 1994/95 Oh Dear and Back Down We Go . . . 91
9. 1995/96 A Close Thing but Two New Stands 99
10. 1996/97 Not Much to Write Home About 115
11. 1997/98 The Waddle Season. 122
12. 1998/99 Stan the Man and a New Era. 131
13. 1999/2000 A Stan Ternent Promotion. 141
14. 2000/01 and a Near Miss 150
15. 2001/02 Stan Ternent and Me 160
16. 2002/03 Juggling with Finances 168
17. 2003/04 and 2004/05 Goodbye Stan, Hello Steve, and Financial Woes 177
18. 2005/06 and 2006/07 Getting the Motorhome 192
19. 2007/08 A Season of Huge Change 201
20. 2008/2009 and Wembley 209
21. 2009/10 The Promised Land and Exit Owen Coyle. . . . 219
22. 2010/11 Exit Brian Laws. 229
23. 2011/12 An Average Eddie Howe Season 239
24. 2012/13 and Big Changes 250
25. 2013/14 Who Expected Promotion? 259
26. 2014/15 Relegation but Only Just 268
27. 2015/16 A Wonderful Promotion 278
28. 2016/17 Now Just an Onlooker 288
29. 2017/18 and 2018/19 The Peak Years? 299
30. 2019/20 Tensions at the Top 315
31. 2020/21 Takeover 327
32. 2021/22 No Longer on the Board, Shares Sold, Goodbye Sean and Relegation 339
Final Thoughts. 346

This book is dedicated to my wife, Sylvia, my constant companion at games home and away and a great support during all my years as a director. I will never forget her reaction when, at our very first away game together at Hereford, in the dark days of the old Fourth Division, the wilderness years, they paraded a very lively, two-ton Herefordshire bull around the pitch perimeter before the game.

'Good Lord, what's that?' she said in astonishment and has accompanied me ever since.

Clive Holt

Acknowledgements and Thanks

WE NEED to thank several people for their help, books and support.

Sean Dyche for the foreword.

Mike Garlick and John Banaszkiewicz for reading the draft and making comments.

James Mossop, formerly of the *Sunday Express*, for the use of his article about the Sherpa Van Trophy Final.

Tim Quelch for the use of interviews he conducted in 2017. They first appeared in his book *From Orient to the Emirates*.

Roger Eli for his account of the away play-off game at Torquay United in *Thanks for the Memories*.

Clarke Carlisle and *A Footballer's Life*.

Robert Smith for yet again digging into his vast collection of memorabilia and finding old newspaper articles and match reports.

Rebecca Bridges Photography

Various writers from the *London Clarets* magazine *Something to Write Home About*, and their permission to use their match reports.

Julian Booth for the report of Plymouth 1, Burnley 3. Stephen Cummings for his report of Burnley 1, Portsmouth 2. Andrew Firmin for his recollections of various games.

Steve and Jane at Tubbs Restaurant Colne, as this became the third book to be written there.

The *Burnley Express* for the use of articles and reports.

Tony Scholes, Dave Roberts, Josh Butler, Andrew Greaves, Winston Sutcliffe, John Gibaut, Clive Lawrence, Chris Gibson, Amber Corns, Rocket Ron Jenkins, John Sullivan and Harriet Thomas.

Steve Lockyer, Craig McNulty, Andy Pritchard and Gary Jenkins, the *Burnley Express* and Burnley FC for photographs.

Foreword by Sean Dyche

I HAVE known Clive Holt since 2012 when I first joined Burnley Football Club and I know he became a director at the club as long ago as 1986. He resigned at the end of 2020. That is one impressively long time to be a director of a football club.

It is somewhat disconcerting to think that back in the 1990s Clive probably saw me when I was a player. I can vaguely remember playing against a lad called Roger Eli in the Burnley side back then. I wonder if Clive can remember that game when we kicked each other black and blue.

Being a director of a football club for as long as Clive takes dedication and loyalty, not to mention staying power and a thick skin. When he first began, Burnley were one game away from demotion to non-league football and abuse was heaped on the boardroom back then. But over the years, through the hard work that he has contributed, he has seen the club rise to the very top. I am pleased that I was the manager who helped him to achieve that dream of Premier League football.

It was thanks to Clive that Barry Kilby eventually joined the club and helped it achieve promotion to the Championship with Stan Ternent.

It was thanks to Clive that the club built two new stands and he made sure that they did not cost a penny more than the contractors quoted. Someone told me that were it not for Clive the old stands would have remained, with benches bolted to the floor. For several years he was company secretary, unpaid I might add, and that was his role when I joined the club. As such, he had an eye for detail, and an eye for where every penny went at the club. We had the occasional tussle over expenditure. There was a time when I wanted something for the training ground. For the life of me I cannot remember what it was but it was rather expensive. Clive looked at the cost.

'What on earth do you want to pay all that much for?' he remonstrated.

But that was Clive, always working on behalf of the club and looking after its best interests.

He was always there at youth games at the training ground and I know of no other director who travelled to away games in a motorhome, or carried a stopwatch for that matter. He and his wife, Sylvia, were inseparable.

Of course, we had some great times together after my early initial period at the club when it seemed we were hanging on by a shoestring. But then came that magical promotion season, and the famed win at Blackburn Rovers. It might have been Clive that said to me, 'Whatever you do, just beat Blackburn Rovers.' And we did.

We won at Old Trafford, Chelsea, Arsenal and Liverpool. We played in the Europa League. All magical occasions. Those celebratory gala dinners at the club were memorable.

It gives me great pleasure to write the foreword for this book. I view him as an old friend. He has some great stories to tell, and many that he cannot possibly tell. Having said that, they always come out in the end.

Enjoy,
Sean

Introduction

I'D FINISHED the latest book, the story of John Bond and Derek Gill at Burnley FC. It had always been on the long list of titles I'd drawn up some years ago. You finish a book and you inevitably think, 'What's next?' Writing is addictive, stops the brain from seizing up; it's an escape, especially when you have a little office you can head to, and Burnley FC has such a long, rich history, with so many great players and managers that for 20 years there had never been a shortage of material.

Writing the Bob Lord book with Mike Smith, not one thought had ever been of the club being sold to Americans. It had always been a local club run by local people, all but one of them Burnley born and bred. It was part of the appeal of the place – small, homely, endless local connections, not just the directors but the staff as well in all departments. Players of course were from everywhere, the manager was from the Midlands, the days long gone when managers had come up through the Burnley ranks, Stan Ternent and then Brian Laws being the last. But until the end of 2020 the club's directors were Burnley through and through. Only one was an 'outsider', Clive Holt, but he had been in the town since 1976, well before the days of John Bond and then the Orient season.

'Clive Holt?' I thought. 'Now there's a topic worth pursuing. A director since August 1986, and then bought out by ALK, along with other directors, in 2021.' We'll cover that story later. I'd already met Clive several times back in 2013 when we'd done a series of articles for a Burnley website and had learned quite a lot about him. We'd met in the Burnley boardroom, a wonderful panelled room, with prints, pictures, photographs and framed shirts hanging on the walls. When old Bob Lord had reconstructed the stand that lined what is now Harry Potts Way, he had tried to preserve some of the oldness in what was a basically stark new building.

On the table in front of Clive were piles of old ring binders and documents, plus minutes of old board meetings. He was then responsible for them, unpaid company secretary and as such knew all the ins and outs of all the goings-on at the club, behind the scenes, all the minutiae of running a club. Sean Dyche had been at the club for just about a year, still to make his mark as a candidate for one of Burnley's greatest managers. When Clive and I met, that first time, nobody could possibly have known that season 2013/14 was to be one of the best in Burnley's long history, with promotion to the Premier League at the end of it.

His first board meeting was in August 1986, and he remembers expressing the view that the club needed to improve its public relations image. Nobody knew then that season 1986/87 would be a season to remember, for all the wrong reasons. It was a time of turmoil, boardroom tensions, relegations and the aftermath of the John Bond season. Supporters fumed, the local papers were filled with rancorous letters and accusations; the club AGMs were heated affairs with real bitterness surfacing. Criticism of the club and its then directors and chairman filled the town. After John Jackson, Frank Teasdale had taken over as chairman, a decent, well-meaning man, but with little money. Managers had come and gone, Bond, Benson, Buchan and Cavanagh and the board had turned to former manager Brian Miller again. The word chaos would not have gone amiss.

And into this maelstrom stepped Clive Holt.

His childhood and schooldays were happy ones with a brother who was four years younger. His father was an accountant. Clive left school at age 15; excellent on the IQ tests that were common back then, but he remembers that English and spelling were not his best subjects.

Introduction

He was just 14 when a leg with a severed nerve and ligament damage, following a bad fall through glass, ended all his football-playing days. Hospitalised for four months with his leg in plaster, he then recuperated in Bournemouth on holiday. It was whilst sitting on the beach there with a football magazine or maybe the *Sunday Express* that he came upon the name of Burnley Football Club. If it was the magazine, in all likelihood, it would have been *Charles Buchan's Football Monthly*. It was an article that fascinated him, all about Bob Lord and the club's famed youth policy. It might have been sometime around 1957 he recalls. He had no notion that one day he would end up in Burnley working for an engineering company but does remember that knowing that there was a decent football team was a great attraction. The first offer to work in Burnley he turned down but accepted another two years later. He moved to Foulridge where he has lived ever since.

Engineering has always been his profession, at Vickers and Vokes, starting as an apprentice when he left school, then as a design draughtsman, next as a sales representative, and then running his own companies. It was Vokes that offered him the chance to run their factory in Burnley, although he professes to having no idea why they thought of him as the man to run it.

By then he was married to Sylvia, whom he met in Benidorm. She was from East London and lived very near the West Ham ground. She had never been to a football match so her first-ever game was in 1966 when Clive took her to see West Ham. She has followed him and Burnley ever since he became a director.

Whilst in Kent he watched non-league football at Gravesend, now Ebbsfleet. His father was a Class 1 referee and he followed him around to many of the games. His pipe-smoking grandfather was the one that took him to the games at Gravesend, where he remembers sitting on the low, wooden benches around the perimeter of the pitch. When he was based in Guildford, he was able to watch Aldershot, or get into London to see Arsenal or Charlton. Sometimes he took in a game in the Third Division South, back in the days when there were four divisions – First, Second, plus Third Division North and Third Division South. Only those a bit long in the tooth will remember those.

Once in Burnley, in 1976, having turned down the chance to manage the Vokes factory in sunny Australia, he then attached himself to Burnley FC and has never watched any other team since. One of his first recollections is seeing Steve Kindon, one of the great Burnley heroes, return to Burnley in the late 70s whilst Bob Lord was still chairman and Harry Potts was manager. Kindon as good as single-handedly rescued one season when relegation was a clear possibility. Kindon was in the side that faced Glasgow Celtic at Burnley one night in a cup competition. The rioting that took place has gone down in Burnley history. By then Clive had his first season ticket and sat in the Cricket Field Stand. Take away the promotion season of 1981/82 and these were not the best of times at Turf Moor, with an immediate relegation following that.

From the Cricket Field Stand he progressed to the Bob Lord Stand and the rather more exclusive 100 Club and from there became a vice-president. The 100 Club was always a bit of a misnomer as it never had 100 members and the title vice-president simply meant that Holt had the privilege of stumping up a bit of extra cash at a time when club and Lord were skint. He can't remember what it cost him but he does remember getting a little vociferous at one of Bob Lord's dinners for the VPs. It was when Lord announced a huge price rise for being a VP and Clive remembers all 60 of them being stunned. It was he that the others voted to act as spokesperson and tackle Lord about the increases. He got nowhere, but found Lord for once jolly and amiable. Interestingly he does think that by then Lord was showing clear signs of fading interest and decreasing energy. At that point no one really knew just how bad the financial situation was. That knowledge would soon emerge.

The next few years, until he became a director in July 1986, were marked by the death of Bob Lord, promotion in 1981/82, then relegation, then the John Bond season, and then John Benson took over as manager. Things were becoming worse and worse at the club and by now he had taken to writing critical letters to the local press. He was now reasonably well known for his forthright views about the lack of any ambition or competence at the club. Looking back, all these years later, he sees that period as a time of inertia, when directors were drifting, unable to see how bad things were, with the boardroom becoming more and more just a cosy place to have a drink. Never a thought was given to things getting even worse at a club without money, prospects, or any quality players.

And so he was invited to put his money where his mouth was (his words). Accordingly, he put £20,000 into the club and joined the board under the chairmanship of Frank Teasdale. John Jackson had resigned and the club by then was mired in the Lowerhouse Land controversy that became public.

Full accounts of this are in other Burnley books (such as *Bob Lord of Burnley*, published in 2019) but the brief summary is that Lord had owned a useless piece of land behind his meat factory and he persuaded the club to buy it from him when he was struggling financially. When the decision was made to build the M65, this land suddenly became worth six times as much, so Lord dragooned the club into selling it back to him so that he could then sell it on again. After all manner of legal wrangling and threats, Lord got his way and it was decided that a third of the proceeds would go to Lord, a third to the club and a third to the taxman. Lord indeed got his third, but the club kept all the rest of the money in what was possibly a highly dubious transaction. In the sale of the club to the Americans it came to light that the club still owned a small amount of land in the area but split down the middle by the motorway.

It was before Clive's time as a director but he wonders today if one of the reasons Jackson, a barrister, resigned as chairman was in connection with this deal becoming public.

So there he was as a Burnley director in 1986/87 having come a long way since he had sat on a beach reading a football magazine. The first ever board meeting he attended was when the board consisted of Frank Teasdale, Basil Dearing, Bob Blakeborough, Bernard Rothwell, Doc Iven, who had been there for years, and cricketer Jack Simmons, whom he thinks only ever attended one meeting. One of Clive's first meetings was a humdinger. Basil Dearing announced that the club was insolvent and Clive wondered what on earth he had let himself in for at a club that was trading illegally. What am I doing here? he thought. The problem was solved quite simply. The ground was re-valued and the new value wiped out the insolvency in the stroke of a pen. Plus, Frank Teasdale was excellent at holding off creditors and even sent flowers to the tax lady one day. He was excellent at finding sponsors who would pay up front rather than spread their money over a whole season.

All this was in the Orient season, at the beginning of which manager Miller had said that the club would not be promoted with the players that they had, but neither would they be relegated. He was correct, just. At the beginning of that season Clive went to watch a pre-season friendly at Wigan at the old Springfield Park and Burnley were so poor he questioned his own sanity at the daftness of becoming a director. He was mindful of the old adage 'Abandon Hope All Ye Who Enter Here.' At Wigan back then, there was a picture of the chairman framed on the wall but it was behind some curtains. If they won, the curtains were drawn to reveal the picture. If they lost, the curtains remained closed.

To this day he remembers the away game at Crewe at the end of the season when the referee blew the whistle several minutes early, fearful that the encroaching Burnley fans would invade the pitch. The game was lost 1-0, putting Burnley in a terrible position. Complaints to the Football League fell on deaf ears. As all Burnley fans know, the last game of the season was won and Burnley survived. Clive said to his wife that the next season they would get to Wembley, to cheer her up after she told him she could not endure another season like this one. And lo and behold it came to pass that they did get to Wembley in the Sherpa Van Trophy Final. The Wembley money was a lifesaver.

Until the promotion season of 1991/92, the club lurched along in Division Four. There was a desperate need for injections of new money, or new directors, or the issue of new shares. Clive offered to put £250,000 into the club if there were changes to the board, since the cosy drinking-club atmosphere remained, with some of the members quite happy for things to carry on as they were. He put it in writing to the chairman that he intended to buy shares on the open market and accumulate enough shares to stage a takeover. Eventually there was a big row across the boardroom table and he was accused of going behind their backs; nonsense, of course: everything had been done openly and the plan had been put in writing to the chairman. Next, he was threatened with being voted off the board if he continued in this way. At the AGM, Basil Dearing demanded his resignation but he responded by saying he would not resign there and then but would consider it. He stayed and stopped buying shares. At least as a board member he would be aware of what was going on and might retain some influence, however small.

The board remained the same but minus Jack Simmons and Basil Dearing, the latter surely having decided he'd had enough of the arguments and aggravation. And so the drift continued until an awful game at Scarborough that Burnley lost. It was a defeat that brought matters to a head, with supporters livid at the whole state of affairs and the endless decline. Frank Casper resigned as manager whilst Holt was away in Singapore on business where he heard the score on the World Service. Jimmy Mullen took over and won promotion with the same players that same season. Joy at last and supporters were wild with jubilation.

By 1998 there had been another promotion and an immediate relegation back to the division below. Mullen left to be followed by Adrian Heath and then Chris Waddle. The latter lasted just one season and next in was Stan Ternent. Money was still a huge problem and the strange affair of the Peter Shackleton offer to find vast sums of money for the club came to naught. Clive had made it his job to dig into this and see if there really was any money. He decided there wasn't and told Teasdale not to touch it with a bargepole. Ray Ingleby with his own offer came into the picture at the same time. Quite simply, the place was in a mess, with Stan Ternent tearing his hair out at all the problems he faced.

By now, most of the board wanted out and would have been happy to sell their shares, but Clive Holt wanted to stay involved and so did another director, Bob Blakeborough. They put their heads together and came up with another name: Barry Kilby, another local businessman. Sometime before this, there had been phone calls from Robert Maxwell about buying the club. Barry Kilby had recently sold his company and Holt and Blakeborough concluded that he was both a Burnley fan and now might have money to invest. He had even been a decent footballer and had reached the level of the Burnley youth team.

Barry said yes and offered to buy the shares of anyone who wanted to sell and agreed to carry on with Stan Ternent remaining as manager, also inviting Ingleby to join the board. Little did anyone know it but under Barry Kilby's chairmanship, the club would experience every trial and tribulation known to football, but then reach the Holy Grail of the Premier League.

Stan Ternent provided a learning curve for everyone at the club, from players to directors to the chefs. Prior to Stan, the managers hadn't been particularly demanding, but here now was a man who was focused, intense, knew exactly what he wanted and was what you might call 'old school'. He was a fine coach and took no nonsense from anyone. He was exactly what the club needed and there were no shades of grey. And at last, there was some money to invest. Of course, he was never off the phone to Barry, so much so that Sonya Kilby one morning on holiday was so fed up of these calls that she threw Barry's phone in the swimming pool.

To say that Stan's time at Burnley was eventful would be an understatement. There were two seasons of just missing the play-offs for the Premier League. Ian Wright was signed. Gazza was signed. In London once, Clive had dinner with Stan and Vinnie Jones, and it was an evening when they went down Memory Lane telling endless stories. Then there was the evening that Stan sacked four players live on radio and said they would never play again for him.

Of course, Stan was demanding, but more often than not in the right way. You'd be hard pushed to find any player who did not appreciate what he did for them, the way he wanted to make them better, and the way he had their back. He did well for Burnley but it all went badly wrong with the ITV Digital fiasco when money from an ITV deal was simply cancelled when they realised just how much money they were losing. It totally changed the trajectory of the club, the finances and the ambitions.

Eventually Stan ran out of steam with a bunch of players that could not be refreshed and improved. By sheer willpower he kept the club in the Championship and then Barry decided it was time for a change. Initially Ian Holloway accepted the job but his profoundly deaf daughters were understandably reduced to tears at the idea of moving home and schools. And so, in 2004, Steve Cotterill came in.

His tenure at Burnley may not have been the most memorable, but to his credit he was the man that signed several of the players that went on to win promotion to the Premier League. Owen Coyle arrived and took off the shackles to release their flair and creativity. It was a promotion that saved the club from financial disaster and probable administration. The Coyle period was memorable until 'The Great Desertion', as we might call it. It left the team floundering and new man Brian Laws was powerless to arrest the impending relegation. It was a miserable time.

The club was back in the Championship and Eddie Howe was appointed. The disappointments continued; he had a good eye for a player and brought several in, but overall, there was no sign that this was going to be a promotion side. For reasons of his own, he left. In 2012 it was Sean Dyche who came in to occupy the hot seat and from that moment on the club took on an upward trajectory. The players that Howe had signed, with a few shrewd signings by Dyche, won promotion back to the Premier League at the end of Dyche's second season.

An undeserved relegation back to the Championship was followed by an immediate return to the top division and consecutive seasons of success and survival followed. In the background, chairman Barry Kilby had relinquished the chairmanship because of ill health. There was then a joint chairmanship for a while of Mike Garlick and John Banaszkiewicz. Mike Garlick, who had joined the board in 2006, eventually took over as sole chairman, but on buying the bulk of Barry Kilby's shares, and gaining the majority shareholding, Garlick eventually set about selling the club to an American group. Clive Holt was one of the group of directors not entirely comfortable about this sale, but it went ahead at the end of 2020 with the American's investment company, ALK, giving those directors who did not wish to sell their shares the option of selling them or holding on to them. But hold on to them and we would be voted off the board at an emergency general meeting that would be supported by all of the new board. Others who would sell them shares would bring up the agreed percentage in the sales-and-purchase agreement. Clive had little choice but to sell.

He had served it as a director for nigh on 35 years. He had served it as company secretary for eight years. He had served it as the club representative on the LCC Safe Advisory Committee for nearly as long as he had been a director. He had been the watchdog and the realist, and the one who was always able to see what was coming round the next corner. He was the one, as company secretary, who saw to all the legal problems. One day when I was interviewing him, I had asked him if he saw himself as the club rottweiler. He merely smiled.

Of all the directors of the club, either past or present, it is unlikely that any of them ever knew as much as he did of all that was going on behind the scenes. The list of people, from the good to the scoundrels, that he met is a long one. The number of boardroom meetings, planning meetings, safety meetings, legal meetings and financial meetings that he attended runs into the hundreds. The number of games he has attended, and still does, both as a Burnley supporter when he arrived in Burnley and then club director, is well past the 1,000 mark.

The number of miles clocked up in his motorhome, travelling to away games, likewise runs into the thousands. It tows a small car that he and Sylvia then use to travel to the actual football grounds. On one occasion down in London it was used for a telephone board meeting. It is unlikely that any other club can claim this little piece of history. One of its first journeys was to Crystal Palace in August of 2006. It was used during lockdown for a game at Norwich when there were no spectators but directors were allowed to attend. Sylvia was not, and watched the game on TV in the motorhome.

Confrontations, consultations, disagreements and negotiations have filled his life, as well as running his business. He retired from that in 2000, having been stricken by but recovered from bowel cancer. Despite that, he had no intention of retiring from the football club. The two newest stands at the club built in the late 90s are his legacy. He watched every penny spent as they were erected and challenged every deviation from the agreed plans and costs. Challenging unnecessary or extravagant expenditure, in any area of the club, has always been his forte.

It is not unreasonable to say he knows the secrets of the club – some of them must remain secrets – and where the skeletons are buried. And there, too, some must remain buried. Unafraid to confront people, to argue or to point out problems, he has upset quite a few people in his time at the club, simply by pointing out a few truths or listing obstacles and extravagances. People don't always want to hear them. It was the chairman Mike Garlick who relieved him of his duties as company secretary when Matt Williams was appointed, along with his involvement with the recent developments at Turf Moor in the new disabled areas in two of the stadium corners.

The way he left the club provided a sad end to a distinguished time serving the team he loved. Other attempts had been made, but this time there was no way he could stay. If anyone had said to him at the end of the Orient Game, in the old Fourth Division, his first season as a director, that all these years later he would leave the club whilst it was in the Premier League, I doubt he would have believed it. You could sum up his time at the club under the heading 'From Orient to Emirates,' But this is already the title of a Burnley book by Tim Quelch that he contributed to. He has given his money, his time, his devotion to Burnley Football Club. It has consumed him. Such is his support, he was even there for the pre-season friendly game at Shrewsbury in July of 2022, travelling down in his motorhome with Sylvia. That takes a special kind of fan, and fan he is, as much now as he was all those years ago when he joined the board.

It is a thankless job, being a football director; only a small handful generate affection. He thinks there should be a placard above the door of every boardroom that reads 'Abandon Hope All Ye That Enter Here.'

This, then, is the story of his four decades.

Dave Thomas
October 2022

CHAPTER ONE

1986/87 Nearly the End

FOUR DECADES at Burnley Football Club. Just where do I begin? We decided the simplest way was to go through all the personal records, notes, clippings and files that I had kept and select all the interesting and key events that I had been a part of. They go back to season 1986/87.

It was the season when the Football League had decided that the bottom club of the bottom division would be relegated to non-league football; and the season every Burnley fan will remember that the final game was against Orient, that Burnley won to preserve their Football League place. Of course, that game was memorable for all the right reasons but there was one just prior to it that compounded our predicament. We lost a miserable game at Crewe having just given ourselves a lifeline by winning away at Southend. It is that Crewe game that is still imprinted in my mind just as much as the final one.

This was my first season as a Burnley director. For the first game I ever attended as a director, knowing no better, I wore a smart jacket and an open-neck shirt. First mistake, and I was told that I must wear a collar and tie to all games. Secondly, we should not stand up in the directors' box to cheer, but must remain seated at all times. But we could clap politely. I seem to remember my first away league game as a director was at Torquay. The old chairman John Jackson wished us luck and told me something I will always remember: that being a director was the best way not to enjoy football. It would always be spoiled by the problems – gate money, attendances, injuries, manager demands and all the other 101 irritations along the way. Oh, and all the abuse and criticism. But, fortunately, I have always been able to separate the football from the business side of things and so survived 35 years as a director. Now that I am no longer a director, I miss the involvement terribly.

At the very first meeting that I attended I'd told the board that this club had to improve its public relations. I have never had any trouble with speaking my mind, saying what's what, what's needed, pointing out things that might work and things that definitely won't. There have been many times when this capacity to say things bluntly has not endeared me to various people. It meant that for the first few matches I was not exactly made welcome. One of the directors, Doc Iven, was particularly unfriendly towards me but eventually became a great friend once he realised that all I wanted was the best for the club.

It was a time when directors did put money in to help pay the wages, at that time about £5,000 a week. The £20,000 I had put in helped keep the place afloat that season. It did not buy luxuries, just the bare essentials. It was useful to be a millionaire, but I wasn't one. Twenty years later it helps to be a multimillionaire, and today a billionaire, if you want to be up in the top six of the Premier League.

The coach firm we used was called Jones Coaches and our driver was usually Hughie Jones. It was the same company that took Manchester United around and if our games did not clash, we got the best coach. The Manchester United players in their unwitting generosity would often leave various items on the coach which our players found most welcome. Goodies such as Mars bars were quickly eaten. Roger Eli, I do believe, once found a pair of boots that belonged to Steve Bruce.

It had been clear to anyone on the outside for some time that things were not right at boardroom level. Criticisms in the local press appeared on a weekly basis. A leading and vociferous supporter, Harry Brooks, was incandescent. There was an inertia, a lack of positive decision-making, but above all there was no money. And here was the club with three games to go one point adrift at the bottom of the Fourth Division table.

That great man Jimmy McIlroy was indignant and pessimistic. Only 25 years earlier he had played at Wembley for the club. Now he was present at what he thought would be the end of the club. 'How has it come to this?' he asked in his press articles.

During that season I could only wonder, what on earth was I doing there? How had I got there? What had I let myself in for? At one of the first board meetings Basil Dearing outlined that the club was insolvent. There was a deathly silence and a sort of 'what the hell do we do' reaction. It was solved by revaluing the ground and in a stroke the problem went away with the new increased value. Who thought of that? Probably me.

It had started well enough with just one defeat in the first seven games but then the rot set in. By the end of the season and the great escape, fans and press talked of the 'miracle'. But what miracle? It was no miracle, it was simply a mess, a time of tension and aggravation and real, deep anxiety.

Brian Miller was the manager following the retirement of Tommy Cavanagh due to ill health. One of the players I remember was Leighton James who had returned to the club. He was 33 and back in the 80s this was certainly regarded as the veteran stage. Today, with sports science, diet and training techniques, it is common for many players to play to this age and beyond. By now he was the wily old fox, rather than the devastating attacking winger of the 70s, when he came into the team.

Joe Gallagher played his part and I remember this tall, commanding player because, prior to this season, he had been as good as ignored on account of his gammy knee that limited his mobility. This was now his fourth season and, with an inflation pay increase clause in his contract that went back to his arrival at the club in the Bond season, he was on a very high wage that dwarfed what some of the younger lads earned. Don't forget this was a time when the club hadn't two pence to rub together. He had to play, with the squad so small.

Ian Britton was the player who was carried off by fans on the last day with his winning goal. Sadly, he passed away some years ago. Ray Deakin, alias 'Whoosh', another one that passed away too early, occasionally drove the team bus. Under a PFA programme, players could train to complete HGV and public-service vehicle tests. So, as we could not afford hotel stays or the luxury of two coach drivers, our captain stepped up to allow the driver his rest time and get us home at reasonable hours. Billy Rodaway was another, one of the last of the crop of good players that the club produced at Gawthorpe in the 70s – solid, tough, from Liverpool. Holly Johnson, lead singer of the 80s pop group Frankie Goes to Hollywood, allegedly was a bit of a fan of Billy.

Knowing that they and the club faced disaster, in a desperate 11th-hour measure, the directors asked the Football League to reverse the decision to relegate the bottom team of the division. We sent them this letter:

> The directors of Burnley Football Club have been concerned for some time that the club, which is a founder member of the League, and which has not during this century ever had to apply for re-election to the Football League, is faced with the prospect of automatic removal from the Football League if it finishes bottom of the Fourth Division at the end of this season.
>
> The directors believe that the present regulations, which were only implemented this season, are both unfair and inequitable.
>
> As we believe that the management committee is committed to the principle of automatic promotion of one club from the GM Vauxhall Conference, and as the clubs in that Conference have been playing this season with that automatic promotion in mind, we accept that it would be

wrong to suggest that Scarborough should not now be admitted to the League.

However, we believe that it would not now be in the best interests of the Football League if our club were to be relegated. We are sure that the management committee are already aware of the reasons, but we will set out a few of the matters that we believe to be material.

1 ... We are founder members of the Football League.
2 ... We have never had to previously apply for re-election.
3 ... It is only last season that we were in the Fourth Division for the first time.
4 ... Our stadium is probably amongst the best 20 in the country.
5 ... Our average attendances over the last few years have always been higher than the average attendance for the division in which we have been playing at the time.

We now request the League to take urgent steps to reconsider the current regulations which provides for the bottom club in the Fourth Division to be replaced by the champion club of the GM Vauxhall Conference.

We accept that this request is principally motivated by the position in which we find ourselves. However, we believe that it has support from many clubs, in all divisions.

We have today spoken to the four other clubs who still face the prospect of automatic relegation, namely Lincoln, Rochdale, Torquay and Tranmere. They are unanimous in joining with us in making this request. They all believe that the present system is unfair and inequitable.

We further believe that the vast majority, if not all, of the clubs in the Fourth Division believe that the present regulation is unfair and inequitable.

> We would like the League to seriously re-consider the proposition that none of the present clubs in the Fourth Division is automatically relegated at the end of this season and that, if necessary, there be 25 clubs in the Fourth Division next season.
>
> We would all like there to be a full discussion and consultation as soon as possible with a view to a more fair and equitable method, if there needs to be one, of automatic relegation being resolved.

The letter and request, drawn up by director Basil Dearing, was rejected.

The Football League had never envisaged when they decided upon this new relegation system that a club so illustrious as Burnley might be affected. The ruling was aimed at clubs like Rochdale, Halifax, Torquay and Crewe, the perennial strugglers. But here were Burnley, this once top club in the top division that had won titles and played at Wembley and in Europe. The appeal fell on deaf ears. It is true to say that the football world waited to see the outcome, with the press descending in droves, all the great names of reporting in attendance.

My recollections of the Crewe game and what happened around it are already on paper and I have managed to fish out the copy of the interview I gave to author Tim Quelch some time ago.

> The penultimate game was at Crewe. We were losing 1-0 but pressing hard for an equaliser. Then, with what seemed to be several minutes left for play, the referee blew the final whistle. I think he was bothered by the large number of supporters preparing to rush on at the end. I turned round to see the Football League assessor sat behind me, to complain at this blatant injustice. He waved my protest aside, kidding me that he did not have a watch when I could see that his match record of refereeing decisions had their respective

timings. Since there was not a clock inside the ground it was obvious that he had access to a watch or a small clock. But he refused to address my objection. From that match onwards I have always had a stopwatch which is now approaching 34 years old.

Our collective protest that Burnley had been short-timed fell on deaf ears as did a plea to the Football League to reprieve the club from relegation because of its historic founder status. We were almost out of time and running out of ideas to save the club. We had considered the ruse of buying the almost bankrupt Cardiff City and bringing it back to Turf Moor in what would have been the Football League's first franchise operation. It looked as if Cardiff might enter administration but nothing came of the idea.

So, we were destined to go to the wire, a last chance home game with Orient who were expected to provide stiff opposition as they were pursuing play-off ambitions. I am brought to tears whenever I think of that fateful day. It was like a near-death experience. However, it became the day when folks reclaimed their team when 16,000 to 17,000 turned up at Turf Moor. Before that the average league gate had been around 2,800. It was pitiful. In Burnley's heydays of the 50s and 60s there had been crowds of up to 55,000. Only the threat of losing their club forever caused the local people to return in large numbers. Having said all that, had the worst happened, I don't think the club would necessarily have expired. I think we might have been able to keep it alive. In those days it was possible to buy a club for a few hundred thousand pounds and I was prepared to consider paying that sort of money to save the club. As it turned out it was not necessary.

Ironically it was Lincoln and not Burnley that fell through the trapdoor, but then Lincoln staged a return to the League one year later. So, relegation for Burnley might not have been a terminal disaster; if Lincoln could return from the Conference, then why not Burnley?

Besides, I'm not a pessimist. I held a firm conviction that all would be well. I was sure that if we beat Orient that this would be sufficient for survival although salvation was not solely in our hands. I did not expect that both of our rivals, Lincoln and Torquay, would both win as well. I thought that at least one of them would lose and of course, that is what happened. When we heard that Lincoln had lost their final game at Swansea 2-0, sealing their relegation, I had a wry smile thinking of the Lincoln directors who had smugly presumed that their club would be safe, after our defeat at Scunthorpe.

The truth was it was a wretched time, very much hands to mouth with a threadbare squad, one physio, Jimmy Holland, and a 'bucket and sponge' trainer in George Bray, a former player. I remember George getting fed up with one of our players who kept going down. George's patience finally snapped in one game resulting in him emptying the bucket of cold water over him. It was a rare funny moment.

Threadbare and penniless, scrabbling for cash, economising to the bone just about summed up this season. We planned to have car-boot sales every Sunday in the car park. They would have been a winner but the council intervened. Because we were within two miles of Burnley market, the Market Charter did not allow us to do this. We were seen as a threat to the market and were threatened with legal action if we continued. How could a car-boot sale once a week be a threat to the market? It was nonsense and denied us the chance to run something that might have raised some decent money. The one that Walsall Football Club ran raised them thousands. The other thing we offered to do was let the supporters' club run the club shop at £20 a week. But they wanted the stock for nothing, so that was a non-starter. They did generously offer us an interest-free loan. But, dammit, we wanted donation, not loans.

Meetings with the bank were frequent. The local council had told us they could not help, early in 1987. The Trustee Savings Bank completed another valuation of the ground at £850,000. As a potential supermarket site, it was worth, they said, £1.8m. Read into that what you will. A family member worked at the Midland Bank in a senior position in London. It was not an immediate no. He was an uncle and wanted cash flows and projections. Alas, as soon as he got those it was a polite no. All we could do was to get money from sponsors up front and push all those who owed us money. But there was some good news when I managed to get Barclays Bank to agree to a loan of £50,000. The bad news was it was set against the directors giving personal guarantees.

One way of getting money into the club was to invite new directors to join us, or their money of course. We invited John Wilkinson and, yes, he joined the board in 2004. Harry Brooks was another we invited, but at that time he was wound up in his work at Loughborough University. He would become more and more of a critic of the club and his name would crop up many times. It was a strange refusal because prior to this we had a letter from him asking to become a director. His letters to the local press slamming the club for this and that would become a regular page filler.

The game at Crewe was a sickener. It was a Monday night. We all knew that we had to win two of the last three games to have any chance of avoiding the drop. But the second game, Keith McNee reported:

> A simple goal after five minutes by striker David Platt for Crewe Alexandra was enough to see off Burnley in yet another away performance that wasn't good enough to deserve any reward. The Clarets again received terrific vocal backing in a crowd of 4,175 but failed miserably to produce the goods, especially in attack. It seemed to me that any of

the players were drained from the tremendous effort they put in on Saturday at Turf Moor to defeat promotion candidates Southend.

Platt was left with the relatively simple task of scoring his 23rd goal of the season with a near-post header after fellow striker Chris Cutler found space on the left of the penalty area to provide the short centre. It has been the same sorry story all season, goals given away so easily and often, as last night. Crewe applied all the early pressure in their hustling, bustling style, with the Burnley defence not at all comfortable. But they did not go close to scoring again until near the end of the game when Peter Leebrook kicked off the line from the lively Platt.

The closest the Clarets went to equalising was with a Leighton James free kick that giant goalkeeper Brian Parkin just managed to tip over the bar for a corner. James occasionally threatened but Burnley were badly short of thrust and firepower in attack and Crewe contained them fairly easily. Burnley were nowhere near inventive enough to worry the likes of Steve Davis and Geoff Thomas at the heart of the home defence.

Skipper Ray Deakin battled hard in defence as usual and Leebrook stuck gamely to his task but there was little sparkle from the forward players and even Neil Grewcock had a pretty lean time. This was another sickening result for the Turf Moor club and supporters, and with only one match left, it leaves them in the most terrible situation they have ever had to face.

We were furious at the referee, Ken Lupton, for blowing the whistle early. Maybe he was intimidated by the sight of massed Burnley fans almost encroaching the pitch. Frank Teasdale immediately wrote to the Football League with a vigorous appeal that the game be replayed, and at the very least an investigation on the grounds that this was a result that could decide Burnley's fate that season and that a point gained if Burnley had scored might determine their survival. It fell on deaf ears. It wasn't rocket science to suppose that someone at the Football League had thought to themselves that there had already been nearly a whole season of games that had put Burnley in this position. If the worst happened, it would not be because of one result at Crewe even if the referee had blown too soon. The records say that he ended the game three minutes early. To this day I'll say it was double that.

On the coach back after the game ... can you be sombre and angry at the same time? Yes, you can and that was certainly the mood in the coach on the way back. To lose this game was a stunner. It meant that the final game was all or nothing. We could go down in history as the directors that oversaw the end of a once-great club. To this day I cannot imagine the pressure, stress and anxiety that Brian Miller must have felt.

Brian Miller was furious and a furious Brian Miller was not someone to ignore. He called it scandalous and that the second half did not run for the full 45 minutes. He had been told that the press-box stopwatches had timed the second half at 42 minutes and that the referee afterwards admitted that he had deliberately blown his whistle early because he was frightened of crowd trouble and the crowd getting out of hand. Miller complained strongly that three minutes was a long time in football and a complaint would be made. But would the assessor agree? he asked. The referee later changed his story, saying that he had not said previously that he had blown early. He insisted he had played the full 45 minutes and this was confirmed by his linesmen. Another Football League referee added to the controversy saying that each half had to be 45 minutes long and that Burnley had a good claim to get the game replayed. But this won't be easy for them, he added. And so it proved.

Immediately after the Crewe game I bought a stopwatch – expensive as well; a Tag Heuer 1010 – and used it at every game. Somewhere I still have the old box and paperwork. It lasted until

November 2021, so with over 30 years of use I call that good value. The replacement was just £3.69. Maybe this one won't last 30 years but I'm 78 so one presumes it will outlast me.

To use a well-known phrase, 'drink was taken' after the victorious Orient game, so much so that Brian Miller had to call a taxi to take secretary Albert Maddox home. My own celebration was with Sylvia and friends, but, perhaps with a few too many drinks, I cannot, understandably, remember much about the evening.

At the celebratory meal after the game, I had euphorically exclaimed that there would be no repetition in the next season. In fact, I said we might even get to Wembley. To my astonishment, we did just that.

CHAPTER TWO

1987/88 Into a Final

THE WORD rebirth was used quite often after the Orient game. Over 5,000 fans turned up for the first game of season 1987/88. I spoke to Tim Quelch in 2017.

> Thanks to Frank Teasdale's successful wheeling and dealing, and of course the healthy receipts from the Orient Game, which enhanced creditor confidence, we had the scope to spend more on the 1987/88 team. Manager Brian Miller brought in some good additions. Paul Comstive, a tall skilful midfield player from Wrexham. Steve Davis, an imposing, young centre-back from Crewe (not to be confused with the other Steve Davis that came later from Luton). And George Oghani, a pacey striker from Bolton with a good average strike rate of a goal every three games.
>
> The wage bill for this improved first-team squad was about £5,000 a week. Which is of course a fraction of the current weekly cost of employing just one first-team player.
>
> 'It was in this season that we did something quite radical and introduced an optional admission charge of £5 for some games. The usual entrance fee was £2.50 but the optional charge was introduced to raise funds for team strengthening. Over time at least 7,000 fans chose to pay the extra admission fee and this raised around £20,000

extra. There was one particular loan player that we were really keen to keep. This was David Reeves. Unfortunately, Sheffield Wednesday would not let him go.

I was frustrated at our failure to land him. When the Reeves loan spell expired, the board agreed to make funds available for Brian Miller to attempt to sign him permanently. But when I told this to Brian Miller, he looked dumbfounded, saying that Frank Teasdale had told him that the club could not afford him. I was angry. It had been a collective board decision that we should arrange to sign Reeves and yet Frank had reversed this unilaterally. The thing about Frank was that he was terrific at keeping the wolf from the door but at heart he was a very cautious man. During his time in charge, I think we missed important opportunities to progress the club because he was too risk-averse.

With the club's financial position healthier than 12 months before, our losses had been slashed by over £100,000 to a more manageable £40,000; I confronted Frank concerning his lone stance on Reeves. He was a player that went on to score over 100 more league goals for lower-division sides. I was angry with Teasdale and wrote him a letter stating my intention to increase my shareholding stake, proposing to pay £50 for each share, instead of the existing price of £15, thus posing a direct threat to his position as chairman. This caused a hell of a row and the aggravation was too much for fellow director Basil Dearing who feared that his professional reputation was becoming tainted by the controversies besetting the club. Basil had been badly shaken by the vociferous protests during the previous season. Consequently, he resigned. Although the rest of us managed to patch up our boardroom squabbles, Burnley's promotion challenge faltered, not helped by our failure to sign Reeves.

But, if the league campaign stopped and started and hiccupped again, to our surprise and satisfaction, progress in the Sherpa Van Trophy went well. You may ask what on earth this competition was. In short, it was for the lower-league sides and gave them a chance to appear in a Wembley final. You may remember that I had told my wife, Sylvia, at the end of the previous near-disastrous season, that this season we would play at Wembley. We beat Halifax in a penalty shoot-out in the northern-section semi-final and this gave us a two-legged northern final against Preston. The first leg at Turf Moor was goalless in front of an astonishing crowd of over 15,000. We could be forgiven for thinking, 'Ah well, that was it,' especially as at Preston the pitch was one of those infamous plastic things.

I'm not going to include every word Granville Shackleton wrote about the win at Preston, but the best of them were:

> Ray Deakin was two years old when Brian Miller last walked out proudly onto the Wembley pitch as a Burnley player for the 1962 Cup Final against Spurs. Now, five weeks on Sunday, Miller the manager and Deakin the skipper will tread that glory path together as they lead out the Clarets in the final of the Sherpa Van Trophy against Wolves. And no other two men deserve to share that great honour under the twin towers of this famous stadium than Miller, who was sacrificed on the altar of the wild and impossible dream that an outsider would be good for the Clarets and was then called back to sort out the mess. And Deakin, a replacement skipper when he took on the job from Tommy Hutchison and is now enjoying the greatest days of his career.
>
> It was to them that the Burnley players, managers and chairman paid glowing tributes as they savoured the moment of victory in a jubilant dressing room at Preston that resembled a vineyard as Preston's chairman Keith Leeming sportingly swallowed his disappointment. He sent the victorious Clarets a case of champagne immediately

they returned to their dressing room after being besieged by their fans.

As at Turf Moor the previous week the foundation on which Burnley's success was built was a courageous and at times brilliant goalkeeper, Chris Pearce, and a back four of Steve Gardner, Steve Davis, Shaun McGrory and Deakin. Pearce paid a heavy price for his courage and returned from Deepdale strapped up and in considerable pain from body blows taken as he dived in the fray. It was from the first of these clashes he had that the Clarets were able to get the first all-important goal. George Oghani scored, this was now his 17th and he was now the hero.

It seemed that Burnley were going to rue a lost chance when Comstive put the ball wide; following a free kick Preston pounced for Brazil to flash the ball past Pearce for the equaliser. And so to extra time and with only three minutes of it gone, Burnley fans erupted once more as right in front of them the goalmouth became a frenzy of players as Deakin sent over a free kick and Hoskin at the second attempt blasted a shot past Brown. The Clarets became stronger, physically and mentally and a huge banner with the words 'Wembley 1988' appeared in the midst of the mass of Claret fans who were now celebrating in style. Their now incessant roar was suddenly intensified three minutes from the end as Burnley caught Preston coming forward and with Brown out of his goal, Comstive charged forward and smashed the ball into an empty net and the Clarets really were going to Wembley.

Unbelievable scenes followed the final whistle as the Clarets ran to their fans, many of whom had now got onto the pitch, and it was difficult to sort out who were the players and fans as scarves, hats and caps were showered on the Burnley players. It was a scene reminiscent of last May against Orient, but now for so many different reasons.

To me, the Preston game was the most important game of the season, even more so than the final. Win it and the income from the final would see us through the summer. A final you can lose but the finances are the compensation. Having drawn the first game at Turf Moor 0-0, we heard that Preston fans and club were already booking coaches and measuring up for club suits. It was usual at the time to split the prize money 50-50, but whether we did so with Wolves I can't remember. Whatever we did, the money would be there to comfortably keep the club in business. We felt relaxed in the final. It would have been splendid to have won but just being there was an occasion after what we had been through. I compare that today with the pressure, anxiety and tension of the 2009 play-off final against Sheffield United. The prospect of promotion to the Premier League and the money it would generate was dazzling. You don't enjoy a game that you need to win, that you absolutely must win, in order to avoid administration. That is pressure.

The directors, as surprised and joyous as any supporter – don't forget we were supporters too – met very soon after the Preston game to plan for the visit to Wembley. So much to plan and organise – tickets, transport, hotels, souvenirs, the 101 little things and details. At last, what you might call nice problems and happy decisions. We were already assured of 25,000 tickets, so in theory that was plenty. But this was a cup final and we knew that overnight there would be more than 25,000 people wanting tickets. We had to contact British Rail and a dozen coach companies. It would be a spring bank holiday weekend, which added to the complications. Looking back, the ticket prices make me smile, with seats at £12, £10 and £8. Standing was £5. The club shop swung into action with two sorts of T-shirt, at just £5. Scarves were £2, or £3 for something a bit fancier. We had five types of hats all at £2. A flag was £2 and a metal badge was just £1. Today, prices in the club shop are enough to make your eyes water. Details of a list of souvenirs were posted to members of supporters' clubs, with no internet and websites back in those days. The most difficult part was deciding on a list of civic dignitaries and town worthies to invite. And then prune that list. Top of the list was the Trustee Savings Bank top director. Without the TSB we were sunk. Then, of course, people like the mayor and mayoress. After the game the local councillors clamoured to be included on the open-top bus ride and raise their PR level. Ask the town councillors for help with the financial situation at the club and they did not want to know us. In the Premier League, kudos being associated with the club is huge. Back then there was little advantage in helping a struggling club.

One of the top reporters of the time, James Mossop, had this to say. Features about Burnley had been in short supply since the deluge of words that came at the time of the Orient game.

> Between bookends of old gold on one side and claret and blue on the other, a volume of football history comes alive this afternoon. Wembley Stadium could be renamed Memory Lane for a day, as Wolves and Burnley contrive to roll 'All Our Yesterday', 'Where Are They Now' and 'Fancy That', into 90 minutes. Such is the affection for these Fourth Division clubs that Wembley had to print extra tickets to accommodate a full house crowd for the Sherpa Van Trophy, an event that normally ranks with hop-scotch and rounders in sporting significance. This time, the finest footballing stage in Britain is taken by two of the clubs that helped us fall for the old game in the first place.
>
> They were the giants of the 50s and 60s. They were Football League champions, FA Cup finalists and England representatives in the European Cup. Then they fell on hard times. Beneath a proud coat of arms, there is the inscription 'Out of the darkness cometh light.' As words of faith go, there could be nothing more fitting. Wolves and Burnley have both kicked the lids off their coffins to be where they are.
>
> Burnley's stumble through the divisions was especially severe. The Lancastrians only retained their league status,

winning the very last match of the season a year ago. Wolves salvaged some pride when they won the Fourth Division Championship last month but Molineux is an echo chamber compared to those days when 30 years ago 50,000 plus got behind the team.

Can anyone outside Burnley and Wolverhampton name the players likely to start the game. I struggle with that, but like a whole generation I can name the Wolves and Burnley teams in 1960 when Burnley pipped their old rivals to the title by a point, although Wolves won the FA Cup beating Blackburn by 3-0. They were great days. Burnley were managed by Harry Potts who had been one of their post-war inside forwards, and had Jimmy McIlroy, Jimmy Adamson, Ray Pointer, Alex Elder and today's manager, Brian Miller.

Miller will lead out his Burnley boys and is as close-cropped and rugged-looking as he was 26 years ago when Burnley lost 3-1 in the Cup Final to Spurs. He could have been speaking for Wolves and present manager Graham Turner when he said: 'It is a boost for the club and it gives everyone a lift. It is wonderful for the town and everybody is getting involved. They are buying rosettes and scarves and streamers. All the old memories are being stirred.'

These days both clubs have to rely on cheap purchases, free transfers and a few local lads but there are a few who could surprise any neutrals in the crowd. The partisans will not need their excitement fanning.

The man deserving sympathy is Burnley's Neil Grewcock. He injured knee ligaments in the semi-final and has not played since. Neil will be just a face in the crowd that should come together to make Wembley a happy place to be. It is a day created for memories, an occasion for wallowing in nostalgia and a reminder to all those other clubs, the fallen giants and those that seem to be forever on the wrong side of the tracks, that 'out of the darkness, cometh light.'

The town went mad, of course. The lads from the Hour Glass pub on Leeds Road, Nelson made a banner that was 26 metres long. The banner, made by Mark Fitzpatrick, was one of many that were taken down to Wembley, but this one was a monster. Local travel agents Althams announced that at least 60 coaches and two trains had been booked to take over 5,000 fans to London. Others had booked weekend hotel packages. Burnley and Pendle Transport were taking another 28 buses down. Thousands were going by car. It was the biggest exodus since the cup final of 1962.

A few more wins might even have made this a double celebration had promotion been won as well. Maybe that would have been a wish too many. Brian Miller was asked what he would have chosen, Wembley or promotion.

The gist of his answer was that promotion might have been a year too soon with the club still stretched for money. After the win at Preston, Ray Deakin had said they had to forget Wembley and concentrate on a promotion run-in.

The Football League were delighted since this was their centenary year and here were two big clubs with fabulous histories, and founder members of the Football League. This could not have been a better written script. They also knew that it would be a sellout. Some previous games had seen attendances of under 40,000.

And if you didn't fancy the football, in Burnley there was Austen Brothers' Circus, 2,000 seats in the heated big top. At the cinema you could see *Broadcast News*, *Fatal Attraction* and *Nuts*. At Chalker's Cabaret, they had top names lined up: Billy Pearce, Marty Wilde, Vince Hill, the Eric Delaney band, Martha Reeves and the Vandellas, and Edwin Starr. Sunday dinner at the Rosehill Hotel was just £5.95.

On the day, I have to admit that Wolves were much the better side, with two great strikers in Bull and Mutch. We made a weekend of it, went down with Basil Dearing and his wife, saw a great show,

Cats, but lost the game 2-0; it hardly seemed to matter. Thanks to this competition we were over £200,000 better off.

And for George Bray it was truly special. In 1947 he had been a member of the Burnley side at Wembley that lost 1-0 to Charlton Athletic. In 1962 he had been there as a member of the Burnley coaching staff. Now he was there for a third time as kit man.

CHAPTER THREE

1988/89 Miller Resigns

COACH TRIPS could be a joy or a punishment, depending on mood and results and distance, but it is no longer the practice for directors to travel on the coach with the team. Steve Cotterill eventually put a stop to that. I always tried to remember that in fact I was a guest on a coach in just the same way that we were a guest in any hotel we stayed in. Normal procedure in a hotel was that the team would eat first, quite early, so that they could then get an early night's sleep. It was most pleasant after that for the small group of directors to eat later with a drink or two. The problem was that chairman Frank Teasdale, once he'd had a couple of drinks, liked to have another couple … and then another couple. More often than not, when it was time to retire, he'd grab the manager on the pretence of discussing the game the next day. A whisky bottle usually went with them. It took fellow director Bob Blakeborough and I a little while to realise what was going on, that chairman and manager would simply continue drinking, with the sad effect that on some occasions the manager the next day was simply not fit to do his job, refreshed after a good night's sleep, and with a clear head. We tackled Frank about this several times and in our opinion two managers were affected by this habit. Bob and I even listened outside his bedroom door on occasions to confirm our worst fears. We confronted him with this in boardroom meetings, with a huge row on one occasion. The other directors remained silent.

At the start of the season, I was really keen to improve our PR with the fans. It was poor at the time but the rest of the board seemed not to be too bothered about this. My frustrations fell on deaf ears and my habit of telling the truth, tell it all and, most important of all, tell it first was something else that didn't go down too well. Too often, other board members would simply say 'no comment' in answer to a problem that was raised. The only success I had was in persuading the board to support my attempts to join the largest supporter group and get on their committee – the intention being to act as a go-between, and how beneficial that might have been. Alas, it did not go down too well with the supporter group when at their AGM in 1988 the idea was turned down flat. Today the club still says it wants to get closer to the fans but liaison groups have been tried over and again and failed. The group I spoke to made it clear they did not want what they thought would be a club spy on their committee but what an opportunity they missed in terms of communication.

Hooliganism was something that would not go away and the previous season we had introduced a scheme that would ban for life any person convicted of a football-related offence. It was widely publicised at the time and did have an effect but it was a long time before it was completely eradicated. The government wanted membership schemes but these were impractical and would have been costly to implement. It opened up the whole chicken and egg argument: did football cause hooliganism, or did hooligans simply attach themselves to the nearest football club in order to cause mayhem? It was decided at this time to attach 'cacti spikes' to the perimeter fencing to deter vandalism inside the ground. Then we looked at the cost. So, the existing spikes were painted with anti-vandal paint. A few weeks later we got a letter of complaint from a Mrs Jones that her little lad had got this paint on his trousers. I think we replied to ask her exactly what was he doing trying to climb up there in the first place?

The Hillsborough disaster was on the same day as our home game against Darlington and the membership scheme was something we were still fighting against. Burnley was elected to host five or six EEC (now the EU) officials, plus a couple of UK MPs, plus FA and League representatives on a fact-finding trip. Two things went horribly wrong that day. On our own terraces we had a running battle between opposing fans with police involvement and unpleasant scenes. And then at half-time we came in to see scenes of the Hillsborough disaster on our TV screen. The room went silent with little interest after that to discuss football and the English game. It was not a day to remember.

But there was one weekend that was memorable for the right reasons even if we did lose. Endsleigh, the club sponsors, had invited us to stay in Cheltenham for a weekend at their HQ after we had played Exeter (and lost 3-0, by the way). On the Sunday we had arranged to play the Endsleigh staff in a football friendly, with the Endsleigh side aided by a sprinkling of Burnley players. To my great surprise I was elected to be manager for the day, perhaps because I was the only one there with a stopwatch. The first team won, of course, so I have often wondered, am I the only Burnley manager in history with an unbeaten record?

In hindsight all these years later you can look back at a period and think, well, nothing much happened there then. But at the time, a season doesn't drift while its actually happening, not for a director anyway. No matter that little happens on the pitch, life in the directors' box and boardroom remains eventful. There is just too much to do and think about. Especially when the fans are unhappy, which is exactly what happened as the euphoria of the Wembley visit faded and mundane life returned. The lot of the Burnley supporter for the next two or three years was not a happy one.

Season-ticket sales had doubled, optimism was high, Miller signed new players, the mood was buoyant and chairman Frank Teasdale announced that promotion was the target. I thought then that this was a half-reckless thing to say and over-optimistic. I was proved right.

As we start to write this book in autumn 2021, here we are in the Premier League, albeit by the skin of our teeth and by the time of publication we may well be back in the Championship, but years ago Burnley rambled around the Fourth Division, regularly losing to the likes of Tranmere, Rochdale and Torquay. It was in just such a game at Prenton Park in January 1989 – a defeat, of course – after which Brian Miller handed in his resignation.

Frank Casper was his replacement, having been approached by Frank Teasdale, but there is the story that Brian actually approached Frank and asked him, 'How do you fancy being manager at Burnley and taking over from me but I'll stay on as chief scout?' He had been assistant manager at Bury, but his heart was at Burnley, where he had been Bob Lord's first buy in the late 60s. John Jackson had discarded him in his pursuit of John Bond, who came for a year and by and large was a disaster for the club. Frank knew talent when he saw it and was a great coach but set a trend, since the players that he brought in were the team that someone else took to promotion – in the same way Owen Coyle took Steve Cotterill's players to promotion. Likewise, Sean Dyche took Eddie Howe's players to promotion. If you analyse just how this happens, that one manager succeeds where his predecessor did not with the same players, you would have the formula for the magic of football.

The striker George Oghani's punch-up incident with goalkeeper Chris Pearce at Gawthorpe has gone down in folklore, although Chris may not care to remember it, being on the painful receiving end. If I am correct, then the origins of this lay in something to do with the purchase of an item by George, sometime earlier when he was wrongly accused of walking out of a store with an ironing board that he hadn't paid for. At the training ground Pearce and Paul Comstive were making unkind comments about it, so George whacked Chris and broke a bone in his face. After this he was 'quietly moved on', as they say. Even before this we had been at a hotel overnight and, in the morning, I think it was Paul Comstive walked in carrying an ironing board, and then walked out of the hotel with it. Huge laughs all round. To be fair to George he had paid for the ironing board but not the packet of screws he had unthinkingly put in his pocket while looking at the board. Security stopped him on the way out. Newspapers made a big thing of it. The moral, I suppose, of the story is that footballers have to live with banter and should know how to put up with it. The dressing room can be a cruel place, but you either ignore it, or laugh along with it, or wait patiently and get your own back when no one is looking.

It was a season of crowd problems and demonstrations. Last-day cries of 'sack the board' rang round the ground. It was Frank Teasdale who bore the brunt of it, of course, and got a truly rough ride from the fans. Make no mistake, he was a Burnley fan himself but he really took a lot of flak for the club's slow drift. The club had been in a bad way when he took over from John Jackson and so he was always the punchbag and target for disgruntled supporters. The fact that he had little or no money of his own did not help. He endured some awful abuse and fans saw it as his fault that the club had no money.

After one game there were over 500 fans demonstrating outside the ground. They were fed up of what was on offer and wanted change whether it was the board, the chairman or the manager. Maybe it was at this point that I had written to various people and clubs in Saudi Arabia to try to raise investment. I had the board's agreement to do this and also wrote to Robert Maxwell via his right-hand man, whose name I forget. I actually got a reply to say, no, he was not interested. Knowing what we know now, perhaps that was just as well.

Abuse is never pleasant. I put up with bullying at school and laughed it off and the bullies soon got fed up. Easier said than done, I know. It does get a little more serious when you are assaulted, which has happened to me, once at Crewe and once at Turf Moor. The latter was when, after a game, three or four lads decided to have a kickabout on the pitch, so I asked them to leave. One of them took a swing at me. The police wanted me to press charges, but I decided not to. It was a poor swing. The PR for the club would have been poor, it would have dragged on, so I settled for the lad being given a good talking-to by the police. The other occasion was when I had my car windscreen smashed with a brick when it was parked outside

Turf Moor. It was hard to understand that one, because we had just won and gone top of the league.

On the day 500 fans demonstrated outside Turf Moor, we were asked to wait in the lounge with our cars under the Bob Lord Stand while they worked out a plan to get us away. So, we all got in our cars, lined them up, got the engines running, revved them up, and swept out of the ground like some sort of presidential cavalcade while the police cleared a way through.

In the press there had been regular headlines such as 'Sad Clarets' or 'Shambles at the Shay'. A poem was doing the rounds:

> The boy stood at the pearly gates. His face was worn and old.
> He stood before the man of fate, for admission to the fold.
> 'What have you done?' St Peter asked, 'to gain admission here?' 'I've been a Burnley fan,' the lad replied, 'for many and many a year.' The pearly gates swung open wide; St Peter tolled the bell. 'Come in,' he said, 'And choose your harp. You've had your share of hell.'

Money-raising schemes were always at the forefront of our minds and discussions. The council did provide £10,000 but it was only a loan. Of course, you accept it and worry later about how to repay it. We'd tried American football one weekend with two Lancashire teams. It was an abject failure and nearly drove our groundsman, dear Roy Oldfield, to suicide. They'd promised him all kinds of help setting it up and clearing it away. That never happened and Roy silently fumed, not just at the extra work but the ruination of the pitch.

I would imagine Roy was secretly delighted one year when Bernard Rothwell found himself without a seat at the top table at the Wembley Sherpa banquet after the game. Bernard was not best pleased. I remember a board meeting when Bernard listed all the things that Roy hadn't done and had accused Roy of being disrespectful to him. Did Bernard ever realise that Roy's priority was the pitch as well as the pitches at Gawthorpe? As a director, Bernard had always given Roy a hard time – 'Do this, do that, mend this, fix that.' Bernard seemed to think he had time to sweep car parks, paint woodwork, fix doors, mend windows and 101 other things. The last straw for Roy was when Bernard told him to empty a skip of all the cardboard boxes that someone had dumped, flatten them, and then put them back in again. Roy fumed and by all accounts told Bernard what he thought of him, and left a few weeks later. He was a lovely man but, with such a shortage of money, had to work more or less alone. He scrimped and scraped and when we were quoted £80 for a molecatcher to come and trap the creatures, Roy used the good soil from the molehills to repair the pitch at Turf Moor. His delightful book, *Mud, Sweat and Shears*, is an education.

Bernard really put his foot in it one Christmas when giving a thank-you speech at a cabaret evening we held for staff. The main lady who had prepared the meal was Mrs Denwood, a stern, straight-faced lady, first employed by Bob Lord. Her nickname was Mrs Demdike, which was based on the name of one of the Pendle witches, old Mother Demdike. Bernard, by mistake – or was it deliberate? – in his speech thanked Mrs Demdike and it got a good laugh but was not best received by the good lady herself. Shortly after this she tendered her resignation. So that was two employees Bernard had managed to get rid of.

He was never the easiest of chaps to work with. As the football authorities became more and more strict about ground-safety work, when they actually wrote to the club to suggest that Bernard was not fully cooperating with them, it was then me that was instructed to go to all the meetings in future and take over the role of safety officer, a bit of a misnomer in fact as I was simply the director responsible for ground safety. It was a role that needed someone who could see to every detail. Up to this point I had overseen the catering side of things and overhauled the system of appointing outside caterers. It became very much an in-house thing and began to earn far better returns for the club with profits coming to us, rather than the contractors. Today it is a huge part of club business.

We tried making video recordings of our away games and then showed them in the Centre Spot in the Bob Lord Stand. There were two problems: the first was that the first films were made on a recorder that I had bought, a great huge thing, and believe it or not I still have it somewhere at home; the second problem was that some of our performances in away games were so poor that nobody in their right mind would actually want to see them. The theory was that watching these games in the Centre Spot would increase the drink sales. Maybe they did, but perhaps only because people couldn't believe what they were seeing.

Another big fundraising idea was to hold pop concerts at Turf Moor. It was left to me to investigate the possibility, so I worked on a three-day event, with Simply Red headlining one of the evenings. Naturally you had to run all this by the local council and the police chief. It went down like a lead balloon but what a moneymaker it would have been. There were worries about behaviour, drug use and fans sleeping in the streets for two nights. We had three meetings with local officials but they refused to grant any licences. A one-night event they would have approved, but this was simply not financially feasible and not something that we could have made pay.

We had the usual sportsmen dinners to raise funds; Ralph Coates offered to bring a Spurs XI to play a friendly. We applied for planning permission to build houses on one of the top fields at the Gawthorpe training area. It was refused. We appealed. It was refused again. But, somehow, we must have had some success with money-raising and paying the bills, as the 30 June 1987 declared loss of £41,000 was £100,000 less than the previous one of 1986.

Match sponsorship today is a huge business and highly lucrative and it was certainly something we did back in the 80s. In its infancy it raised but a fraction of today's huge sums. One of the perks of being a match sponsor when we had away sponsors was two tickets on the team coach. Harry Brooks was just such a sponsor one weekend and it was a game just before Christmas at Wrexham. On the way back Harry rose to give a speech of thanks for the players' efforts during the season so far. Alas, it all began to go wrong when he began to tell them how they could have done better and how they should be playing. Brian Miller, who could blow a fuse when angered, was incensed and was within an inch of putting him off the coach to make his own way home. The players were in uproar. The next week was the directors' Christmas lunch to which Harry had been invited. It fell to me to uninvite him since Brian Miller had said he would not attend if Harry was there. Brian, meanwhile, had a new two-year contract. Harry was a lovely and well-meaning man with Burnley blood flowing through his veins, but he could upset just about anybody, including the local cricket club and the town council – and us. His angry letters to the local press were frequent and a treat to read.

It was no luxury life for the players at that time and on overnight coach journeys we had this system of ordering fish and chips for the journey home and then collecting after the game. Eventually we managed to bring frozen meals on board if there was a microwave. In charge of 'cooking' were Jimmy Holland, the physio, and George Bray, the trainer. They were the best of pals and sat together, talking and telling endless stories. But on kitchen duty they were priceless, endlessly falling out until it resembled a pantomime. The laughs we had were welcome.

CHAPTER FOUR

1989/90 Just What Am I Doing Here?

THE VERY first game of the season and we lost it 2-1, away at Rochdale. The word depressed was inadequate as I walked round the perimeter of the pitch after the game, unable to face the directors' lounge. The ground was empty and silent. Our club's problems were going round and round in my head, not the least of which had been over-optimism during the summer. Add to that a board of directors mostly unable to see the problems and how our approach needed to change. It was almost back to square one, when I had asked myself, 'Just what am I doing here?'

What makes a good board of directors? How long is a piece of string? Is there a perfect answer to the question? A director will have a different answer than a manager. Supporters will have their own ideas. Bob Lord's idea of a good director was simply one that did as he was told and never argued. Brian Clough thought they should keep quiet and out of the way. He saw them in three groups: duplicitous backstabbers, feckless sycophants and desperate egotists. Len Shackleton wrote a book and one chapter was dedicated to directors and their place in football and what they knew about football. He simply left a blank page. I think he and I would not have got on. Some of us do know a bit about the game. To any manager who questioned whether or not I could recognise a bad game, I would simply ask him if he could recognise a bad meal? If he said yes, I would then tell him I could also recognise a bad game.

A manager might simply say that all the directors need to do is give the money I needed for players. It was ever thus. John Bond in his time spent every penny he could until it dried up.

Most directors at Burnley, certainly in my latter years there, were always mindful that we were custodians of the club; there to assist, to make it better if we could, to communicate with supporters, to assist and support the manager (although more will be said about that later). We were there to protect it financially. We always knew that it was the heart of the town, it fitted into the geography of the town like a piece in a jigsaw, less than a mile from the town centre. The relationship between small town and small club was unique; it was a name known throughout the football world since the days of Bob Lord when it first played in the European Cup. It had existed since 1882, its history punctuated by titles, runners-up places, promotions, cup finals, great players, and all kinds of drama. It was and is the town's ambassador. Our job was to cherish it. In the Coyle promotion season, the police chief, I believe, contacted the club to say, 'Please keep it up, crime has gone down.' Bob Lord always used to say that when the team won, factory production went up in the town the following week. A winning football team brings smiles. Sadly, as we began this book, wins were few and far between and the manager had been short of funds to seek new players and strengthen the team in the seasons preceding the takeover.

Did the new ALK American owners know all this history and tradition when they bought the club? Or at least have they come to appreciate it?

My own view is that a board of directors should not exceed six members. Above that, it is cumbersome, discussions can be too lengthy and time-consuming, decision-making can be slow. But an even number of directors can present problems since, if a vote is split, it gives the chairman the casting vote. Too many members and cliques develop, which is far from good and healthy, or constructive. A board needs a range of skills, someone who understands legal background (John Jackson was good at this), someone who understands business finance (Derek Gill was good at this and so was I). A medical expert can be useful but not easy to find. Doc Iven, as his name suggests, was a medical man but blotted his copy book in the John Bond season when he pronounced Joe Gallagher fit even though Joe had a gammy knee. For ground maintenance and construction, a civil engineer is useful but uncommon.

At Burnley, directors have always been self-made men (Jack Simmons was not but hardly attended anyway). Money helps but none have ever been in the billionaire class. Some of them, if not most, have been millionaires or almost; some of them with very large businesses, but all of them well used to running a business and making decisions. They have run very successful companies but have done it one way, their way. Put six such people on a committee, each with strong views and opinions, and there can be many a disagreement. Yet they have to be a team player, willing to listen to the views of others, although I am not sure that this was the case in my last couple of years as a director, when the club was being sold. If a board is democratic then all members will accept the majority view, though they may not agree with it. But was it a democratic decision to sell Burnley Football Club? No. Three members were in favour, but three were uncomfortable. But those in favour held the bulk of the shares. On any board, he who holds the share majority is king, as Bob Lord will attest.

My own background helped me as a director. I was used to working as part of a team working for public companies. I was on technical committees, ran my own successful company for years, learning about employment law, accountancy, the tax system and finance.

I learned about life and people from an early age, leaving school at 15 and then going to night school to learn more and more. Nothing ever came to me on a plate or with a silver spoon. I was a grafter. And never suffered fools gladly. An ability to see where things might go wrong, an insistence on dotting every 'i' and crossing every 't' has not always endeared me to people.

Different circumstances need different directors to handle them, so into the mix comes the art of delegation by a chairman. When the club was at rock bottom financially after the collapse of ITV Digital, Barry Kilby was skilled at juggling the finances, and organising a way of protecting the club. A cautious man, as I am, never willing 'to bet the ranch' as he put it. Brendan Flood, on the other hand, had a different skillset. Using his own Modus company's money, he funded an ambitious drive to move the club upwards. You could perhaps class Brendan as a blue-sky thinker but he pulled it off, energising the club and seeing the reward of promotion to the Premier League in 2009. It so nearly went so very wrong, but we'll come to that later.

The right man at the right time is the way to see Barry and how he 'saved' the club. The right man at the right time is the way to see Brendan and his drive to promotion. But all the time you need other people to see problems, pitfalls, consequences, to provide balance, caution and input their own expertise. But above all you need a chairman that will not go against the wishes of his board. I worked for four chairmen and as we journey through my story, we'll meet each one of them.

* * *

In 1989/90 the drift continued.

But from somewhere we found £90,000 to sign John Francis and what a significant signing that was. I can still see him two years down the line scoring the winning goal at York to enable promotion out of the godforsaken Fourth Division. How did we find that sort of money? By paying it over the period of his contract so it wasn't all up front. I doubt we could have found it in one lump sum. We found his wages by offloading another player to Preston who had been fined a week's wages for something he did.

The one highlight had been a 5-0 win over Scunthorpe in an FA Cup replay and it was the game that Roger Eli announced his arrival as a striker when he scored two goals. I remember Roger because he was always selling gear from the back of his car, shell suits one year if I remember rightly. Sometime later when we played a couple of games in Russia, nobody had a bigger holdall than Roger stuffed with all kinds of food.

The Graham White saga took up a huge amount of our time and energy. He was a local businessman and boss of neighbouring club Colne Dynamoes, a club that had been formed for his schoolboy friends years earlier. With his financial backing it grew and grew, became hugely successful, won promotion after promotion until it was refused entry to the Conference league, from where they would have joined the Football League. It had the makings of a real fairy story as it became more and more successful, eventually employing professional players, several of whom were former Burnley players. He had ex-Burnley manager Harry Potts working for him as well as ex-player Paul Fletcher as commercial manager, and Burnley's future CEO. There was one problem, however. Their ground was deemed unfit for the Conference.

In November 1989 the board discussed a letter from Graham White, written to each of them individually, in which he explained he was keen to hire Turf Moor to play his Conference games if he was successful in gaining promotion. Pendle Council would not, reports say, play ball with him in the building of a new ground that would have held 10,000 fans. All this was to be the start of a drawn-out exercise that involved a legal libel action, Blackburn and Blackpool. I also seem to remember him saying he was willing to become a director of Burnley FC and made a verbal offer of £1 million to join, and he wanted to be club manager. Clearly this was unacceptable to the board.

We were not keen on him playing any Conference games at Turf Moor due to the poor state of the pitch, and the idea of doubling the number of games played would have presented huge problems. White made our discussions public, made some derogatory comments, and these we deemed libellous. We issued proceedings.

We did agree to meet White and discuss his requirements and what he was prepared to pay, but there could be no agreements until the libel case was resolved. He explained he would like a seven-year lease to play all his first-team games as he knew the Conference Ground Committee would likely not pass his Colne ground fit. It was an amicable meeting and a public statement said as much.

But then another complication arose when Blackpool asked us to ground share for at least 18 months so that they could redevelop their ground. Meanwhile, we put terms to Colne Dynamoes to share with them; negotiations re-opened and White offered to pay for a new pitch. However, complications struck at his end when the Conference wanted certain guarantees from him, which we believed to be financial, with the background suspicion on our part that Colne Dynamoes were too far financially extended. They seemed to be spending money like there was no tomorrow with a full-time squad, including some from the Brian Miller family. The average gate was just around 1,300 and it was rumoured that White was putting £10,000 a week in himself.

The next communication from them was that there would be no need to ground share with us. With everything at a full stop, and White saying that none of this was the fault of Burnley FC, plus an apology that ended the libel case and payment of our legal costs, the whole thing came to a close, as did Colne Dynamoes eventually. This to the relief, I suspect, of some members of the Burnley board who regarded White as an upstart and were indeed worried that their cooperation would help Colne overtake Burnley one day. There were stories of unpaid bills and wages so that our own hero Brian Miller, it was said, threatened to go and see White and sort out the money owed to his family. I never heard what the outcome of that was.

Somewhere along the line, chairman Bill Fox at Blackburn Rovers had said that ground sharing with Colne would help them financially. And nothing came of the suggestion about ground sharing from Blackpool. The time we had spent on all this had been extensive, for no end product. Life in a boardroom consists of many things that are time-wasting and this had been the perfect example. Meanwhile, the fans that knew nothing of all this energy and effort spent on fruitless matters continued to abuse and complain and criticise.

January 1990 saw the ignominy of losing to nine-man Rochdale at home. There have been some low spots in Burnley's history but this was one of the worst. For years Burnley fans had looked down their noses at lowly nearby Rochdale. And now, here we were on a level footing in the Fourth Division. Our fans had seen them as a joke club, apt enough since Tommy Cannon had been their chairman. Now it was their turn to laugh at us – oh, how are the mighty fallen, and all that.

Rochdale: the home of the Co-op and the birthplace of Gracie Fields, birthplace of Bill Oddie. Once, in distant times, a place of sweet meadows, streams and quiet agriculture. It became a sleepy market town and then, when the Industrial Revolution arrived, one of the first boomtowns, but living hell for any factory worker. In some ways it was like Burnley – street after street of substandard housing, both clubs struggling to exist. Re-election was an oft-used word in that neck of the woods.

Rochdale: where some fans had scarves that said 'better than Burnley', a club with pitiful gates and a primitive stadium almost falling to pieces, a club that forever propped up the rest of the division. It is not untrue to say that Rochdale fans hated Burnley to a level that was almost irrational. That dislike was fanned by the apocryphal story that we at Burnley in our panelled boardroom had argued with the Football League that the new demotion plan of 1987 was to catch out ‹the Rochdales' of the football world. I can't remember anyone actually saying those exact words, but Rochdale fans convinced themselves that this was true.

The Rochdale main stand had less than 1,000 seats; the roof collapsed with alarming regularity and Coventry once refused to play because the lights were so bad. Oh God, how were the mighty Burnley fallen and they at Rochdale resented us with our illustrious history, the remaining delusions of grandeur, the horror we felt, our expectation that this was just a temporary blip, and our clear feeling that we just didn't belong there. We could have said the same about so many clubs in the Fourth Division and felt just the same.

In truth, both clubs were now pygmies at this time, but whilst Rochdale knew that, we didn't, as we filled their ground and took it over, the gate receipts then keeping them ticking over for a few more weeks. The club's one distinguished claim to fame perhaps was that Alan Ball's father had once managed there, and Charles Hurst, father of Geoff Hurst had once been on their books. Not a lot of people know that. A few ex-Burnley players had made their way there in the twilight of their careers – Doug Winton, John Deary, Colin Waldron, Doug Collins and more recently Paul Weller. Mick Docherty had managed there for a year, a near-impossible task back then. Like all Rochdale managers he inevitably got the sack but his optimism and stickability earned him great kudos. Some people are heroes and gluttons for punishment, being a director at Rochdale for example.

It might have been just a few miles over the hill from Burnley but this was a trip to the dead as far as we were concerned. 'Just how is it possible we are here?' we asked. 'Just what are we doing here? How many more years of this must we endure?' We begrudged going to places like this and the distaste might well have showed on our faces. And how did they feel as we visited there, honouring them with our presence with 'we don't belong here' printed on our foreheads. But how good did they feel on the occasions they beat us? How sweet it was for them when they punctured our conceit. And how demeaning for us.

For seven seasons we had to play them and on the first occasion we beat them 3-0 and thought, 'Thanks very much. We won't be seeing you again. We won't be in this division long.' Alas, we were over a seven-year period, and in the return game that season we lost 1-0. What a wake-up call that was. Oh, the dejection we felt that here was the stark reality of the bottom division. In 1986/87 they thumped us 3-0 at Turf Moor and for good measure knocked us out of the League Cup. This was my first season as a director. 'It isn't meant to be like this,' I thought. The irony is that if Rochdale had beaten us in the return game that season, we would have been demoted. The Orient game would have been the performance of the last rites. To Rochdale might have fallen the honour of kicking us out. But they blew it and the win we had there late in the season was crucial. After that calamitous season, never again did we sink so near to such a dramatic exit. The games with Rochdale continued until 1992, but yet again they managed to kick our feet from under us when in 1990/91 they drew the penultimate game to end any hopes of automatic promotion.

Years later Rochdale had just lost 1-6 to Blackburn Rovers and the club were appealing for a new Desmond the Dragon inflatable mascot because the original had just run out of puff. Don't laugh. Remember how Burnley's claret-and-blue blimp flew away and vanished.

So: 1989/90 and Burnley 0-1 Rochdale at Turf Moor on a dreary January day. They were reduced to nine men and Rochdale fans exited the ground scarcely believing they had held out and won. Burnley fans (and directors) exited the ground utterly depressed. How on earth do you lose to a nine-man team? For Mark Hodkinson, a very fine Rochdale writer, it was one of the greatest moments of his life. He remembers Burnley fans hollering for the dismissal of the two Rochdale players and then Burnley raining shot after shot at the Rochdale goal. He remembers some Rochdale supporters crying with joy at the end at the absurdity of what they had seen. Burnley had already lost to Rochdale on the opening day of the season, 2-1. Now they had done the double.

We had just lost to another side whose supporters, for reasons no one really knows, also used to view us with distaste and dislike. This was Stockport County, who won 3-1. Five defeats in the space of six games and the knives were out for Frank Teasdale. Some idiot, or idiots, decided they would block the flue of the gas heating system of his ground-floor flat where he lived alone. Mercifully, it was seen and he was spared the possibility of being poisoned by carbon monoxide.

The police when they got involved classed it as attempted murder. The culprits were never found and what utter imbeciles they were. I had my differences with Frank, in fact there were many of them, but make no mistake he saved the club when it was down at its lowest financially. He was superb at keeping the creditors at bay during the worst of times. When he at last retired as chairman we formed a good and amicable relationship. His heart was in the right place and like all directors and chairman he was a Claret through and through. Frank in later years was able to appreciate and share the joke that younger fans came to believe his name was Teasdale Out, after they had seen old videos of games when it was a frequent and loud, prolonged chant.

Frustration and irritation on my part grew and at an end-of-season board meeting, I dropped a bombshell when I announced that the chairman should consider his position. I was utterly fed up of the lack of progress and initiatives on the part of too many others and, as the second-largest shareholder, was in a strong position. We needed more investment and new directors, I argued, new people to provide new funds. And: I myself was willing to invest new funds. I should have known (and probably did) that it had little support and would be kicked into the long grass. But there was agreement to discuss it again at a future meeting. It was a meeting that followed remarkably quickly. It was clear that the chairman had no intention of stepping down and he announced that he would put forward a 'grand plan' to take the club forward. After yet another meeting nothing happened. There never ever was such a thing as a grand plan. Frank Teasdale's life was the club and no one was going to threaten to undermine his position. There would be no new directors, no new investment, and I was told I would not be able to buy more shares, with any available shares being split among the existing directors.

Impasse. There would be no real progress or improvements to the status quo, with me seen as the irritating troublemaker. Truly, this was a season to forget and, sadly, there was more to come.

CHAPTER FIVE

1990/91 A Bit of a Spat

ONE OF the great perks of being a director is being able to visit other clubs and enjoy their hospitality and see how they operate. Sometimes you learn things and sometimes you don't. Some clubs are a pleasure to visit, and others the absolute opposite. Remembering the spat we had at Scarborough is a reminder of this. But other clubs certainly spring to mind.

Hartlepool was where we were incensed at the behaviour of their chairman behind us when an Owen Coyle team was winning by the odd goal in a cup tie. The game was petering out and we were playing keep-ball, or 'game management' as they call it now. So, he's up behind us shouting abuse and calling us cheats. We turned round astonished and getting angrier and angrier with him. At the end of the game, we marched into the boardroom to confront him for his lack of etiquette, but he had disappeared. Mind you, it was in another game at Hartlepool that I was so fed up watching a dismal game from my seat – and I seem to think it was the game when Alastair Campbell brought Tony Blair – that I went down to stand by the dugouts. Jimmy Mullen took great exception, maybe because we were losing, and yelled at me with some prime language to clear off and stop spying on him.

Former director Chris Duckworth was involved in two stories. At Arsenal when we lost a cup game our boardroom table was labelled with a 'Burnley' card. The young lass waiting on us afterwards asked

Chris if he would like the card sign as a souvenir of the visit. She must have thought we were just a small town from the backwoods and this was a very special visit for us. Chris laughed, 'No, keep it, luv, for next year. You'll need it when we come back again.' And we did. We won the play-off final against Sheffield United and joined the Premier League. Mind you, Chris also nearly got us lynched years earlier at Bradford City. It was a time when they were really down and struggling and as we were about to win this game Chris was laughing at Bradford supporters around us. I had to tell him to shut up before they lynched us. They really were ready to leap over and have a real go at us but we got into the boardroom in record time.

West Ham were less than hospitable, or at least the supporters were when we went down there in the Prem and beat them 3-0 in their new stadium. It was memorable not just for that but also the dreadful crowd scenes when West Ham fans demonstrated against their board and club in their hundreds. They surrounded the directors' area, they got on to the pitch, they marched around the gangways; it was getting more and more serious. Then they started throwing coins at the West Ham directors. Some of those coins were coming in our direction too, which was funny in a way until Sonya Kilby, Barry's wife, stood up and yelled at them to stop with a loud, 'Hey, we're from Burnley!' Unfortunately, that had no effect seeing as we were winning at the time and the abuse hurled at her was less than polite, shall we say.

One positive visit was up to Glasgow Rangers at the time we were doing the new stands at Turf Moor. It was very much a fact-finding mission and one thing that impressed us was the standard of stewarding provided by Rock Steady. Ours at the time was not particularly satisfactory, our stewards being mostly local people, some of them more interested in watching the game than the crowds. When we got back it was one thing that I insisted on, that we must improve our stewarding now that we had these new stands with all the extra exits, stairs, concourses and gangways. So, we got Rock Steady in. Initially they were bussing teams down from Scotland until they got themselves established in the north of England with a base in Sheffield.

* * *

Two clubs spring to mind looking back to this season. Scarborough and Torquay. Neither provide the best of memories. I've already said what it was like visiting a place like Rochdale, and these two clubs were on a par with them. Ironic that both places as holiday resorts are very pleasant; Torquay is sometimes seen as the south-west answer to the Riviera, and Scarborough up in the north of England, on the east coast, a decent place with a nice harbour area. In days gone by, it was Yorkshire folks that went to Scarborough whilst Burnley folks trekked to places like Blackpool and Morecambe on the west coast. But their football teams and stadiums were anything but picturesque.

Scarborough had joined the Fourth Division in 1987 when Neil Warnock was manager and we crossed swords with Scarborough several times during our sojourn in the Fourth Division. Today they are Scarborough Athletic, run by supporters, having dropped from the Football League in 1999 with huge debts and then vanished completely in 2007. For some reason it always amused me that at one time their ground was called the McCain Stadium, funded by a frozen-chip tycoon. Perhaps this was the reason it was dubbed the Theatre of Chips by one supporter.

Anyway, in this particular season we actually beat them twice, 2-1 at Turf Moor early in the season and 1-0 at Scarborough, and it is the latter that provides one of my abiding memories. Their chairman then was a certain Geoffrey Richmond. He is perhaps better known as the chairman of Bradford City during a time when they were in the Premier League and were spending heavily. They ended up in administration and, to be fair to Richmond, he blamed himself entirely for what he described as six weeks of madness. He had also spent time as a boardroom adviser at Leeds United during their difficult years.

My confrontation with him at Scarborough, I seem to remember, was my first experience of a real set-to in a boardroom, with a humdinger of an argument. He had requested that the 7.30 kick-off time should be put back to eight o'clock. Our assistant manager at the time was Jimmy Mullen and he was immediately scornful and dismissive, suggesting that it was bad enough trying to keep players attentive and concentrated at the best of times before a match, without delaying the kick-off to eight o'clock. So, we turned down the Scarborough request.

Lo and behold, when we arrived for the game and looked through the programme, what did we find but a page of notes from Geoffrey Richmond grumbling at Burnley Football Club and the board of directors. We were incensed. 'SPECIAL APOLOGY' it began, in heavy, thick lettering, and went on:

> We have received numerous telephone calls from Burnley supporters during the course of the last week asking us to have an eight o'clock kick-off time to enable them to attend tonight's match. Burnley fans have pointed out that an 8 o'clock kick-off would allow many of them to attend, whereas a 7:30 kick-off would not allow them sufficient time from finishing work to arrive in Scarborough for kick-off time.
>
> We promised all the fans who took the trouble to ring up that we would do all that we could to change the kick-off from 7:30 to 8 o'clock.
>
> The Scarborough police agreed to an 8 o'clock kick-off. The Football League had no objections. But unfortunately, Burnley Football Club refused, and when pressed said that it was a decision by the Burnley board of directors.
>
> I find great difficulty in understanding this refusal. I apologise to all those Burnley fans who would have been here tonight who will miss this important match, but I do think that it is important that the record be set straight and

that the Burnley fans should know where the responsibility lies. *(Geoffrey Richmond Chairman)*

I was livid, and not the only one, when we saw these programme notes as we picked up a programme in the boardroom at Scarborough. I seem to remember I was first into the room and a furious row erupted. Richmond's wife suggested that I should be ejected. Other Burnley directors arrived, to which they suggested that if that was the case they would leave as well. It was suggested to him in no uncertain terms that the poor publicity that would fall on Scarborough the next day would not do their PR any good. Common sense prevailed and tempers cooled. We won the game 1-0 with a John Francis goal. It felt rather good. The boardroom afterwards was quiet, perhaps because we had won.

The next game we played there later in the year was hugely significant for us, Frank Casper and Jimmy Mullen. But we shall save that story for the next chapter.

In the Rumbelows Cup there was a meeting with Brian Clough and Nottingham Forest. After a Stuart Pearce tackle, one of our players, David Hamilton, was badly injured and we seethed afterwards. Brian Clough would have none of it and, in fact, when our criticisms were made public, he threatened legal action. It came to nothing but left us with a player whose career was as good as ruined. When it came to us wanting to sign one of his players, Andy Marriott, a superb goalkeeper, it came to nothing after the loan spell, when Brian wanted the proverbial brown envelope to be exchanged at a convenient motorway service station. It was kept well quiet at the time, but fans today may be interested to hear that this is why he was never signed permanently.

A game to remember was versus Manchester City in the FA Cup third round, when we played really well but lost 1-0 at home. Twenty thousand fans might make for a financial windfall, you might think. But no. Back in those days the gate was shared 50-50 and a percentage also went to the FA.

Four games to go and third in four automatic promotion places. Eighteen thousand vs Blackpool at Turf Moor, a 2-0 win and the directors began to really think that automatic promotion was possible. But no, there was a poor defeat at Maidstone. Funnily enough the game was played at Dartford, which seemed no better than Maidstone. But Dartford I knew well, having been born at Gravesend just a few miles down the road and where my grandfather took me to games in the Southern League. A player I used to see was Jimmy Logie, a Scottish international who was being paid £25 a match. Jimmy died in 1984 and by then was reduced to selling newspapers from his stand in Trafalgar Square, London. How times change. Today he would be a millionaire, set up for life.

All this was back in the days when football was played on Christmas Day and the next game was on Boxing Day, the day after. I went to two such games, one at Gravesend and the next at Dartford when the referee abandoned the game because of the number of players he had sent off. Today, managers talk about rest time between games, overworked players and burnout. They have no idea of what football was once like. Player welfare is the hot topic – to a degree rightly so, since the top footballers are supreme athletes, much more so than many years ago. Today there are counsellors, psychologists, nutritionists, dieticians, personal chefs, physiotherapists; the top players have their every need taken care of. A top tennis player can play two five-hour games in the space of three days and no fuss is made. For a footballer, two games in three days or even two games a week is seen as too demanding. Plus, they play on perfect pitches rather than the strength-sapping mud of yesteryear.

Disappointingly we had to settle for the play-offs with Torquay. You probably could not find a quainter little ground in the whole of the UK. In theory anyone can walk across the pitch at any time because when the land was bequeathed to the council, it was deemed it should be open for recreation at any time to the public. It's a good job our fans didn't know that at the time of the game when we were losing 2-0. The main stand had been purloined from Buckfastleigh

Racecourse ten miles away. Where once it saw thoroughbreds, it now saw not quite the opposite, but almost. The ground was surrounded by neat little streets of houses and what a hospitable homely place it was. Some of our supporters had been to the social club at the ground the night before the game where the chairman paid for their drinks and sausage sandwiches. Alas I wasn't there but was at Turf Moor supervising the big TV screen for home fans to watch the game. It was a huge, heavy thing that had to be craned over the Cricket Field Stand roof. The picture was poor and it made us very little money after the costs, and the share of attendance money we had to give to Torquay and the Football League.

Roger Eli wrote about the game at Torquay, when we lost 2-0, in his book *Thanks for the Memories*. Promotion hopes were dashed where it was a game of nasty challenges and bad feeling. Close-ups of manager Frank Casper showed him to be really unwell. In Roger's book, Frank explained that it was a bad reaction to medication he was on at the time. To this day Roger wonders if they were ever in the right state of mind for the game, with Casper so indisposed and Mullen doing little to remedy the situation. Frank looked ill, he wrote, but by half-time looked a whole lot better. They played badly but had no idea why they were so poor. During the whole of the journey home, they felt utterly miserable.

The game at Turf Moor was an anticlimax, even with a 1-0 win and the feeling afterwards of just how did we not score more? The team gave everything but it was to be another year in Division Four. To make it worse, it was the game when some bright spark from Blackburn hired a plane to fly over Turf Moor bearing a derogatory message. We followed the golden rule of all boardrooms: say nothing for 24 hours. Let tempers cool and grumbles subside. It doesn't always work.

But at the next board meeting we did decide that discipline at the club had to be tightened. The players were accordingly instructed that any player booked would be fined, but instead of the money going into a players' pool for use later in the year at Christmas parties or end-of-season events, it would come back to the club. It did not go down well. Despite the disappointing end to the season, Frank Casper was awarded a new one-year contract at £25,000 a year with a promotion bonus of £10,000. And so we awaited the next season with little idea of what it might bring, more in hope than expectation.

Meanwhile, in 1990, the Taylor Report on stadiums was published. It was to have a huge impact on us and football as a whole. It was finally published in response to the Hillsborough disaster that resulted in 97 deaths and over 700 injuries. The main recommendation was in connection with standing and it had to be abolished by 1994, with all grounds expected to be all-seater by then. This meant that two areas at Turf Moor were affected. Whilst stating that standing was not intrinsically unsafe, the government decided that it was. Other things affected were the sale of alcohol and where from, crush barriers, fencing and prices. In all there were 76 recommendations with the government eventually easing the need for lower-division clubs to become all-seater by the stated date. It was from this report that it became clear that there needed to be drastic changes at Turf Moor.

The impact on clubs like Burnley was immediate with the need now for safety certificates issued by Lancashire County Council to be absolutely bang up to date. Without this there was no way that any ground could be opened up to spectators. It was my name on that certificate and my responsibility, with me in court facing charges in the event of any incidents or disasters. My name was on it until 2020. If you'd let it, you could have had sleepless nights. My spotless record went for a Burton when the parachutist landed on the Cricket Field Stand roof.

We knew that complying with the report would cost the club a lot of money, and police charges didn't help, with a charge of £39 an hour for each one on duty on a matchday with a minimum charge of five hours. In terms of the report and its implications, we now knew we had some serious thinking to get down to about what to do. Two of the biggest stands were affected and would need seating.

It would be me that sorted it, and not without a few battles.

CHAPTER SIX

1991/92 Light at the End of the Tunnel

BY NOW I had gotten rid of the responsibility for catering and functions, a merciful release. I can boil an egg but not much else and here was I in charge of catering. But I had to take up another role when I was nominated to go on a resuscitation and emergency first-aid course. Me of all people, in charge of resuscitation and first aid. Fortunately, I suffered no embarrassment on the course or ever had to carry out emergency resuscitation, although I do recall the story of one bloke on such a course who, during a bandaging exercise, bandaged his patient's leg to the chair he was sitting on. Neither he nor the guinea pig knew, of course, until he tried to stand up, took a step forward and fell flat on his face with the chair on top of him.

One big disappointment was being unable to sign Nigerian international Folrunso Okenia, who had played in the Africa Cup and was a decent player, because of work-permit problems. This, by the way, was at a time when racial abuse at football games was widespread.

I doubt that any season can have two games that contrasted more than those away at Scarborough and then York City at the very end of the season.

It all began with a trip to Russia, of all places. Doc Iven, a fellow director who had been at the club since time began, had actually fled from Russia as a boy and he refused to go back. He still spoke Russian. The trip was brought about via the head of languages in the department at Liverpool University. His Russian was good, so he came with us as interpreter. I still wonder if we were the poor man's alternative to Liverpool or Everton. The funding was a simple one; the Russian teams would fund us – hotel, team bus and pocket money. Back in those days the PFA had an agreed rate of money to be paid to staff and players on overseas trips. Even the four directors got spending money, but, alas, we had to pay for the privilege of going: £500, a sum not to be sneezed at back in those days. If you were a foreign visitor, you could stay in what were classified as international hotels and pay in hard currency like dollars, pounds or marks. But because we were being funded by the Russian clubs we were booked into local hotels of a different, lower standard altogether. If a Russian club came to us, we would fund them in the same way, the difference being we had decent shops in which they could spend their money. Plus, they stayed in far better hotels.

On the outward journey we were halfway down the runway taking off when suddenly the plane screeched to a halt and had to return to the terminal. What a great start that was as we missed the connecting flight in Moscow. Waiting around in the airport lounge in Moscow, we'd gathered to wait for the flight to Stavropol. Outside it was pitch dark and raining, taking gloom to a new level. Russia in the early 90s, not the jolliest of places. Suddenly, as we sat there thoroughly fed up and some of us nodding off, a voice called out, asking for two volunteers. Joe Jakub got up and grabbed someone to go with him. This is Russia, we thought; should we be worried? No, just amused, for as we boarded the next flight, the two of them were loading all our luggage.

The plane was old and creaky; a very slow turbo-prop. This will be a three-hour flight, we were told, but three and a half hours later we were still flying. It was me that was delegated to visit the cockpit and ask, 'Where the hell are we and how much further?' To my astonishment there were five people crammed in there. In poor English one of them told me there was still another two hours to go.

Tired and worn out, we landed in darkness to find power cuts. The hotel was awful and my room was on a floor that was being renovated, with building gear everywhere. The players were up in arms at the state of the place and were ready to head straight back home (assuming there had been a plane available) but Frank Teasdale managed to talk them round. It helped that it was also a beautiful, sunny morning.

There was a KGB officer with us all the time. We named him Vodka the Lodger and when the players somehow managed to steal his pistol there was uproar. The poor bloke must have been terrified he'd be sent to the nearest gulag in disgrace if it wasn't found. Yes, he retrieved it; and he and the directors were mighty relieved. Having travelled abroad a bit and done my homework I knew there'd be shortages and it would be a good idea to take jeans to trade and food for myself. The latter would make up for what was on offer in the hotel. For some odd reason, my room had a huge fridge, one of the biggest I'd ever seen. It was where the players kept the food that they had brought.

We played two games and after one of them everyone stayed behind, including us, and watched the draw for a grand raffle where the prize was a car. When it was a police officer that won and the crowd saw him coming down the steps to claim it, there was a near riot. Simple programmes had been printed for each game but the picture was not us; it was the 1959/60 title team – Jimmy McIlroy, Adamson and Pointer and all the rest.

The first game in Stavropol was a 1-1 draw on a pitch that was far from good and we had to clear broken glass from one of the goalmouths. So too was the second, in Kislovodsk, another long journey away up in the mountains, and this too was a 1-1 draw. The road to the ground was so steep. The battered old coach in which we bumped and rattled round on dreadful roads would not make it, so all of us got out and tramped up the hill. The other route was by a dodgy-looking cable car. None of us had any intention of using it.

The hotel in Kislovodsk turned out to be part of the Russian Olympic summer training camp and, being there for a few days, we had use of the pool and facilities after the Russian team divers had finished their training. It was a joy to watch. We would normally watch them for an hour or so before it was our turn. The abiding memory is of the high-dive board; in fact, the very high-dive board. The players were betting who would be brave enough to get up there and dive in, with Jimmy Mullen betting that he would certainly do it. I think it was Joe Jakub who took up the challenge, with our physio Jimmy Holland shouting at the pair of them to get back down and not be so stupid. The players, of course, happily egged them on. Jakub was first. He seemed OK and climbed out, not letting on that he had hurt his shoulder and then missed the start of the season. Jimmy Mullen was next. Now, unfortunately, the week before, he had had the snip, the gentleman's operation that does leave you in some discomfort for a while. In he jumped. He had to be carried out. He should have listened to Jimmy Holland. Joe Jakub was involved in more merriment when we met up with the Russian women's basketball team. Joe, who was 5ft 5ins, stood next to one of the girls who must have been nearly 7ft tall. We could only stare and grin.

All of us had pockets full of roubles but there was simply nothing to spend it on. Russia at this time was beset by all kinds of shortages, but at last we found a shop with huge queues outside. Bernard Rothwell went in and came out quite beside himself. It was a state-controlled shop of the kind that every now and then was fully stocked with some product that might just have arrived. Normally the shelves were empty, but with no warning, stocks of something would arrive and on this occasion the shelves were filled with toilet plungers. Another week it might be tins of paint or shoes and, if they were lucky, food. But Bernard ran the James Hargreaves plumbing merchants back in Burnley and was hell-bent on buying up all the plungers and shipping them back to Burnley in a huge container because they were so cheap. I managed to talk him out of it.

After the second and final game in Kislovodsk there was a grand celebratory dinner in a very grand dacha, one of the fine country houses that wealthy Russians used to own before the state took over their lives. Mind you, today, wealthy politicians now inhabit them. The food this time was endless. Life in Russia was clearly good if you were one of the lucky ones that ran the country. The plane that took us back to Moscow, we were told, was the official Stavropol plane. Once in our seats we looked on in astonishment as more and more people got on until it was standing room only. The word backhanders sprang to mind. But when crates of chickens were brought on and stacked up down the front of the plane we really did wonder what kind of world we had landed in.

On our final day in Moscow, we wandered round for a while and wondered what we could do with the roubles we had left. Vodka the Lodger was sure we'd give them all to him but instead we gave them to a little old lady, clearly impoverished, who was collecting empty bottles. She took them from us, in fact almost snatched them, and then ran off as fast as she could in case Vodka the Lodger took them from her and confiscated them.

The season drifted along until it was time for Scarborough again. What was it about that place? It witnessed one of the worst-ever Burnley performances, after which Frank Casper called it a day. Roger Eli, in his book *Thanks for the Memories*, remembered it vividly. It was a desperate game that was a 3-1 defeat on a wild, wet and windy day. Frank Casper described it afterwards as just 'horrible'. It was truly appalling and this despite Scarborough being reduced to ten men. How different it might have been if Roger Eli had not been pulled back as he burst through and nearly had his shirt ripped off. Chance gone; the foul was successful. After this the play got worse and worse, the howls of abuse became louder and louder from the Burnley fans. The players said afterwards that it affected them badly; the negativity was draining. The longer the game went on, you could see that the Burnley players wanted only to get back in the dressing room and a warm bath.

I was not at this game, being in Singapore on business, but heard the result on the BBC World Service and with the time difference went to bed immediately thoroughly depressed. I could well imagine the surprise on Geoffrey Richmond's face afterwards as he enjoyed the result. What's that old saying? What goes round, comes round.

I remembered Doc Iven's old advice to me – 'In this game, you need to learn how to lose as well as win.' Never a truer word.

I'm sure that the players afterwards sat numbed in the dressing room, depressed at the scoreline and at how badly they had played. They said that they could hear the abuse continuing as the fans left the stadium, every bit of it: the catcalls, the shouts and the insults. The fans went home just so angry at this capitulation, bitter and furious at the prospect of yet another season in the Fourth Division. It wasn't just the players that were subjected to this tirade of anger. It was also the directors, the chairman and the manager. All of us.

And yet it was a turning point in the season. Frank Casper called the players together at Gawthorpe the next day and quietly and briefly told them that was it, he was leaving. There was no great long speech, just something short and dignified but emotional. Football can be a cruel and heartless business, taking its toll on mind and health. The pressure of constant criticism and displeasure from the fans brings a pressure that is sometimes unbearable. He'd had enough. The previous season he'd got to 79 points and that in any other season would have been an automatic promotion. It was sod's law for Frank that this was the occasion that it wasn't enough; the next club above had 80 points. You could torture yourself looking at games we should have won, or points we let slip, when a defeat should have been a draw. Such is football. Then there had been the debacle of the play-off game at Torquay. He had clearly looked unwell at that game. But astonishingly his resignation was to be the start of something extraordinary. A strange thing happened. With the same players, Mullen began to win games, and win again, and keep on winning.

The plan was to interview other candidates for the vacant post but what surprised us all was the success that Jimmy had almost overnight. First game was a 2-0 win, second game an astonishing 6-2 win away at Wrexham and what made that all the more special was a hat-trick from one of our own young lads, Graham Lancashire, who had come up through the youth ranks. Going home that night on the coach after that was a great journey. And Wrexham were such a good club as well, with a very friendly board and chairman. Let's just say they liked their whisky, but, while they had a few nips to get over the result, we had a few to celebrate.

By the time the board met to discuss the manager situation, he had played two and won two and the players clearly wanted him to stay. Nevertheless, we interviewed two other candidates, Frank Stapleton as player-manager and Don McKay. Jimmy's confidence and cheerful disposition won the day and we let him know by telephone that he had the job. His appointment was the start of something extraordinary. Just sometimes, directors do get decisions right.

What praise the club and fans got for their performance in a cup replay at Derby. After the game, even though we had lost, the fans stayed to chant and sing and it went on and on until the Derby staff began to worry that they were never going to go home. It reached the national press and became a lead story that this was what football was all about. We had to ask Jimmy to leave the dressing room and go out and acknowledge this support, such was its passion and intensity. Some things in football you never forget, and this was one of them.

There are plenty of accounts of the game at York, when we won the title in several other Burnley books. The chairman of York City, when we finally left the directors' box and the fans on the pitch, presented us with a case of champagne. Let's just say that a good time was had by all to celebrate our last night in the old Fourth Division.

But the significance of the date when it was actually played relates to a real tragedy that took place at the club. On 9 March 1992 Ben Lee died. During the week there had been an under-21 international match at the Turf playing with a new type of ball. One of the balls ended up on the Longside roof and Ben, one of our youth team, went up later to retrieve it. It was a tragic decision, when he fell through the roof. The match at York the next night was postponed. I always remember Ben because the season before I had been asked to meet his parents for them to sign his YTS papers. I've said before, football gives you lasting memories. Some good, some bad and others just terribly sad, and this was one of them.

Ironically that same day I had been asked to go on a scouting mission. Good Lord, what would Brian Clough have said about that? Would I take in the Stockport versus Cambridge game? A very unusual request for a manager to make. I came back with a rave review about one of the players, Dion Dublin, but he went on to sign for Manchester United eventually, not Burnley. Who says I don't know my football?

And some things years later are just plain amusing, although maybe not at the time. Scarborough were due at Turf Moor for the April return game and the normal arrangement was that we gave the visitors complimentary tickets for the directors' box. In those days we had very posh white seats that had been installed by Bob Lord, rather like armchairs, and 12 complimentary tickets for visitors in red ones at the front that were not quite so luxurious. The chairman of any club always sat in one of the white seats. Visitors always managed to compliment us on the comfort of these seats, although years earlier the Cobbold Brothers from Ipswich, no great fans of Bob Lord, had commented on their ostentatious vulgarity. It was always the custom to advise the visiting club as to who should use which seats so that there would be no embarrassment. Directors and their partners always got the best white seats. What could go wrong?

Mr Geoffrey Richmond, the Scarborough chairman, was due. For whatever reason, and I really have no idea whether it was a mix-up on our part or the Scarborough people could not read, Mr Richmond ended up in an inferior red seat. Bearing in mind all that had gone on before between the two clubs, you could have forgiven Mr Richmond and his good lady for thinking that we had put him in the red seats as a deliberate snub. Far from it. It was a genuine mistake, but by whom we have no idea to this day. Frank Teasdale, our own chairman, was a dab hand at smoothing troubled waters and was always ready with a bunch of flowers when the occasion arose. Mrs Richmond was presented with a bouquet after the game by way of an apology. It was a 1-1 draw. Probably the best thing that could have happened, I suppose.

CHAPTER SEVEN

1992/93 and 1993/94 Back to Wembley

THERE HAD been a couple of friendlies, one against Ajax in May and one against Dynamo Moscow in August. Ajax had won the UEFA Cup just seven days earlier and had several big names in the side, including Dennis Bergkamp, goalkeeper Edwin van der Sar, and Frank de Boer. At the AGM later in the year, Frank Teasdale was proud to mention the visit, as we all were, but neglected to mention the slightly embarrassing moment that the Ajax manager thought that Frank was the commissionaire. He was wearing his very official-looking club blazer, with the club badge on the top pocket and bits of gold braid here and there. When Frank held out his hand to shake it and welcome them all, the manager handed him his bags. It was a priceless moment.

The visit of Dynamo Moscow was memorable for the trip that the players made to our local Marks and Spencer's. During their stay we put them up in the local Endsleigh Insurance training centre, which was in Burnley at that time, before it moved to Cheltenham. The custom was to present a visiting team with spending money that they could use in the local shops. Being Russian in the early 90s, they were totally unused to going in shops like Marks and Spencer where there was such a range of goods on offer. They were well and truly dazzled. Unfortunately, they thought they could just wander round, pick out the items they wanted and just walk out with them, largely because back home you paid at a counter, and in M&S the counters were not that obvious. We had to round them all up, take them back in and explain that they actually had to pay. There was much confusion, and there were apologies all round, not the least of which were to M&S management. Fortunately, we kept it all out of the press, something that today would be impossible, and there was no diplomatic incident.

During September of 1992 the chairman and myself began the long process of getting Turf Moor to be an all-seater stadium when we met with the Football Trust and their chairman and secretary. It was the beginning of a long, hard road; it would cause arguments, differences and a huge workload for me. Just getting planning permission was an arduous process, with meetings and presentations to shareholders and a separate one for local residents who were far from happy at the proposed size of these buildings. When they went up, TV reception went haywire and this was something no one had foreseen. The letters of complaint came in like an avalanche because for about three months there was no TV signal to many homes around the ground. 'We can't watch *Coronation Street*,' was one of them. As a goodwill gesture we added a TV repeater station to one of the stands at our expense. We were under no legal obligation at all to do this; in fact, there was a London legal case where some new building went up, TV reception went haywire, the building owners were taken to court, but the residents lost. But there was no way we wanted to lose all the goodwill of local people.

Still, the letters of complaint flooded in to the local press, with many local people around the ground writing to say that whilst they were prepared on matchdays to put up with crowds, noise, litter, bad behaviour and the like, the loss of TV pictures and *Emmerdale* was the last straw. Pictures now consisted of snow and candy stripes. The local MP at the time, Peter Pike, also got a pile of mail about it. Despite the club putting up the new repeater system, residents still had to pay for their own new aerial in some cases and tuning. It was a big problem.

At pre-building point, chairman Frank Teasdale was getting distinctly cold feet because we knew by now that the grants would only cover half of the costs. His concern was cash flow. 'Just how are we going to pay for all this?' he would repeat. I battled on and got the green light and the development was approved by Burnley Council in February 1993.

Chasing money was the name of the game for me and it was a Sports Council grant that enabled the setting up of an artificial pitch at Gawthorpe. This was my first major achievement and success at the club and I can assure you, you feel damned good when you do something like this.

The main sponsors at this time were Endsleigh, the insurance people, with their name on our shirts for a number of years. It was good to have such a long-standing sponsor, but there was also a drawback. Sponsors receive benefits at the clubs they support but whilst our commercial director, Bob Blakeborough, was always pressing Endsleigh hard for more money, they always had a back door to the chairman via the friendship between their MD, Mike Naylor, and our chairman, Frank Teasdale. Mike Naylor had always supported the club financially in times of need but the relationship between club and Endsleigh did result in some heated boardroom discussions, with Endsleigh often wanting more from us in return for their sponsorship, and Frank in the middle in a difficult position. Sadly, Mike was killed in a road accident in France and soon after we ended the relationship with Endsleigh.

Suffice it to say precious little else happened and Burnley finished 13th in the table in the Second Division following the promotion the season before. In the trade they call it consolidation and if Burnley fans feared that the next season would be more of the same, there were even better times to come. Jimmy Mullen's Claret and Blue Army was destined for another triumph.

* * *

Despite a very average away record we inched towards a play-off place in 1993/94. Sixth place saw us face Plymouth Argyle, managed by Peter Shilton, no less, and the first leg was a 0-0 draw at Turf Moor.

To say Plymouth were rough is an understatement and they had a man sent off. We seethed in the boardroom afterwards but tried to make sure we were restrained and respectful when we went down to Plymouth, despite being incensed at the way they took victory for granted in this game. I have to say, I was not particularly restrained and had words with their chairman about their discourteous attitude to us and the assumption they were on the way to Wembley. Their chairman was Dan McCauley and only passed away, aged 84, in 2020. We had become quite good friends, despite the spat at Plymouth. He told me one story that he used to get a lift on a matchday to the ground from a friend who was a funeral director, who one day turned up in a hearse to collect him. In the back was a coffin, which Dan assumed was empty but was never too sure. Years later Dan would ring me up for advice about a manager they were interested in. I think I said 'don't touch him', but will refrain from saying who it was.

One of our players, Ted McMinn, was kicked mercilessly at Turf Moor and their gamesmanship had been appalling. It was to the great credit of our supporters on the night that there was no trouble. With that result Plymouth thought they were in the final at Wembley already. You could see it in their directors' smug faces. Their thousands of travelling fans were beside themselves with satisfaction. Jimmy Mullen really did put copies of press cuttings up on the dressing-room walls at Plymouth before the game. They were as good as a team talk.

After the game at Plymouth, of course we took delight in their boardroom of reminding them who was going to Wembley. It was poor manners on our part but who could blame us. To make it even better there was a representative to hand us our share of the tickets for Wembley. We accepted them gleefully and then one of the great pleasures of the journey home was meeting our fans at various motorway service stations. It was one of the best-ever long-distance coach drives.

The second leg down at Plymouth was a win for us, but it was a game marred by blatant, raw, crude racism. It still leaves a bitter taste. I am indebted to Julian Booth for allowing me to dip into his memories of the game that he wrote for the *London Clarets* magazine.

This was one of the most traumatic, memorable, nail-biting, exciting games I have ever seen and will live in my memory for a very long time. At Burnley the Plymouth fans had sung 'We're better than you with ten men,' and had finished ahead of Burnley by 12 points. Our away record was dreadful and by the time the second leg came, they had booked every available coach in the west country. As far as they were concerned it was a foregone conclusion with the tannoy announcement before the game telling fans where to get their tickets the next day.

Something like 2,000 fans were in the away end and bearing in mind the form of the two teams few were expecting the win that was to come. Burnley had won just one of five and had been thrashed at Exeter. There had only been four away wins all season so that when Plymouth went 1-0 up as a brilliant right foot strike from a free kick found the top corner, we feared the inevitable.

But over the next quarter of an hour Burnley upped their level and improved. The behaviour of the Plymouth fans did not as they directed the most offensive chants towards Super Johnny Francis I have ever heard, every time he touched the ball. These idiots seem to forget the colour of their own striker who had just given them the lead. It was disgraceful and an act that was to bring shame to the Devon side but a huge grin to the face of John Francis by the end of the game.

Burnley by now were making a fight of the game but Plymouth continued to push forward looking for the second goal to kill off the game but then the ball fell to the feet of Inchy, Adrian Heath. His first-time ball down the centre of Home Park found the run of Francis perfectly. His pace was electric as he ran past the hopeless defenders as if they weren't there and stroked the ball past the advancing keeper and into the net. He stood there in the middle of the pitch dancing up and down mimicking the obscene monkey chants from the Plymouth fans. As the celebrations were dying down exactly the same happened again, the defence-splitting ball coming from Heath and again Francis ran at the defence with no fear as they fell over in his wake. He evaded the last desperate attempt to stop him and smashed the ball past the helpless Nicholls. There was delirium on the terraces.

I'm not sure what Peter Shilton said to his team at half-time, because they never really appeared for the second half. They produced one of the most abject performances I've ever seen from a team on the verge of a Wembley appearance. As the minutes ticked by and Burnley confidence grew, the sweet song 'you're better with ten men' began to ring across the ground. Except this time, it was the Burnley end singing.

Warren Joyce had come in for his fair share of stick in both games. He started the second match warm-up with Mark Leather's 'Judas' training top as a message to the home fans as to why he had left the Devon side earlier in the summer. On 80 minutes he finally got his revenge. Ted McMinn, Tinman, attacked down the right, turned three defenders inside out, before reaching the touchline and laying the ball back for Joyce, who gleefully tapped the ball home and sent us all to Wembley. The celebrations started; a conga line began to work its way round the terraces. The final whistle blew. It was a glorious performance that night.

Julian was one of the 2,000 that had enjoyed one of those great Burnley nights. The players were ecstatic and shook the hands of Burnley fans who were hanging over the perimeter fencing. They sang their songs; some had managed to get on to the pitch. And we the directors were as jubilant as they were. Directors are fans as well.

The play-off final was on Sunday, 29 May and it was agreed that directors would go on the team coach, with directors' wives on a second coach to a different hotel on the Saturday. Their hotel, by all accounts, was rather like *Fawlty Towers* so that when secretary Mark Blackbourne, who had travelled with them, made sure they had all checked in, he then disappeared as quickly as he could before the complaints came his way. My wife still goes on about it to this day every time that match is mentioned. No one has ever owned up to making the booking. For us, directors and players, it was a relaxing journey down, despite the enormity of the game the next day that could make or break the season. Our hotel was close to Wembley, the evening meal was most enjoyable, but tension and atmosphere was beginning to build.

To break that tension, the next morning the directors took a walk around the hotel gardens; conversation was light-hearted, on anything but the match. The tension was certainly broken by a simple thing. Director David Iven decided to have a sit down on one of the garden chairs without noticing the large puddle that filled the saucer-shaped seat. Overnight rain had filled it so that when he sat down, within a few seconds he stood up groaning 'oh no' loudly and with very wet trousers. His misfortune relaxed us, although maybe not him, as we headed back to get the trousers dried off. The players were in there having their pre-match meal. Ours was at Wembley – one of the perks of being a director, I suppose. All of us, directors and players, travelled in the one coach to Wembley, still the old one, and I will never forget the legions of Burnley fans clearly outnumbering those from Stockport. It's a cliché, I know, but it was just a sea of claret and blue.

Burnley won the game 2-1. Stockport were 1-0 up in minutes but let themselves down with two players sent off. Even so, they had us chewing our fingernails for much of the game. The best accounts of the game are in the Tim Quelch book *From Orient to the Emirates*.

Burnley's fans outnumbered Stockport's by at least four to one and the Burnley end was a mass of flags, banners and colour. David Elleray was the referee, a public-school headmaster, and refereed like it; a good referee who stood no nonsense. Our lad Ted McMinn certainly knew how to wind players up so that when Stockport's Michael Wallace spat at him, Elleray sent him off. Then they had a second player, Beaumont, sent off in the second half for stamping on Les Thompson. The Stockport players hadn't finished letting themselves down and were clearly upset at the refereeing and the result. Our coach was parked inside the stadium near the dressing rooms and got a real kicking and the result was several thousand pounds' worth of damages. We sent the bill to Stockport and I have always hoped it was the players that were made to pay for it. Perhaps the saddest thing of the day was seeing John Francis limping off the Wembley pitch very soon after kick-off, the result of treatment he had received in the game at Plymouth. Sadly, it was pretty much the end of his career at Burnley.

Success: we had done it, the celebrations in the evening were long and loud, all of us together this time and a night to let our hair down before the job of planning for the new season. And we knew there would be a lot to do to be ready for life in the higher division.

Board meetings during the year had covered a huge range of subjects. We'd signed David Eyres from Blackpool, in the days when there were no agents creaming off the millions they do today. It was a time when the PFA acted for the player and seemed to work so much better with none of the manoeuvring to get players a big payday. How much simpler life was back then. At the beginning of the season Oldham wanted a friendly and it reminded me of a first meeting with Joe Royle years earlier – it might even have been in the late 60s. We were on holiday in Elba and I was swimming when Joe Royle asked Sylvia if she would kindly look after the Royle clothes whilst they too had a dip. She had no idea who this was so when I came out to dry off, I had to ask her, 'Have you no idea who that is?' He was quite famous at the time as a player. Anyway, here we were in

1993 and he swears blind he remembered when I reminded him at a reserve game. Back then in the 60s you couldn't take piles of money abroad and there was, if I remember rightly, a £50 limit on what you could take overseas because of the controls.

The details of running a football club are plentiful. Arguments with Endsleigh Insurance continued about their terms but we continued the deal for another year. HMRC investigated our finances as part of a routine sweep of many clubs. Give Frank Teasdale credit: he ran a tight ship with everything above board and no shady corners. Lord knows what they would have uncovered in the Bob Lord days. But well done to Bob Lord for getting a right of way signed and sealed to the training ground at Gawthorpe, using the shared drive to Towneley Hall. It was a Lancashire County Council responsibility to maintain it. This would surface years later, when Barnfield upgraded the Gawthorpe training complex. There were issues with the TV gantry, floodlight towers and health issues in the dressing rooms. As ever there were player contracts to deal with, player discipline – one player had been sent off three times. We were fed up of postponed games because of frozen pitches so we invested in pitch covers. Today, games are more likely to be postponed if it's the public areas around the ground that are frozen, pathways and car parks. The pitch might well be perfect but the police can still insist that a match is called off if access is made dangerous by ice and snow. All we could do was make sure that we were able to call in a snowplough and gritters if needed. Calling off a match at short notice is hugely costly.

Taylor Woodrow was keen to be involved in ground redevelopment, in fact the whole of the ground, not just the two stands that we wanted to replace but as ever there were problems with cooperation from the cricket club behind one of the stands. Taylor Woodrow had themselves contacted the cricket club without informing us. They envisaged a shopping development but on this the town council were not keen as they wanted to keep all retail development in the town centre. I thought it was short-sighted and still do. So, yet another plan to redevelop the ground on a grand scale failed. Bob Lord's plan had been the first and Brendan Flood much later would submit another that involved buying the cricket ground. Whilst Taylor Woodrow was trying to get involved with us, Paul Fletcher, our ex-centre-forward, was involved in building a new ground for Huddersfield Town, so off we went to see what he was doing and to see if we could pick up any ideas. MP Peter Pike and members of the town council came with us. It was important that the council were supportive of our own building plans.

Perhaps the most fanciful item ever to be discussed at a board meeting was the proposed player trip to Hawaii to be sponsored by Endsleigh if we ever won promotion again. We actually did, but there was no trip to Hawaii. In the summer of 1994, we signed Mark Winstanley, something I mention only because he would be one of the four players that Stan Ternent would later dispense with so publicly. He was an interesting character because his wife was a keen horsewoman and I heard that Mark's job at home was to look after the horse, or horses (I never did find out if they had more than one). There were big arguments around the boardroom table about how much to increase admission and season-ticket prices, plus how to fit in all the extra people who wanted corporate facilities, or wanted to be vice-presidents or members of the 100 club.

Taylor Woodrow sent me a beautifully produced brochure of all their plans. It made me all the more determined to get these new stands built with all the extra facilities. But sadly, it would not be Taylor Woodrow and a new shopping centre.

CHAPTER EIGHT

1994/95 Oh Dear and Back Down We Go

THE SUMMER had been a whirlwind of things to sort out and we hadn't finished; there were still player contracts to be signed, Granada TV wanted to televise two games but we were unhappy at the level of payment and resultant lower gate money, Bernard Rothwell was unhappy at the way Jimmy Mullen had spoken to him, there were still arguments with Endsleigh and we faced the prospect of no sponsor name on the shirt, there was a long list of injuries following the pre-season friendlies, the players wanted increased match bonuses, and the floodlights were not bright enough for the new division.

We spent £130,000 on Jamie Hoyland, the Endsleigh sponsorship seemed to be fading and ending, matchday expenses were a huge £120,000, there was still the new stadium design to finalise, and a presentation to give to the board. I wanted a start date of May 1995. At last, I got the go-ahead and was able to proceed with the necessary grant applications. Meanwhile, Jimmy Mullen wanted more players to secure the place in the new division. We splashed £250,000 on a new striker, Kurt Nogan. Tender documents for the new stands were burying my desk at home in paperwork. On top of all that was the paperwork that grant applications had generated. Paperwork, endless paperwork, and I was also running my business.

At a special board meeting in June, we had Booth King, structural engineers, and our quantity surveyors, O'Neil and Partners, but Frank Teasdale had been holding up progress worrying about costs.

Getting someone new on the board with money was a no; this would threaten Frank's position and might upset the cosy drinking club that was still flourishing. By now we had three suitable tenders, from Mowlem, Linpave and Relkin. Only a few thousand separated them but we discounted Relkin because we didn't like the roof design and we wanted a cantilevered roof. All three contractors insisted we would never get a better deal but Frank was worried about hidden costs. The Longside and Bee Hole End were built on old waste from coal pits and the tenders were based on uncontaminated materials. The other worry was what was underneath them but test bore holes I had done eased worries on that score. Frank wanted more tests and in the background was the Football Trust urging us to make a decision, plus Bernard Rothwell suggesting at the Bee Hole End we could just bolt seats on to the concrete and stick a roof on top. A May 1995 start was looking impossible. Was I just batting my head against a brick wall?

What's that saying? A week is a long time in politics. Well, a relegation season seems like a lifetime. Not one person might have expected the end product of this season, a season that was to be an exercise in willpower, gritting teeth, and failed hopes.

When it began there were increased season-ticket sales, new players. One of them even cost £200,000, when Chris Vinnicombe signed, and then an even higher one when Liam Robinson was signed for £250,000. If memory serves, we spent over £1.3m during the season. But sadly, there were no highlights as this particular season ground on and on with an eventual run of eight consecutive defeats providing the foundation for eventual relegation.

It was the home game against Portsmouth on 22 April when relegation was confirmed. An immediate relegation, it was something we had never expected. The grim account is in Stephen Cummings's *Burnley Were Back*.

> No more reprieves, no more chances, no more hope. The slender thread that had kept the Damocles sword of relegation suspended menacingly overhead, finally

snapped in the howling gale that gusted round Turf Moor. Burnley were down. It was perhaps appropriate that it was Portsmouth who finally sealed our fate and consigned us to Division Two football for the 1995/96 season. After all it was at Fratton Park that our disastrous and ultimately decisive run of eight consecutive league defeats had begun. 21 league games later, I cast my mind back to that afternoon and remember how we stood contracting hypothermia on the south coast terraces, as the Clarets folded in the face of adversity. Looking back, it was as if the Pompey Chimes had rung out as a form of warning to Burnley. Four months down the road, those same chimes sounded more like a death knell.

This was the game when all our chickens came home to roost. The points thrown away in our first two home games against Stoke and Bristol, the sloppy goals we had repeatedly conceded from set pieces on our left, the games we should have won against the likes of Wolves and Bolton, our profligacy in front of goal and most tellingly the months of January and February, during which we failed to pick up a single point from a possible 24.

But hope had sprung eternal. In the light of recent home form, five wins out of the last six, we felt not unreasonably optimistic. Why not? We'd seen off better sides than Portsmouth in the past few weeks and the players were sure to be fired up for this one.

'Portsmouth won't like this,' said a chap next to me as the teams ran out and the rain took on such biblical proportions, that just standing up became an achievement of some merit. 'They're southern softies.'

He was right. The southern softies didn't like it. But the problem was, the northern softies liked it even less. The Clarets soon became dispirited as it became clear that Portsmouth weren't going to do a Charlton and throw in the towel. This clearly didn't suit some of the players who seemed to give up halfway through the first half. Instead of going down fighting, we were going down sulking.

One person who was actually going down fighting was Steve Davis. He proved this nine minutes before half-time, bringing down Alan McLoughlin with such a vicious challenge that had it happened off the field, it would have earned our skipper a stint behind bars. Durnin smashed the penalty into the roof of the net, to the delight of the away fans, who celebrated with their bloody silly hornpipes and cowbells, which had proved such an irritant at Fratton Park.

The tannoy announcer after half-time announced in suitably funereal tones that Sunderland were 1-0 up against Swindon. To the majority of football supporters this was just another scoreline; to Burnley fans it meant that we had just 45 minutes to save the season. The first half hour of the second half was all Burnley and had Mr Winter not played silly buggers with a perfectly legitimate penalty appeal, we may well have been level. But then disaster struck. For the first time in the half, Portsmouth managed to get the ball over the halfway line which would not have been a problem had not every Burnley player been stranded in the Portsmouth half as Kit Symons bore down with only Marlon to stop him. The Pompey number 5 rounded him with an ease which bordered on contempt.

All I could then hear was the loudest MULLEN OUT chant of the season. It was hardly surprising. The fans had stood by their side through thick and thin over the last few months, and now they'd had enough. Enough appalling performances, enough apologies, enough promises that things would get better. Next was WE'RE GOING DOWN 'COS OF MULLEN, as a season's worth of frustration, impatience and bitter disappointment oozed from the terraces and across to the manager's dugout. This was the sound of a season that had finally, perhaps inevitably, come apart at the seams.

David Eyres strike, nine minutes from time meant too little for it to be described as a consolation goal and the dismissal of Jamie Hoyland in the penultimate minute seemed a perfectly terrible ending to a perfectly terrible afternoon. At a quarter to five, Mr Winter blew the whistle on Burnley's hopes of survival. The tannoy announcer's news that Sunderland had hung on at Swindon solicited more calls for Mullen's head.

Sunday morning was hideous. The newspapers reported the facts in cold, bold, black and white. There we were, eight points adrift from safety, third from bottom of Division One with a capital 'R' for 'RELEGATED' next to our name with a thick black line separating ourselves from the rest. *We were relegated.*

I still say to this day that maybe two of the most significant games were both against Bolton Wanderers. The home game was as early as October and fans then could have been forgiven for thinking that the final result would have been of no great consequence. It ended 2-2 but it was a contentious scoreline. Bolton equalised when John McGinlay scored but it came after a Bolton player had been injured and a Burnley player kicked the ball out so that he could receive attention. It was a well-respected convention that the ball would be thrown back to Burnley, but not in this case. Bolton ignored it and from the resultant throw-in scored. Such things leave a sour taste. And then there was the very last game of the season away at Bolton and a 1-0 win was thwarted by a last-minute Bolton equaliser.

Back on the coach after that last Bolton game, there was a mixture of anger at the whole situation, and deep disappointment at results of individual games. If you get on a coach after a game and feel furious, the sensible thing is to button your lip and say nothing. But this time it all came out when I shouted angrily down the coach, 'Another bloody last-minute goal. If we had stopped them all, we'd be staying up.' Mullen heard it and turned round and shouted back. 'Yes, and don't I bloody know it.' It had been a horrendous season of last-minute goals for the other team, and a dreadful disciplinary record; someone told me it was the worst in the Football League that season. Not only that, we had the worst defence in the division.

Their last-minute goal in a way summed up the season. A cross was swung into the Burnley box, someone headed goalwards; our keeper, Marlon Beresford, soared like an eagle through the air acrobatically and saved. But no, the ball hit the post and then trickled over the line. A last-minute goal to the opposition is a sickener when it robs you of a win. Until that equaliser our fans had roared their support and chanted their love for Burnley, despite the impending relegation. I, too, felt a small measure of pride in this heroic resistance to a side in the play-offs. But that goal just sickened us. To make it worse, Blackburn Rovers were the champions of the Premier League, bankrolled by the Jack Walker millions, and didn't they let us know it.

What I'm saying next is what I said to author Tim Quelch for his book *From Orient to the Emirates*: 'The solitary season Burnley spent in Division One was a disaster. Jimmy Mullen seemed to struggle with the extra pressure. It was said to me on one occasion that he had absented himself during one home game, only to be found later fast asleep in a Turf Moor toilet cubicle. It gave further cause for doubt whether we now had the right man for the job. But at least this "one-season-wonder" allowed us to avail ourselves of the Football League Foundation grant which met 50 per cent of the costs of erecting the two badly needed all-seater stands on the sites occupied by the Longside and the Bee Hole terraces.'

To go back a bit, we had started planning the redevelopment of Turf Moor six years before it began. It was when we had five MPs here as guests of the club on their fact-finding mission for Margaret Thatcher's doomed ID card scheme in connection with the investigations into the Hillsborough disaster. But things slowed down after that and it wasn't until 1993 that a suitable design and workable financial plan came through that seemed viable. We still didn't have much money so we concentrated on coming up with a scheme that was self-financing, and that takes time.

It was a capital project that we estimated would cost £5.28m and had we not been promoted in 1994 would never have been able to afford it. Our one-year stay in the second flight allowed us to qualify for this grant, which was allocated to help all clubs at this level to build all-seater stadia with the recommendation from the Taylor Report. We were certainly in the right place at the right time but not all board members were enthusiastic. The club would still have to find £2.64m from its own resources to supplement the Football League grant.

Fellow director Bernard Rothwell continued to suggest putting seats on the Longside terraces as a cost-saving measure rather than building a replacement stand. I opposed this suggestion vehemently. I insisted we needed two new, purpose-built stands on a larger footprint to accommodate the new revenue-earning functions that a modern club was expected to provide, such as banqueting and conference facilities, plus executive boxes. There was no way we could do that if we retained the old terracing.

I am not a construction engineer but I am a very experienced mechanical engineer, having successfully run my own company. This has taught me that whenever it is necessary to embark upon a development of this size and importance, it is imperative that the client is totally conversant with each of the project details, being integrally involved in drawing up the specifications, and in the appointment of the contractors, ensuring that throughout the project that the contractors are held accountable for the delivery of every specified item and that the required quality standards are met. So, while these stands were being constructed, I scrutinised every aspect of the development, making sure that if the contractors attempted to depart from the original specifications that prior approval was sought, and that it was done on the understanding that each variation incurred no extra cost to the club. I maintained a comprehensive record of each of the written communications with Linpave, the contractors.

We are jumping ahead now into the next season, 1995/96, when construction actually began, and at the end of building, Linpave attempted to add around £0.5m to the final bill. I went through every item listed in that bill with a fine-tooth comb to ensure that no unauthorised extras had been slipped in. As it happened there were several, therefore we disputed the charge. Linpave tried to take us to court but thanks to our rigour through the process, including the maintenance of a comprehensive record of all communications with the builders, the High Court judge determined that the final bill should be £0.28m less than the original estimate and that the £0.5m unauthorised additions should also be deleted.

Some people expressed disappointment with the new stands, regarding them as too clinical and unadventurous. Maybe that's true. We'd have liked to have done more, but I defy anyone to get better value for money than the end product that we got. What we have is what we could afford at the time and they have helped set up the club into what it is today: six seasons in the Premier League. I remain proud of what we achieved here. The alternative was simply to bolt seats on to the already crumbling terraces. To me, that was unthinkable and unacceptable and I had to really argue to get my way. It is so important to get the infrastructure of a club on a sure footing so that when there is success on the pitch, it can be maintained with the revenues from such constructions. Not every club can have benefactors like Jack Walker and if Blackburn Rovers had not had his involvement, they would always have been in a similar position to us. His money enabled them to get into the Premier League long before us and funded new stands and facilities. Their rise did not last, however, but that is a story for them to tell.

Meanwhile, here we were planning on two new stands with fans as well worrying about where the money was going to come from, but back down in the lower leagues again. Stability at Burnley Football Club at this time was hard to find.

CHAPTER NINE

1995/96 A Close Thing but Two New Stands

The chairman's statement for the season just gone was bland to say the least.

> It is my sad duty to record for the first time during my tenure of office as chairman, a relegation season. Despite all the efforts of the board, management, playing staff and last but by no means least our supporters, we were unable to hold our place in the First Division. The very considerable expenditure on players which is the sole reason for the loss on ordinary activities revealed by the accounts was not successful in the short term. However, the board believes that the playing strength of the club is far greater than it was when we were last in the Second Division.
>
> The success of the youth team in winning the Lancashire Youth Cup, and the current position of the reserve team at the top of the Pontins League, cause us to remain optimistic that success will return.
>
> As I reported last year, the development of the ground was an urgent priority. Legislation left us with no option but to proceed with the development as soon as practicable. Grants were made available by the Football Trust that had to be taken, or a significant portion may well have been lost forever. The board therefore made the decision to

go ahead with the development of the Longside and the Bee Hole End.

The chairman's report went on for three more paragraphs but I have left it there to enable myself to say that it was largely me that dragged the board, in particular Teasdale and Rothwell, into opting for complete rebuilds of the two stands. Left on his own, Frank would not have sanctioned the costs, despite the grant from the Football Trust. And as I cannot say often enough: Rothwell would have simply bolted seats on to the terraces. Teasdale added that by the start of the next season, the fans would have a stadium of which they could be proud. What he would have preferred was something makeshift and Heath Robinson that would have been an amateurish mess. In later years something new would have been utterly essential, but without the grants.

About to embark on the new building, we also wanted to improve the Cricket Field Stand so I agreed with cricket club chairman, Peter Lawson, to buy a five-metre strip of land behind the stand. The proposals were circulated to the board but there was no approval, and certainly it was one cost too many for Frank Teasdale. It was so short-sighted and today the new owners, I believe, are once again trying to buy the same strip. On the other hand, Frank was keen to sell the car park along Harry Potts Way, the large area of land that Bob Lord had once bought to enable his huge retail scheme. With Frank very much in favour, there was a bid of £800,000 for it but sense prevailed and the majority of the board including me were against it. It helped that the TSB Bank agreed to fund our share of the costs for the new stands without it affecting our normal overdraft. Thwaites Brewery supported us as well with a loan of £400,000 as long as they supplied all our beers and drinks. Supporters might, or might not, like to know that the unpopular increase in our prices then helped pay off the loan. How much to charge for the new boxes? It was £14,000 a season for the middle ones and £8,000 for the side ones and a minimum two-year agreement.

All kinds of problems had to be decided in the boardroom. The police wanted payment for being on duty on the highway outside the ground. We refused. Inside the ground it was £39 per hour for each officer. Few fans would have known that. The Football Association were unhappy with Burnley's disciplinary record and so were we. Not only that but was Jimmy Mullen still the right man? There were discussions on the renaming of Turf Moor but nothing settled. Coral Bookmakers occupied a building in the corner of our building and we wanted them out. They were making good money and refused until the lease ran out. What does help enormously is if you have a fan who is also financial director of Readymix Concrete. This was Derek Jenkins, who lived in Surrey at the time. We were able to do a deal with him for a discount to be given on all the concrete used, and believe me it was a huge amount for the two stands. Into the new North Stand we would also place plaques in memory of the two people who had died as a result of falls through the roof.

Also, at this time we were bedevilled by complications between myself and director Basil Dearing. With no secrecy I had been trying to buy more shares, but I was accused of going behind people's backs. For the first time ever, Frank invited Radio Lancashire to an AGM, presumably because he expected an explosive meeting. I had no awareness of the plan to demand my resignation. Unprepared, I said little, only that I would consider my position. But Basil offered his resignation and the origins of that seemed to be my attempt to buy more shares, plus an attempt to improve things for the ladies with a mixed guest room instead of just a lady's room. The ladies could then choose from either on a matchday. How could that cause friction? But it did.

On top of all that, Frank expected that I could resign as a director but carry on working on the two new stands. 'Get lost,' I said, or words to that effect. Could there be anything more ridiculous? Come January and there were indeed fireworks at the board meeting. There was me thinking that Basil had resigned but in fact he was at the meeting suggesting that I was trying to increase my shareholding behind the chairman's back. So, I said what I thought: that this was rubbish, that I had spoken and written to the chairman. Then, more furore when I told the directors sitting there that they had not got the wherewithal to contribute to the club in a way that was needed. None of them had any real money. And I was certainly not resigning. But Basil eventually did, effectively, from February of 1996.

As I began the laborious job of ordering new floodlights, carpets, kitchens, kitchen equipment, tables and chairs, everything down to knives and forks, I could only marvel at Frank Teasdale's absurd suggestion that I should resign but carry on and organise the new stands. And, alongside that were plans to completely refurbish the sports centre for the general public to be able to use – new changing rooms, a weight and fitness room, along with the Café Claret. The players would use them two days a week and the public the rest. Would I do all that as well if I was no longer a member of the board? No, I would not.

To cut a long story short, it was Basil who eventually resigned, me that stayed on and Frank explained to one and all that this was a difficult situation but there needed to be continuity in the boardroom, where Mr Holt had managed the development programme since its inception. But still it wasn't over. Basil wrote to the *Burnley Express*. It was agreed that I should reply. I never kept copies of these letters and I'd love to see them again.

* * *

The date of 16 September 1995 was the historic occasion that the last game was played in front of the iconic Sanderson Ford Longside Stand. An eight-minute YouTube video records the day and the emotions. The closure prompted a deluge of reminiscences as everyone took a journey backwards to remember the great nights, the great events and the great occasions. There were memories of wonderful games, the players we had seen, the goals that we had witnessed. We had seen both triumphs and heartbreaks.

Demolition began after the Hull City game in September but there was no carnival atmosphere or sense of occasion, and we were now back in a lower division. Burnley won 2-1 but it was as if it meant nothing. It was joyless, almost an anticlimax. Would we have a team the next season to match the splendour of two new stands? Disaffection, this season, was the word of the day.

The Hull manager insisted that Hull were by far the better side. Burnley fans responded by wondering if they had been at the same game. Nevertheless, fans left with lumps of concrete from the terraces and some of the signs, even light fittings, they had managed to pull down. Some had even taken hammers to chip away at the brickwork. Some fans chalked farewell messages on the walls. Director Bernard Rothwell had stood on the Longside when it was just a bank of earth and ashes. It was his suggestion that all we should do was bolt benches on to the existing terracing. Now he was saying in the press, what great progress this was, the building of these stands. I shook my head in astonishment.

With just three games to go, relegation was still a possibility yet again, back down to Division Three this time. Two wins in the last three games saw us safe. The two promotions with Jimmy Mullen now seemed a lifetime ago.

A crowd of over 10,000 turned up for the Hull game, but we thought there might have been more for such a historic game. Maybe the absentees were somewhat disillusioned with the club. Who could blame them? Relegation turns people away. The special programme produced for the game was a splendid commemorative edition. Club chairman was still Frank Teasdale, Doc Iven was vice-chairman and the remaining directors were Basil Dearing, Bernard Rothwell, Bob Blakeborough and myself. The groundsman was a former player of some distinction, Arthur Bellamy. It was an especially poignant occasion for him having played on the turf so often in front of that stand. Bit by bit he would witness it being torn down. So would I, clambering up ladders, or climbing up the debris-filled remaining terraces on several occasions to take photographs that I still have today. More than once as I got up to the top of a precarious ladder I thought, 'What on earth am I doing up here?' But what I also did was watch the contractors with the eyes of a hawk.

Teasdale expressed his support for the manager, Jimmy Mullen, and added it was the job of the board to back him. But this would turn out to be a season when not even Teasdale's fierce support and loyalty could save the manager. He wrote in his programme notes that he would understand if a few tears were shed during the afternoon; hundreds of people had stood in the same spot on the terraces for decades.

Dave Thomas wrote his appreciation some time ago for a small publication that was produced to mark the ten-year anniversary of the end of the Longside. His father had taken him way back in the 50s and that was where they stood through the 60s, and then he stood with his wife during the 70s.

> The Longside was my father's place, roundabout the halfway line and then when my own regular visits began in 1959/60 it was always the same place near the front and you had to pay a bit extra for the privilege of being in the Enclosure, as it was known. Little lads had stools to stand on, carried in for them by their considerate dads. Today you wouldn't get one past the first steward.
>
> 1959/60 wasn't a bad season to start and one vivid memory to this day is a 2-0 win over Tottenham Hotspur and a goal from Ray Pointer; a goal I have never forgotten, a bullet header from a cross by John Connelly. In those days the din was incredible, the roof of the stand acting as a lid on a soundbox, and with those old-fashioned wooden rattles that we all had, the sound was thunderous.
>
> Somewhere up on the moors high above Todmorden was a pub in the middle of nowhere where dozens of us would meet up after a game to relive the moments that had us enthralled. There was always pie and peas to accompany our

good humour, because back in those days we always seemed to win, including European games against Johnny Foreigner on foggy nights. Funny how it was always the misty evening games that seemed most vivid. The floodlights made for pure theatre, a wet pitch would glisten and sparkle, unless it was midwinter and it was six inches deep in thick black mud. We watched Brian O'Neil take to it like a duck to water. Was it the mist or was it the steamy breath from 20,000 fans, mixed with cigarette smoke that drifted out from under the canopy of the Longside? Whatever it was, the atmosphere was inimitable and the noise just awesome.

People who are old enough to have stood on the Longside in the 60s and 70s are so privileged. Not just to have stood there but to have been able to see the procession of great names and players that came our way. Not only did we have our own great players, Jimmy Mac, Adamson, Pointer, Connelly, O'Neil, Irvine, Lochhead, Coates, Morgan, Dobson, Flynn, James and so many more we could fill the page; but there were visitors as well, Blanchflower, Mackay, Ball, Best, Charlton, Law, Greaves, Bremner, Summerbee and dozens more. You stood on that Longside feeling such pride, a little team amongst the city giants; it was just such a marvellous feeling.

If you were there on the night that Celtic came to town in the Anglo-Scottish Cup you witnessed mayhem and the Longside was a terrible place to be. By then it was divided by railings to separate the home and away supporters. But on that shameful night, the rioting and violence was abhorrent, with the fencing used as spears and the bricks that were hurled causing injury and bloodied heads. The police were overwhelmed and it became national news.

Of course, the good years couldn't last and the demise of the Longside and the gradual dwindling of the regulars, mirrored in many ways the decline of the club through the 80s, until at last it came to the last game of that awful season when the club was about to implode. Thank goodness it scraped a 2-1 win to save itself from non-league football and there is no doubt that on that day the crowd really was a twelfth man as it urged, cajoled, willed the team on with an endless volume of noise, passion, fervour, support and desperation, as the river of noise cascaded down from all around the ground, but none more so than the packed Longside. It transformed limited players into winning ones. It infused them with a passion that lifted them; our will to win became their will to win. It is doubtful that never has such a crowd lifted and carried a team to a victory in the way that it did that day. There is no way that this was a great game but it was certainly a great sporting event.

I'm lucky, this was about the only game I saw there in the 80s, so I never saw the Longside forlorn and dilapidated in that decade when crowds were down to a mere handful, the empty spaces were embarrassing and we even lost to teams like Rochdale and Hereford. Lord knows how Bob Lord must have felt as he looked across from his comfy seat in the stand opposite and saw the lack of spectators and the prairie like spaces. He must have known the game was up, his day was done, and that the great club he had once chaired and created, was now crumbling before his eyes. From Hamburg and Naples, it was now Shrewsbury and Newport. From riches to rags, from delight to dross.

With family and a career, the 90s were nearing the end when on a rare journey through Burnley we decided to stop and take a look at the ground for old times' sake. We looked in amazement at the two, towering blocks. I was actually numbed with shock it was so totally unexpected. The Bee Hole End and more significantly, the old Longside where I had grown up, were gone. The car as good as stopped itself, my mouth dropped open. Gone.

But the memories remain in scrapbooks, old newspapers, and albums of cuttings and pictures. They remain on websites such as Stuart Clarke's Homes of Football, on video and broadcasts on TV of old games. It is in the mind and memory, however, where the best of them remains.

The old Longside eventually became the James Hargreaves Stand and the corporate area was filled with sponsors, diners – not quite a new breed of support but almost. Waiters fussed around them and the carpets were deep and plush. But something was gone forever – that sense of camaraderie, standing shoulder to shoulder now that it was all-seater. Something died when standing was ended. Only on the very rarest of occasions did the noise from the stand ever match what it had produced before. As we write, it is simply called the North Stand, but the diehards still call it the Longside.

Nothing surprises me in football – doesn't now and didn't then – so when a letter appeared in the local *Burnley Express* having a go at the club, and me, I wasn't unduly perturbed. It was from former director Derek Gill, passionate about the club but always disappointed that he had never become club chairman. He was certainly no friend of the current board and Frank Teasdale. His book, *A Director's Tale*, is well worth reading. Anyway, his letter resurfaced as we wrote our own book.

> For some years now, I have watched without comment, the fluctuating fortunes and attitudes of the men entrusted with the running of Burnley Football Club. I do have some sort of axe to grind, as it may be recalled that for three and a half years, I was financial director and later on the nominal managing director of the football club.
>
> It was, has been since, close to my heart and I grieve for its misfortunes. So why should I bother to write? Although I have ignored various matters arising from time to time, it

is a relatively trivial matter that has tipped the balance. In November last year, I made a nominal share transfer to a friend of mine and businessman who is also a season ticket holder and keen supporter. The board of Burnley Football Club have refused to register the transfer and this is not the first time it has happened. On January 23, I wrote to the chairman but sadly, and I am afraid predictably, I have had no reply.

Coming on top of a revelation that at least one director was actively seeking to mop up shares, there is only one conclusion to be drawn. On that particular subject, a perceptive party might well conclude that the whole story, and indeed the truth has not emerged. The facts, as half presented do not stand up to examination. The irrefutable fact is that Mr C Holt wrote to a number of shareholders. In my opinion the letter was a misjudgement and not well drafted, but it was certainly not illegal, nor as far as I can see was it harmful to anyone.

The only matter of issue would seem to be whether or not other directors were aware of the intention to solicit shares. On the one hand we have Mr Basil Dearing announcing his resignation as a matter of 'high principle', honour and integrity and all that, while it seems to be accepted by other directors that they were at least aware that something was in the offing. At best, there is economy with the truth and I find it difficult to believe that Mr Holt could continue as a director if he had acted in isolation. The truth should be told but perhaps this is not currently possible as it may disclose serious differences on the board and ultimately lead to its disintegration.

Because of this I am glad that Mr Mullen has retained his position, however tenuous that may be. This is very different from saying that I think he is the right man for the job; I am not in a position to know. What I do know is that a combination of Kenny Dalglish, Jimmy Mullen and Brian Clough could not bring success on the back of a divided board.

When I resigned all those years ago, I went in print to state that there were directors at the club to whom 'I would not give a job'. This is just as true today but I suspect there might be one or even two directors capable of bringing some improvements. I am glad Mr Mullen holds on because his is not the prime responsibility. If my own firm, Lupton and Place failed, then blame me as chairman and controlling shareholder, not the storeman or even the production manager. The same principle applies to Burnley Football Club. I will not embarrass Mr Teasdale by relating here the 'last straw' that brought about my resignation from Burnley Football Club, he knows it well enough, but the time is overdue for he and Dr Iven to move aside.

I went into the club at a time when bonuses for home wins took the entire gate money and crowds of 5,000 were considered to be a luxury. I have a documented history of those dark days; the full story has never been released and while I do not wish to be pulled into a slanging match, I can divulge more than enough if the chips were ever down. There is reason to think that much could be brought to the club if Teasdale and Iven moved on. At a recent AGM, Mr Teasdale said that 'he would do the job as long as people wanted him'.

Come in Frank Teasdale and Dr Iven. Your time is up.

Coming across this, all these years later, I am reminded that there was nothing underhand in my attempt to gain more shares. Frank Teasdale, the chairman, was certainly made aware and when Derek Gill writes that there were one or two directors capable of bringing some improvement, I would count myself one of them. Like Derek Gill himself during his time as a director, I would have loved to have been in a position of strength to have more influence. And, like Derek himself, I was fully able to see that Frank and the Doc were unable to take the club forward. Eventually Derek did release all the facts when his detailed diaries were translated into book form in March of 2022.

As 95/96 dragged on with precious little to enjoy or celebrate, Jimmy Mullen continued to struggle until it all became too much and he was relieved of the managership. The defeat at home to Crewe 1-0 was the catalyst. It was a sad end to a term of office that had seen two promotions including the all-important one of getting us out of the Fourth Division. For that he must be remembered in the history books with gratitude. But even before this parting of the ways, directors had discussed his results and whether to dismiss him, but with a vote of four to two it was decided to retain him.

The last straw for him must surely have been the occasion when his wife was abused one Sunday evening by a group of youths. It left Jimmy angered as much by the sensationalised newspaper reports and headlines as by the incident itself. He and his wife and son had gone to collect a Chinese takeaway and it was Mrs Mullen who was abused. First stories said that she had been set on fire in a restaurant as they dined and one story included the words 'fire horror'. But, according to police, a group of youths had congregated outside the takeaway premises and whilst one group abused Jimmy and his son in the car, another turned on Mrs Mullen outside the shop as she walked back towards the car. Somehow a cigarette lighter was involved. All of us were horrified and ashamed at the behaviour of these youths. MP Peter Pike expressed his sadness, and said that it brought shame on the town and reflected badly on the thousands of genuine fans. On the morning after the Sunday-night incident, Jimmy went to see Frank Teasdale and they both agreed that enough was enough. In the boardroom, we wondered what effect would this have on prospective new managers thinking of applying for the Burnley job. It was an appalling way for Jimmy's time to end.

Jimmy Mullen was put out of his misery when Teasdale met him and they decided it was time to call it a day. There had been so many protests at his management, and Frank Teasdale's chairmanship for that matter. At the Crewe home game on 10 February there had been a protest that has since gone down into Burnley legend, when spectators, at 3.33, turned their backs on the game and at us, the directors, as we sat in the Bob Lord Stand. The national media had a field day with this, especially as Burnley lost 1-0. Two days later, Mullen was gone.

The directors were not the town's favourite people at this time, with the accusation that we treated fans as third-class citizens. Fans printed 5,000 leaflets urging that there should be a silent protest during the game. The fury of the fans was fully evident in their accusations that we were ignorant, patronising and dismissive. They got together and made their plan to turn their backs on the directors at 3.33 exactly. It was a simple but effective ploy to make Frank Teasdale sit up and take notice. Fans in the Bob Lord Stand were simply asked to stand and stare at Teasdale during the protest. It was emphasised that this was not a protest at the players or even Jimmy Mullen, but at the running of the club. When Frank was informed of the planned protests, publicly he could only say that he was disappointed, that they were doing all they could both on and off the field and there was no Jack Walker to help them out. The protest organisers bridled even more; this was a patronising answer that simply confirmed their views.

In all honesty I took more notice of what the team were doing on the pitch than in the 3.33 demonstration; that's where my concentration was and that's how it is in every game. I did, however, make a note of the ringleaders around the directors' box. At half-time it was barely mentioned as the pressing need was to look after the visitors.

What I do remember is going into one of the lounges after the game and seeing one of the leaders with his chums. I asked him to leave, commenting that he should not enjoy our hospitality if he had come to insult us during the game. But I did have some sympathy with them. There was a lot that could have been improved. In the end we did improve, but in the meantime, it was important to be a united board, at least in public.

Mullen's departure was hastened by necessity, and that necessity was not just to do with the results he was getting but as much by the awful incident he had faced when he and his wife were publicly abused. Teasdale met Jimmy and his wife at his house to discuss things and Mullen confirmed what had happened. There had also been incidents at Jimmy's house. It was mutually agreed to bring the contract to an immediate end.

We were all devastated. Numbed, in fact. What Jimmy and his wife had endured went beyond all that could be accepted in the football world where we know that derision is part of the job at times. But this was more than derision; it was vicious and bordering on the inhuman. People who had once thrown flowers at him and the players, were now throwing things at him and his wife. Frank Teasdale told the people involved that if they had no regrets or felt no sorrow, then there was something wrong with them.

The atmosphere at Turf Moor was a strange one as the rebuilding took place and games continued in front of stands that were being demolished. Rebuilding didn't affect the size of the crowds as they slowly became smaller and smaller; fewer and fewer people were coming anyway as the team stumbled along.

It was those two new stands that resulted in me needing a hip replacement. As they neared completion and all the stairways were being installed, I was going up and down those steps so often. I always joke that it wore my hips out. Nearly lost my dog as well when he went bounding up the steps one day and we came to a door high up that hadn't been locked. For some reason I pushed it open and the dog ran forward. Only by grabbling him by the tail as he headed downwards did I save him from a long, long drop.

It was a design and build contract that simply meant that a lot of the general design and quantity surveying was done by us not the builders. They did the final detail design. We designed what we wanted generally with Booth King building engineers, and O'Neil the quantity surveyors, and then it went to tender. Doing it this way, I had control over costs and any possible escalation. Six companies tendered and we did not choose the cheapest. Linpave of Lincoln got the job and everything was done in such a way that they had no charge on us for extras as the job progressed. This is what often happens in building and if you are not careful a lot of things can be added without you knowing. We'd kept to a very basic design so that it could be done quickly and without complications, with many of the parts exactly the same as a further simplification. The arguments had continued as to whether we should build or not, but the deciding moment came when the Football Trust told us that if we didn't make up our minds, their grant offer would be lost.

The new Longside Stand opened on 23 April 1996. It was not the celebratory win that we all hoped for but a dismal 1-0 defeat to Bristol Rovers. What an anticlimax and not what people had paid to see. Instead, it was a leaden, ineffective performance unfitting of the occasion. Nine thousand three hundred supporters turned up and marvelled at the stand but grimaced at the result.

As the season neared its end and with just three games to go, Burnley, now with Adrian Heath in charge, were faced with the prospect of relegation again. It seemed unthinkable. Only a 2-0 win at Wrexham finally disposed of that possibility. The relief was palpable. The boardroom had been in a state of real anxiety – did we really want to be the directors that had overseen such a calamity? But the threat was gone and to make matters even better there was a win in the final game of the season at home to Shrewsbury. But even that created a problem in that it was then too easy for some directors to be complacent and to imagine that next season would be fine. A win on the last day makes it too easy to gloss over things and forget the turmoil we had seen.

The season had also seen the removal of the four enormous floodlight pylons that could be seen from miles away, as much a part of the ground as anything else. They had helped create the unique night-game atmosphere, especially on misty nights. And what wonderful games they had witnessed, especially in the Bob Lord era. In fact, it was always said that Lord had them switched on early when there was an evening game so that workers on their way home would know there was a game that night. The bulbs could be used again said the contractors, who used a giant crane to do the job, cutting the pylons into sections to be lowered to the ground. They had stood there since the 50s; an iconic emblem.

CHAPTER TEN

1996/97 Not Much to Write Home About

IT'S 1996/97, and, as ever, never a dull moment. There was continual jousting with the building contractors Linpave – not quite acrimony but almost – as we fended off all their attempts to charge us extra, and we asked them for damages for deadlines and targets not met. Sometime afterwards they went out of business. Dave Thomas jokes that his first-ever book, *It's Burnley Not Barcelona*, put his publisher out of business, but it would be a shame to think that our two new stands put Linpave out of business. We asked for £193,000 when the North Stand was not handed over on time.

Once completed, we had no trouble selling the new corporate boxes in the Longside Stand; 50 per cent were sold almost immediately and then the outer ones gradually went. Frank Teasdale was mighty relieved, since finding 50 per cent of the money for these stands had been his worst nightmare. To be fair to him, the club was his 'baby' and, overall, he had done a wonderful job keeping it going in the years after the Orient game. But I sometimes wondered if, as a single person, he was lonely and suffered from having no one to talk to at the end of the day and go through the problems. I wonder too if he was too protective of his role at the club and feared anyone else appearing to muscle in, shall we say. I suspect he was also fearful of me ending up with more shares than him. I wasn't that far behind him. Unfortunately, he was reluctant to open up to new investors if it meant outsiders coming in. I wish I had a pound for every time I said to him, 'For God's sake, Frank, we need new investors.' Strangely he would never have any kind of a meeting on a Sunday. And we never did find out why.

Some things are amusing when you look back on them: we got the cricket club to pay us £1,300 for damages to the Cricket Field Stand roof, particularly from their cricket balls landing on the asbestos. We heard a story that this was due to players in practice having a competition to see who could whack the ball over the stand roof. Anybody who could do that had my full admiration until it came to inspecting and paying for the damage.

We argued with the police about their increased charges, especially as they wanted to increase their presence on matchdays. Matchday presence was a lucrative opportunity for them and their conditions were becoming stricter and stricter. If the match commander was a young bloke hell-bent on promotion, then he would overstaff to be sure there was no trouble. We later reached a compromise whereby we reduced the police and employed more stewards, who were far cheaper.

The Bosman ruling was about to change player-club relationships forever. It as good as gave the players the winning hand. It originated in Belgium, where restrictive practices still operated and clubs could hold on to the registration of a player. That situation had long since gone in the UK and disputes went to a player tribunal to be settled. Now, the boot is on the other foot: a player can manipulate situations; players run down their contracts to get a move with a free transfer and higher wages and agents hawk their players around like they were products on a supermarket shelf. Contracts in some cases are not worth the paper they are written on if a star player wants to get away.

Keighley Cougars rugby club were in touch with us with a view to ground sharing as their own ground no longer met the standards required now that they were in the Super League. What concerned us was their poor financial situation and damage to our pitch. They could not answer our questions so the request went into the out tray.

As director responsible for ground safety, one of my concerns was crowd scenes when we scored, especially when a player ran to the crowd and joined in with them. Crowd surges at Burnley? You might laugh and think we never got crowds big enough, but nevertheless if someone did this, my first thought was, 'Please, no injuries.' Call me an old misery guts but these were the things you had to think of, so the manager was asked to have words with the players to keep their celebrations on the pitch.

The expected charge for extras came from Linpave – £209,000. In reply, we asked them for another £120,000 damages because the East Stand was behind schedule. For both stands we'll take £250,000, we said.

We had a player with a fractured cheekbone and packed him off to Blackburn Hospital, where there was a facial surgeon specialist. He should have stayed in for 48 hours under observation, before an operation to repair the damage. However, he decided to discharge himself to attend a christening. Doc Iven was far from pleased. This guy could have lost an eye without the necessary operation.

The new floodlights contractors made a mess of their simple job. They didn't build them tall enough so some parts of the pitch were inadequately lit and were in the shadow of the Bob Lord Stand roof. More arguments ensued about getting them done properly and who was going to pay. It certainly wasn't us.

Linpave landed us with a writ for what they said were extra costs incurred by us. I had the paperwork to show that they were responsible not us. There was no way they would win a court case.

Some things were a pleasure to deal with. Did you know that Eric Cantona once played at Turf Moor? It was for a TV commercial and they wanted to hire the ground. It was my job to make all the arrangements and settle the fee – £6,000; very nice, thank you. If I remember rightly, Eric was at the ground for just one day and got a phenomenal fee; something in the region of £1m, I was told. When making the arrangements I had no idea that it would be Eric Cantona who would turn up. Talking of star players, it was round about this time that we signed one too. Glen Little arrived from Ireland where he was playing for a club in the north. I mention that because he went on to become one of our most popular players, and what a player he was. Of course, we all thought he was Irish until he opened his mouth to speak.

We sent Clive Middlemass to Australia, not as punishment but to look at some possible young players that we might be interested in.

Then a real controversy when we had to abandon an FA Cup tie because of floodlight failure. It was against Walsall and they were winning. When we won the replay on penalties, Walsall unhappiness doubled and they complained to the FA that we had done this deliberately. It is unlikely that they knew the story of old Bob Lord, who, in an FA Cup draw that involved Burnley, picked out a ball that he didn't like and threw it back in. It was on the radio, so, somehow, he got away with it. However, Walsall did think that the abandoned game was a put-up job, even though we identified exactly what the problem was in the locked Norweb transformer area and our electrician, Joe Loftus, quickly realised it was a transformer problem with just a tired old fuse. But on the night, there was no way of getting into the transformer room without Norweb electricians. The palaver it caused with Walsall was draining, with us having to provide letters from Norweb, the police and our own electrician. Today, there is a standby generator.

Linpave again: and a meeting in the High Court was looming. It meant that Frank Teasdale and other directors were getting anxious and developing real cold feet. 'Hold firm,' I told them, battling them as well as Linpave. 'We will win.' And we did. Fans today see the two towering stands and will have no idea of the battles we had, the endless negotiations and a court case.

Daley Thompson opened the new sports and leisure centre in the revamped gymnasium, a project that had been enabled by the two huge grants I had worked for. Frank commended it in his end-of-year report now that it was open to the community with its fitness suites, a sports-injury clinic and the Café Claret.

Words always come back to bite on the you-know-what. I'd once said after a postponed game that this was the last time a game would ever have to be postponed by the weather. It would probably have been around the time we got our roll-on roll-off pitch covers. Lo and behold, the home game against Norwich was called off due to a waterlogged pitch with no other game in the north affected. I'd given as the excuse that Burnley probably had more wet weather than anywhere else. Norwich had already set off so they weren't too pleased and it wasn't called off until the final pitch inspection at 2pm. With Norwich supporters arriving, and Burnley fans on their way, my name was mud. And so was the pitch.

* * *

The man now in charge was Adrian Heath, a bubbly character, a nice guy with a nice family, easy to get on with, a leader and he was available. He was a top player and well respected in the dressing room. He was in situ and with money being an issue at that time it seemed an obvious appointment. He had a good assistant in John Ward and we had high hopes that this was going to be a successful appointment. He was given a record £400,000 to buy striker Paul Barnes from Birmingham City. For us that was a phenomenal amount but he was not the answer or the saviour who would carry the team to promotion. He had one bonanza game when he scored five goals but he was never a prolific scorer, although another hat-trick came later. Paul's son Harvey was born in Burnley and now stars at Leicester.

Both new stands were now finished and occupied but yet again this was a mediocre season. There was a brief spell in the top four but it was not to last. The five goals in one game that Paul Barnes scored cheered us up but there were more runs without a win. Good strikers are hard to find, the best ones just have that knack of being in the right place at the right time with an instinct that you cannot coach. From my younger days I always remember Jimmy Greaves:

rarely scored from 20 yards, so many of his goals were from inside the six-yard box. He was lightning quick over the first couple of yards, almost impossible to mark, there one minute and gone the next. I loved to watch Alan Shearer, especially on the odd occasions I had the chance to see him at Blackburn when I had an invite to a game. Gary Lineker and Sergio Aguero, even though they had had a nasty habit of scoring against us so often, and Ian Wright, who of course we had at Burnley for a short spell. Our own recent players include Robbie Blake and Danny Ings. Robbie scored such wonderful free kicks, plus his one never to be forgotten goal against Manchester United, and Danny Ings was like quicksilver, a diving header at Old Trafford an abiding memory. As we write, there is Maxwel Cornet who only seems to score world-class goals but now at West Ham.

Two of the last three games were against the bottom two clubs but we could only draw. Two wins would have made it quite an exciting final day when we beat Watford 4-1, but by then any hope of the top four was long gone. Five points below the play-offs, the season ended in ninth place but with genuine optimism in the boardroom this time that the next season could be a success. One reason for the downward turn in fortunes in the season was said to be the departure of coach John Ward and that may well be true. He was seen as the main tactical brain and team organiser and more than one player attributed the best moments of the season to him. I still think that had he stayed, a play-off place at the very least was there for the asking.

But then Adrian Heath decided to leave, a huge blow.

On his appointment in the previous season, he had made the usual noises about the challenge, the desire to see Burnley back to the top, his confidence, affection for the club and ambition. But when Howard Kendall at Everton came calling, he could not resist the temptation. During his tenure he had placed a bit of faith in younger players and several of them were quite disappointed when he left. One thing he had done was to sign Glen Little, a name that was to become very familiar and popular around the club and town. Of him, we shall speak later.

When he came in, he seemed like a breath of fresh air and, of course, he began with the bonus of being popular with the fans as a player. I thought we might have got somewhere under his leadership but as soon as Kendall came for him, his former boss at Everton, it was impossible to get him to change his mind and stay. I did my utmost to persuade him to stay, using the simple argument that if it was experience that he wanted, it was better to be manager at Burnley and in charge than an assistant to Kendall, even if it was at Everton. I had a huge phone bill that summer, being in Italy and having long telephone calls with him from over there. I have heard that today he does regret the decision he made and wishes he had stayed at Burnley. He left us believing that he would take over from Kendall and assume the manager's place. But that never happened. My hour-long phone calls to him from the dockside in Italy had no effect. Sylvia and I were having a Mediterranean cruise and communication whilst on board cruising around was poor. I could have called using the ship's system but it was something daft like £5 a minute. But once in port, I could use my mobile phone, in the days when they were as big as a shoebox, and call Heath. He was actually in his car on the way to Everton during one call, and I spent another hour trying to persuade him to stay. It was a helluva bill and it was me that paid it. Never claimed it back either.

CHAPTER ELEVEN

1997/98 The Waddle Season

WE'D SEEN how Bryan Robson had been so successful at Middlesbrough so the idea of another player-manager, especially of the player quality of Chris Waddle, was hugely attractive. He was a stellar name, a 'Diamond Light' in fact, an instant attraction and the players were astonished at his arrival. It was an opportunity not to be missed we all felt and I personally had no reservations when I heard of his appointment. But …

'Who is it going to be?' my wife Sylvia asked me.

'It won't work,' she replied when I told her. She was right.

The interest it generated was huge and attracted national publicity. We were congratulated on being ambitious and imaginative and it was double kudos when Glenn Roeder came with him as his assistant. On top of all that, the cash was being flashed: Mark Ford, a midfielder from Leeds for £275,000; Steve Blatherwick from Nottingham Forest for £200,000; and Lee Howey from Sunderland for another £200,000. This was a lot of money and in addition Waddle had brought in Gordon Cowans and Chris Woods as coaches as well as Roeder. None of the actual purchases were a success and ironically it was Cowans and Woods who, when they had to play, were the better value.

My own worries about him did not take long to arrive, however. Being a football manager is a 24-hours-a-day job and the change from player to manager is a huge shock. Players do not live in the normal world, they lead a strictly regimented life, they are told what to do, what to eat. Basically, all they have to do is turn up for training and most things are provided for them. One thing they certainly have to do is be up and get to training on time. I've said to many a player that there are two eight o'clocks in every day. With that and my stopwatch there is the inevitable banter. I eventually came to wonder if Chris was the best early riser in a morning.

The other noticeable problem for him was that he was truly a cut above the players that he managed and I suspect he found it very frustrating trying to get his points across. You only have to read Paul Weller's book *Not Such a Bad Life* to see that. His vision when he had the ball at his feet was superb, but other players did not read the game well enough to anticipate his passes. As a player he was a joy to watch, especially his control and striking of a ball with little or no backlift.

Pre-season was in Northern Ireland and with all the political troubles over there we had quite a few concerns about safety and security. We had a Special Branch officer with us most of the time to add to the general unease. Adrian Heath had arranged it all before he left, so we did wonder if it should go ahead and so asked local MP Peter Pike for his advice. He in turn contacted the Northern Ireland Office in London; they made contact with the RUC over in Northern Ireland, and their advice was that there was no risk to our safety and promised to look after us. The tour went ahead.

Nevertheless, the tour was not without its lighter moments. Heading to one of the games at Coleraine, Chris asked the Irish driver in no uncertain terms to slow down a bit. The driver unfortunately had no idea where the ground was as he careered round the narrow country lanes with us hanging on for grim life.

'But I'm going as fast as I can so I can find it in time, 'cos I don't know where I am,' he answered.

The players didn't waste any opportunity to play Waddle's World Cup song, to his huge embarrassment. And then one night, when we didn't know that Irish favourite Daniel O'Donnell was playing in the hotel, the place was besieged by the women who idolised him. They were, of course, mostly either elderly or middle-aged, and the players coming in from a training session were both amused and horrified when they thought that they had come to greet them and were fans of the team. From a distance, when the players saw this throng of women, they thought they were well in, but faces dropped when they saw how old they were. I'd never seen Daniel O'Donnell so went to see his concert at which the women responded in the same way that you'd see at a Tom Jones concert.

We had a player with us on trial by the name of Gentile, a relation of the great Italian player Claudio Gentile. Frank Teasdale had high hopes for him but it fell to me to tell him that this particular Gentile was not much good, leaving Frank less than pleased.

Andrew Firmin remembers being impressed with Waddle during his first game of the season at Watford, when all seemed so bright and optimistic. Nevertheless, we lost.

> New season, new manager, new players, a new era for the Clarets. A new team, a young team, striving to do their best for Burnley. Opportunities for all players to grow stronger and fitter and achieve their goals. A younger, leaner, fitter manager. People ask me what my priorities are for this new season. I tell them, promotion, promotion and promotion.
>
> Watford manager Taylor had reverted to type. Two big lads at the back kick the ball to two big lads up front with little midfield intervention. Depressingly, this works in this division. Regardless of who the manager is, we can never play against sides like this. Instead of doing what we do best, we end up trying to copy what they do. After a couple of close chances, Marlon parried a shot but sent the ball out to be hit back in to Winstanley on the line, who, amazingly, cleared. Jason Lee scored. Thirty minutes gone. Possibly our defence was still patting Winstanley on the back while this happened.

Waddle did maybe three of four things with the ball that I have never seen a Burnley player do. He put himself in the middle of midfield. He saw things quicker than any other player, found angles, released the ball at the right time. He often looked the only means of relieving pressure on our defence. Of course, he played fabulous balls to unsuspecting Clarets. This was a subtly effective performance; some may have been expecting fireworks, but had this been a young unknown, on loan, we would have been clamouring to sign him. It was a novelty to see Waddle challenging for the ball once or twice, but in general he did not fall into the player-manager's trap of trying to do everything. He did take all the free kicks and corners though and we looked most dangerous from corners. After many years, it is a pleasure to use a sentence like that.

The early signs that Waddle was not going to be answer this season were plentiful. Not that he didn't turn things round and eventually save the place in the division, but the first half of the season was dreadful, with Burnley marooned at the bottom at the turn of the year. The November situation was poor, and we had spent £570,000 on his behalf, and now he wanted to buy another player. We didn't, although eventually arranged an exchange deal that brought proven striker Andy Payton to the club.

We were perplexed and deeply worried. Just how could this be happening? Had we made the wrong decision? Did Waddle have the capability to turn it round? In January we were livid at one stage when he had the audacity to send Roeder to a board meeting.

At this particular board meeting we did something that, as far as I know, has never been done before or since at the club. We demanded that he pick Little and Weller, the latter an impish wide midfielder, for the next game. It wasn't a suggestion; it was a direction. We considered that the club's desperate position called for desperate measures. Waddle was furious, of course, but we were insistent and rightly so; Little went on to play a leading part in Burnley's recovery. So did Andy Payton and Weller and Gerry Harrison.

At nine the next morning Waddle rang me, furiously telling me that we would regret what we had said. The argument that followed was along the lines of he was right and I was wrong, and vice versa, of course, fuelled by Roeder's comments that Glen Little was not fit to tie Waddle's shoelaces. If I remember rightly, we won the next game and none of this was ever mentioned again.

The signs might have been there earlier in the season when as early as September he had requested that we change the date of a board meeting that he was unable to attend. He was still living in Sheffield and stayed in Burnley two nights a week. Of course, we expressed disappointment, especially Bernard Rothwell. Looking back, you might smile at the effrontery of it, but in truth for a manager to ask for a meeting to be rescheduled so that he could attend was new territory for us.

Even after all this there was another meeting he did not attend. Bernard Rothwell was incandescent and thought it an utter scandal. It was decided that if we were relegated, he would be dismissed, but if, somehow, we managed to survive, he would be offered another year with strict conditions. All of us were left shaking our heads at a manager who had missed another meeting.

Just as in the Orient season, nothing was safe until the very last game of the season. And just as in that same season, it was the penultimate game when disappointment was so intensely felt. In this instance, a 3-1 half-time winning position at Oldham Athletic was squandered, which led to such tension in the final game against Plymouth Argyle.

In any other season the Oldham game might have been seen as a classic and the best game we had seen. Waddle was tracksuited on the touchline, saying that but for injury he would have played. Old friend Neil Warnock was on the Oldham touchline. For the neutral, this was a game that had everything, including the weather. Win this game and the situation was simple, we would be out of the bottom group with survival in our own hands, not depending on the results of other teams. The fans came in their thousands, so many that before the game began another area of the ground adjacent to the away fans had to be opened to take the overspill of hundreds of Burnley supporters. The atmosphere was electric.

There are arguments in football regarding if there is any such thing as a must-win game. The answer is, yes, there are at this stage of the season, with this game and just one more remaining. It was to Waddle's credit that he had turned things round from the abysmal first half of the season and a Christmas position of being marooned at the bottom of the division. But here we were still alive – just. Thus, when Burnley took the lead from a terrific Andy Cooke header from a corner, the supporters went absolutely wild. Quietly so did we in the directors' box, if there is such a thing as quiet wildness. Within 90 seconds Oldham had equalised and the Burnley silence quickly turned to groans. The scorer was Ronnie Jepson who would actually join Burnley when he signed for Stan Ternent.

It was Paul Weller who restored the lead. Taking the ball in the middle, he sent a long ball to the left for Andy Cooke to latch on to. Cooke controlled, took a few paces and crossed. It came to Weller, who controlled it on his heel and sent the volley crashing into the back of the net. It was a marvellous goal so that, once again, players and fans went wild. Weller was about to succumb to a debilitating illness that would take nearly two years out of his career. But to his credit he came back to become an integral part of Stan Ternent's journey towards promotion.

When Glen Little scored to make it 3-1 before half-time, and then when an Oldham player was red-carded, all of us thought we were home and dry. How could we possibly not play out the game and win. Little's goal was a strike from 15 yards after great work by Andy Payton. The red card was awarded for an alleged elbow to Andy Cooke's head. Maybe it was harsh, awarded on the recommendation of the linesman, but that was of no real concern to us at the time. We were coasting, tails up, what could possibly go wrong. Everything.

From a classic solo breakaway from the halfway line, they scored; 3-2 and time to chew fingernails. But just play safe, we thought, control the game, they are down to ten men and teams down to ten men do not come back from 3-1 to make it 3-3. Do they?

Yes, they do. By now the rain was lashing down and pools of water glistened on the pitch. To our utter dismay and astonishment Oldham equalised. Now it was Oldham fans and directors jubilant as we sat and silently moaned in dejection. It's football, it's what makes the game so great. But not when it happens to you.

In the background, of course, was the Peter Shackleton takeover story; the takeover that never was. Nevertheless, Frank Teasdale had arranged for him to have two tickets in the very cramped directors' box and a car space at the Oldham game. After the game, to say he was dejected was an understatement. We too were not best pleased, but for a different reason. We had gone over to the game with our neighbour and good friend who had driven us all. After the game, his coat was gone and in it the car keys, of course. The only coat still there was Shackleton's. Frantic phone calls tracked him down and an hour later he sheepishly returned with the coat and the keys. Sometime later, Ronnie Jepson, who had played in that game, told me that even down to ten men, Oldham would have gone on to win the game had there been another five minutes. Burnley were dead on their feet he said, just plain unfit and, it seemed to him, clearly lacked fitness training.

As many a previous Burnley book – Paul Weller's for one – will relate, Burnley beat Plymouth 2-1 in that final game in front of over 18,000 people, twice the season average. The Plymouth manager said it was like a bear pit out there. We stayed up and Plymouth were relegated. It was Burnley joy and Plymouth tears at the end. Considering what was at stake, it was a remarkably physically restrained game, unlike the brutal game against them when they came with Peter Shilton and a play-off place was at stake. Remarkable too, looking back, was the fact that I had given not a great deal of thought or worry to the climactic Plymouth game. At that time, I was still working flat out with my business so that even though Burnley Football Club was my passion, just every now and then there were things that took precedence. Maybe that was not a bad thing in the week leading up to this game. I told Tim Quelch my thoughts a couple of years ago.

> In my opinion, Waddle was still a useful player but not a good manager. He seemed pre-occupied with his media interests, often leaving the running of the team to his assistant Glenn Roeder. As the relegation worries intensified in the New Year, we became increasingly exasperated with the often-absent Waddle and that was the prompt for when he was required to report to the board on how he proposed to overcome the growing danger of the drop, and sent Roeder instead whilst he attended some media event. Roeder had already made himself very unpopular with the supporters at a fans' forum when he disdainfully dismissed their calls for Glen Little's inclusion. Little was an unconventional but hugely talented winger.
>
> Having averted relegation by the skin of our teeth, the directors were undecided about whether Waddle should be retained. I wasn't completely averse to the suggestion that he be given a further season in which to prove himself. We recognised that this first year in management had been a steep learning curve for him, but that perhaps he had learned from his mistakes. However, when I discovered that both he and Roeder were tied up with the England World Cup squad during the summer, Waddle as a media pundit and Roeder in some coaching capacity, I became very concerned about who would take care of the club's preparations for the next season. As it turned out, Waddle took the decision out of our hands and resigned shortly after the Plymouth game. It seemed as if he had lost his appetite for the job.

Problem was, it seemed to me he was still a player, with a player's mentality. So he seemed to work what we might call players' hours, which is hardly a full day. It was me who was seen as the one who provoked him into leaving. We had to ask him what did he see himself as, and did he want to be a football manager, a 24/7 job, or a pundit. And it was me listing the questions that he needed to be asked, so hence it was solely me I suspect he saw as the one who didn't want him there. And that wasn't really true. I had written a list of items where Chris needed to change if we were to continue with him, so that he would be 100 per cent committed to being manager at Burnley. We certainly couldn't carry on with a manager that the players were sometimes baffled by, never knew if he would be in for training with them, left things to Roeder more often than not and seemed just far too cavalier. He even had the builders who were doing our new stands over to his house in Sheffield to do some work. To be fair, he paid for the work.

Frank Teasdale met him after the season ended with the list I had prepared before Chris went off to the World Cup on media duty. It was a forthright meeting and Chris would not agree to it. Frank showed the list to him and it was signed by me at the bottom, because I had written it, but in fact for Frank. But Waddle saw my name at the bottom, so if he blames me for him leaving, this is why.

CHAPTER TWELVE

1998/99 Stan the Man and a New Era

THE MINUTIAE of running a club over 12 months, many things unseen by supporters: shares were being transferred to Ray Ingleby; Peter Shackleton was still insisting that things were in place for his takeover; the club bank account was £177,000 in the red; new man Stan Ternent wanted to strengthen the squad; Paul Weller needed a triple operation; changes to coaching staff; new contracts for players. Doc Iven was made club president, Ingleby was telephoning me asking for a place on the board. The eventual new board later in the year would have just four directors: myself, Barry Kilby, Frank Teasdale and Bob Blakeborough.

We had pipes under the pitch ready for undersoil heating but with cash-flow problems could not afford the boiler and there was no boiler house. We hoped and prayed that until we could get these organised there would be no freezing weather. A constant source of annoyance was the number of complimentary tickets the club gave away. On some days it was over 1,000 – the visiting team and directors, all club staff two each, home players and their families, ex-players, the community people, sponsors; it soon adds up to a huge figure. I always used to argue it should be more strictly controlled and these were views not too popular. Maybe the new club owners have similar problems. Who should get them was always a hot potato? Where do you stop? Who do you include? The mayor? The local MP? The bank manager to whom you owe money? Local celebs?

There were continual discussions with local planners about developing the training ground at Gawthorpe. They would fall on deaf ears. Today there is a training area to be proud of but it has taken years of effort.

Tuesday, 17 November 1998 is a day imprinted on my mind. It was the day we played Darlington in the FA Cup. I was irked to start with because I had to miss the game, being away in Germany on business but was travelling back as it was being played. At Manchester Airport I got into my car with us winning 2-0. The match was on the radio so I was happy enough with this but by the time I got home we had lost it 3-2, with goals in minutes 81, 87 and 90. I got out of the car utterly fed up and let's just say that the car door was slammed pretty hard.

* * *

It was me that was tasked with organising the replacement for Waddle, as a result of Frank Teasdale being away, or at least I was tasked with drawing up the interview shortlist. It might well have been a case of others thinking that it was me that had made the most noise about Waddle, so let him get on with sorting it. So I did, and I had three criteria. It had to be someone who had already been successful as a manager. It had to be someone that we could rely on to work 24/7. And it had to be someone who had been there and got the T-shirt; in other words someone with credibility. There was no way that this time it would be anyone cutting their teeth on their first management job.

For me there was one standout candidate and that was Stan Ternent. He was working at Bury at the time and had got this tiny, penniless club promoted twice. I made the list, did the organising and the list included Neil Warnock, who came over very well at the interviews, a nice man, not at all like the public image you see. He had won a host of admirers and was a known success at getting promotion for lower clubs. Sam Allardyce seemed keen on the idea and, in a telephone call with me, said he would like to be interviewed, but the chairman of his club would not allow any contact or negotiations, not even an interview. He was reminded in no uncertain terms of his contractual obligations. We on our side were not prepared to break the protocols. It was the unwritten rule and gentleman's agreement that you don't poach managers.

But one who did was Phil Gartside at Bolton Wanderers and took Allardyce to Bolton Wanderers from Notts County. Sam resigned and not long later he was the Bolton manager. Gartside would again ignore protocols years later when he took Owen Coyle off our hands in mid-season to appoint him Bolton manager. We shall leave that story for later.

When push came to shove there was not much to choose between Stan and Neil but Stan lived locally and he was an ex-Burnley player. Town and club were in his blood. It wasn't solely me that appointed him; my job was only to arrange the interviews. Appointing him was a board decision. Were we guilty of ourselves poaching? No, Stan was out of contract in the summer and the suggestion by Bury that we pay them compensation was quickly refused. Mind you, I had unofficially sounded him out earlier – tapped him up, as the saying goes. But, unbeknownst to us, Stan appointed Sam Ellis as his deputy and as Sam was still under contract at Bury, we had to find £15,000 compensation. So were we guilty of poaching Sam Ellis? No. But Stan was.

Fifteen thousand pounds? A bargain when you consider what they brought to the club, how they sorted it and turned it round. They turned out to be worth every single penny and Stan would transform our fortunes. But it would turn out to be a rocky ride, with moments of real aggravation and conflict, and other moments of real joy and celebration. If you wonder what kick-started the journey to the Premier League, my money would be firmly on Stan Ternent. He took us into the Championship and miraculously, against all the odds, kept us there and this was the platform from which other progress began.

Stan signed Michael Mellon from Tranmere and this is of current interest because, as we write, his son now plays for the U21 side. I've watched him and even at just 17 he is a big strong lad with an eye for goals. He could well make it into the big time.

It wasn't long before Stan and I had our first set-to. Barry Kilby had yet to arrive and there was little or no money available for Stan. In our talks with Barry, we did actually ask him would he be happy to work with Stan and his reply was yes. A defeat at home against York City had Stan raging, and rightly so. It was the second home defeat in five days and Stan's patience at last ran out with some of the players he had. A bad injury list could have been used as an excuse, but Stan didn't. At half-time he replaced two players with two 18-year-olds and eventually Burnley had five teenagers in the team.

York carved through Burnley like a knife through butter. They got the winner in the first half, and after that Burnley rarely looked like scoring. Even accounting for injuries and valiant teenagers it was a cathartic experience and made Stan's mind up about four players in particular. They were told that they would never play for Burnley again. Steve Blatherwick, Lee Howey, Mark Winstanley and Michael Williams were told that they were not right for Burnley and not right for Stan. This is not personal, said Stan, just business, adding that he would do his best to get them fixed up at other clubs. They were under contract and would remain on the payroll until they could be sold but it was spelled out to them in no uncertain terms, they had no further part to play at Burnley. They had cost a total of £350,000 but it was the end for them at Burnley. All this was said in an amazing post-match press conference and was soon headline news.

It was when Stan said that they could go on the free transfer list that I thought, 'Hang on, you can't say that. These players have cost money. How the hell do we sell them now?' Stan came into the boardroom and gathered us around him as he said he wanted to tell us something. He dropped his bombshell that he had informed the press these lads would never play for him again. My own reaction was one of shock and anger. A manager might well kick players out, but it's the directors that have to fork out the cost.

'Why on earth did you say this to the press?' I asked. 'How do you expect us to sell them now? Free transfers? We need to get some money back for them.'

While all this was going on, in the background was all the palaver about getting more investment into the club. During the York game there were chants against the board as the Ray Ingleby investing in the club saga dragged on. He was sat in the stands watching the game.

The club was losing money and the grants we had received did not totally pay for the new stands. In fact, the debt was approaching £3m. Even Frank Teasdale realised that something had to be done and Stan Ternent was absolutely hamstrung by the shortage of money to bolster the team. His early days at the club were therefore less than impressive, through no fault of his own, and then got even worse. Only a terrific recovery in the last months of the season lifted the club out of relegation fears.

In simple terms it boiled down to businessman Ray Ingleby versus supporter Peter Shackleton, who claimed to have many contacts in the football and finance world. And this had dragged on and on from the previous season and through the summer.

Time and again I told Frank that the Shackleton offer was simply not worth listening to, but he was the man Teasdale preferred for the simple reason that he would have remained as chairman. We asked each of them to deposit £1m with the club solicitors as an act of faith, which is not unusual. As for Shackleton, no money arrived; lots of promises but never any money. Meanwhile, Teasdale just didn't like Ingleby, a New York-based tycoon. Shackleton's promises of up to £12m were so appealing to Frank, who appeared unable to see the wood for the trees. The state of limbo was likened to that of a stricken tanker lurching along from one crisis to the next and supporters' groups clamoured for decisions to be made and for Frank Teasdale to step aside.

With the mythical Shackleton bid the preferred option, though certainly not mine, Ingleby was still waiting in the wings. He told the press he would certainly not go creeping to the board and joked that he was seen as the 'Ingleby Devil'. We were continually told by Shackleton that the £1m was about to be lodged with our solicitors, but time and again it never arrived. Quite what Stan made of all this, heaven only knows, but he arrived at a club that was in a state of near paralysis, with everybody bar Teasdale realising that the Shackleton bid was a sham.

Eventually even Frank realised that this could not go on much longer, with more and more fans urging him to accept the Ingleby bid. The fans, meanwhile, sick to death of the whole lack of action, were now urging people not to buy things in the club shop as a protest. Six months had elapsed since the saga began with the local press accusing Frank of not knowing what was going on. I could have told them. Frank was simply holding on to the slowly disappearing prospect of the Shackleton millions, and Ray Ingleby, who by now had bought something like 30 per cent of club shares but was not yet in possession of the certificates, so could not call an emergency general meeting, was therefore getting more and more frustrated by the whole thing.

I remember that in the press I was calling for patience. I understood fans' anger and could only remind them of the old maxim 'marry in haste, repent at leisure'. It was something we had to get right. What I could not say publicly that this was all down to Frank Teasdale's infatuation with Peter Shackleton. What I could say was that there were background matters that were confidential and that some things were not what they seemed. Again, something I could not say was that in my opinion the Shackleton money was non-existent.

The next thing we knew was that Shackleton's house was up for sale, which made me even more suspicious, and at the same time Ray Ingleby seemed reluctant to further his interest. Fans saw it all as a farce, especially with the new claim that an oil company worth £750m was behind the Shackleton bid. Supporters countered that with the threat of legal action against the board, and their letter had been sent to the club solicitors. Could it get any more complex? Well, yes, it could, when we heard that the Ingleby business, Caribiner International, had been hit by a stock market plunge. But, we were told, this would not affect his interest in the club.

Maybe it did or didn't but with the pre-season under way, and Stan in situ, Ray Ingleby withdrew. 'Totally cheesed off,' said his right-hand man, David Parry. 'He cannot keep banging his head against a brick wall and the Burnley board will not budge.' An offer to buy 20,000 unissued shares for £3m came to nothing. But still the Shackleton saga lumbered on, with Frank setting deadline after deadline, desperately hoping that there was some truth in the deal. With the season in full swing, Shackleton jetted off to France to talk with his mystery backers, with an alleged deadline of 30 September.

If you, dear reader, are bored by now of the whole story, then think how I was feeling. But the trouble was, nothing came from Ingleby officially as it should have done via the chairman; we only heard in the press. And we were still waiting for the real deal to come from Peter Shackleton. Suffice it to say that the latter came to nothing, as I had firmly said months earlier. We had wasted months of time and energy on a deal that was never going to materialise.

So without saying anything to Frank Teasdale, Bob Blakeborough and I spoke to Barry Kilby about joining the board. What we knew was that two board members, Doc Iven and Bernard Rothwell, were keen to sell their shares and the way was open for Barry to buy them. I have to say I took an instant liking to him, plus I remember the excellent coffee in his office. Funny the little things you remember. Bob Blakeborough and I had been talking to him for some time and a new era at the club was about to begin. Even Frank saw sense, gave in, but would stay on the board, and thus a new name appeared in the story – Barry Kilby.

With Stan asking for more money for new players, tell me a manager that doesn't, I couldn't yet tell him that things were about to change with a new chunk of investment, new capital and new directors. If you were on the coach with him and the team on the way to a game, then there was no escape if he singled you out for a talk about money. To say you got an earbashing is an understatement. I would love to have said, 'Stan, the money is coming, it's on its way,' but there were still things to iron out. Tempting though it was, I could not tell him that things were indeed happening in the background but as yet it was not signed, sealed and delivered. It might just have gone wrong at the last minute.

Stan would indeed get some money and the place by the end of the season was far more optimistic, although that was not before there were four consecutive defeats, including two at home, 0-5 and 0-6. There was no talk of sacking him; Burnley directors have never been guilty of knee-jerk reactions. Besides which, sacking a manager is an expensive business. No problem if you are a top-six big club with billionaire owners, but that has never been the case at Burnley. You have not just the manager to sack and compensate but also his assistant and staff. The new man will come in with his own new team and will inevitably want more money for his own new players.

Yet after those defeats, there were no more in a run to the end of the season that went into double figures, including a terrific win over Fulham, bankrolled by Harrods' Al-Fayed. He, by the way, never made an appearance at Turf Moor. Stan had sifted through a total of 38 players in his quest to find the right ones. The following season would justify all his determination and ruthlessness, and the decision to have faith in him. The way he culled many of those 38 players was almost brutal, but in his own words, it was never personal, just business. It was something he was always keen to say.

It was 30 December 1998 that Barry Kilby became chairman, but do not ever think that this was a swift, straightforward, neat, tidy, harmonious process. In my basement at home, I have an old lever-arch file that bulges with all the paperwork and documents related to the Barry Kilby/Ingleby/Shackleton takeover bids. Take it all out and you would have enough to wallpaper a small French chateau. It was all highly complex, time-consuming and complicated, but in the great universal football scheme of things, you could say this was one of the easier ones.

One thing that was always against Ingleby was the lawsuit taken out against his American company, Caribiner, by a firm of San Diego lawyers. In the end it came to nothing but it did nothing for his image. Added to that, Frank Teasdale just did not like him. Meanwhile, he was buying shares on the open market, many from Harry Brooks. Barry Kilby later brushed it all aside, of the opinion that there were no criminal charges and by the time Barry was on the board, he couldn't see how it would impact Burnley anyway.

The complications regarding Barry came from objections raised by two former directors of the mid-80s, John Jackson and Basil Dearing, who, to cut a long story short, didn't like the way the sale of shares to Barry by Bernard Rothwell and Doc Iven was being done. I never did fully understand what their concern was, but I suppose indignation, in my opinion, might sum up their response. There were quite a few 'humphs' and letters flew back and forth, solicitors were consulted, the local press had a field day.

Not everyone is happy when someone increases their shareholding, as I know from personal experience. There were even suggestions that Barry Kilby might become the new Bob Lord if this went ahead. The ensuing clash at the AGM that year was memorable, between Rothwell, Dearing and Jackson, and all was reported in the *Lancashire Telegraph*. In my letter to the *Burnley Express* I described it as squabbling. The gist of the Jackson–Dearing argument was that Rothwell and Iven were not demonstrating fiduciary responsibility, which made it sound highly dubious, although of course it wasn't. I came into all this because I had to set aside my own rights to buy new shares to enable Barry to buy the shares and the money go directly to the club.

The only way that we could get Barry into the club to become a director and then chairman was an agreement that I and Bob Blakeborough made with him that he could buy any directors' shares who wanted to sell at a fair price and we knew that Doc and Bernard would be happy to sell.

And so, on 28 September of 1998, Barry took his seat on the board, our own solicitors having declared that everything was above board. But even then, Ray Ingleby threatened legal action to block Barry from buying more shares. However, Ingleby was invited to join the board and Barry took up another £3m of shares. And so, all was well. Frank Teasdale stepped down as chairman (I had written courteous and respectful letters to him suggesting that this is what he should do) on 30 December 1998 to make way for Barry to take the chair, and then he resigned from the board on 21 July 2000, selling another 1,722 shares to Barry.

The good ship Turf Moor was thus set for new voyages. Quite where to, we weren't too sure, but hopefully enjoyable ones and not too stormy.

CHAPTER THIRTEEN

1999/2000 A Stan Ternent Promotion

I'D BEEN at Burnley on the board of directors now since 1986 – what's that, 13 years? I'd seen so much in that time that drove me mad. Twice I'd seen attempts to get rid of me off the board. I'd been so frustrated by Frank Teasdale at his reluctance to do anything that involved spending money, but even he had to see the sense of funding the two new stands. I could look at those stands and think, 'I did that. That was me. Without me they would not have happened. We'd have been sitting on benches bolted to the concrete.'

Now we had facilities that were comfortable and helped make money. The spaces and rooms inside the stand behind the goal at the old Bee Hole End were unused, however, despite how we racked our brains to think of ways of generating more income from them.

With that end-of-season run – 11 games if I remember rightly – Stan had steadied the ship, and when Barry Kilby had become chairman in October of 1998 and reassured the tortured board, he had put £5m into the club.

In the previous season, before Barry arrived, Stan had been at loggerheads with all of us. But that had been sorted and smoothed and the waters calmed. Barry was good at that with Stan. And he had stuck by Stan at a time when, after those two awful home defeats, some members of the board were urging Barry to replace him. Barry's backing had given Stan a boost and in typical Stan style he had roared his affirmation that he wasn't a quitter and was at Turf Moor to do a job. People could shout at him until they were blue in the face, but it was water off a duck's back.

For now, we were still in Division Two, above us the target of what is now the Championship. By the season's end, we would be in it and with a surprising addition to the squad. For years I had grimaced at things, now there was a chance to smile.

Ray Ingleby joined after investing half a million. He hoped to raise commercial revenue from new sources. I was never quite sure what these were likely to be but there was mention of financial products bearing Burnley's name. He said his involvement with Burnley was like a drug and he did not regret losing the bid to become chairman. Barry had already added John Turkington, persuading him to join and invest. Ingleby told us he planned to move back to the UK so that he could spend more time with the club.

In September Ray Ingleby was made vice-chairman, following the proposal by Barry Kilby. But I had reservations about him. I advised Barry of my concerns. Barry smiled, I remember, and replied that he'd be a millionaire or go bust. 'I guess the latter,' was my reply. His company had a private jet, a Falcon, and Ray had it repainted claret and blue. He set to work, however, producing a three-year business plan and put more money into the club.

John Turkington said he was prepared to put more money into the club and that if they reached the Championship, the club would need another £5m to compete. At the moment Burnley were losing money, he added. This was true enough, despite all the funds from new directors coming in. He was looking at ways of using the empty internal spaces in the Jimmy McIlroy Stand. It would be quite a while before we got them into operation but, for now, they stood empty, wasted, potential revenue untapped.

We looked at ways to raise money with Allied Dunbar, selling their financial services, and selling telephone contracts via First Telecom. Talks with the cricket club about taking over their ground continued and, as ever, came to nothing. Even with new directors putting money in, money remained as tight as ever, with us all giving guarantees to the bank.

With Stan, there was never a dull moment and after a game against Bristol Rovers that we had lost 1-0 he lambasted the referee Keith Hill, who'd had a dreadful game, including a penalty against Burnley. Off Stan went on one of his tirades – that the referee was not up to scratch, that the game had been ruined by a shoddy performance from him, that he was not good enough to referee at this level. If he had to call witnesses, he could find nine or ten thousand of them. That was an absolutely appalling display from a referee. The ref had failed his responsibilities to players, managers and travelling supporters. Stan emphasised that he wasn't allowed to say much, but it didn't stop him on this occasion. When he was angry, he was unstoppable, and once stopped the coach on a journey home so that he could have his say on the sports programme and reporter that were criticising his team and performance after a game.

Then there was the occasion that the fans booed the introduction of Ronnie Jepson during a game. Stan was livid. 'They are morons,' he said. 'Nobody should treat a fellow human being in this way when they are going out to do their best. Morons.'

There are two schools of thought about this: one that it is always wrong to boo the team or players; or, second, the fans pay their money so they are entitled to shout and boo when things are going badly. I always argue that you wouldn't boo your plumber if he was taking an age or struggling to fix your gas boiler. You wouldn't go into a classroom and boo the teacher. So why is it fair game to boo footballers?

Anyway, three days later he was still calling them morons, refusing to retract it, leaving us, the directors, to say to ourselves, 'Please stop, Stan. Leave it now. Enough is enough.'

Meetings between the board and supporters' groups were always interesting. One such meeting was in September, attended by Barry Kilby, myself, Bob Blakeborough, CEO Andrew Watson and Stan himself, along with around 20 supporters. There was no agenda and it was just an informal, relaxed and friendly gathering that lasted nearly two hours in the Café Claret that adjoined the gym. Sadly, by the way, the Café Claret is no more (it did a good bacon sandwich).

There were inherent problems, of course, in trying to improve things at the Gawthorpe training ground and this was a sensitive issue due to the location in open countryside and so close to National Trust property Gawthorpe Hall. There could well be objections unless we obtained local support.

The supporters had weightier matters on their mind. The price of beer had gone up 20p, from £1.60 to £1.80 in the Centre Spot. But, said Barry, the use of the Centre Spot needed a complete rethink. There was concern at the quality of the pies on a matchday. Something like 3,000 were sold every game. Andrew Watson told the supporters that the suppliers had been told to get their act together. And the programmes: fans who liked to make changes to line-ups or tick those that were playing could not do so on the laminated paper. 'Ah, but some people don't want to, anyway,' replied Andrew.

There was disappointment at the lack of proper pen pictures of opposition players in the programme, said one fan representative. Andrew asked for the views of the meeting on this important topic. I remember the silence. I doubt anyone else there had the slightest interest in the matter, and that it was a very rare person that in mid-game would turn to the programme to read the notes on an opposition player. Meetings such as this were, and still are, useful for gauging supporter feelings, but it left me thinking, 'It's all very well being worried by the price of beer and the quality of pies, but if only they knew of the much bigger problems, like how to keep the club settling all the bills.'

There was just one actual football question on the night and that was to ask Stan how on earth he had managed to get Mitchell Thomas, the former Spurs defender, to sign. I must admit, I was intrigued by that as well, since Thomas was a standout defender and a class above what you might expect in our division. Stan beamed. Thomas was part of the same crowd as Ian Wright and Mark Bright and he knew them all from his days at Crystal Palace. But getting Thomas to sign was an absolute coup. Little did we know it, but it was a signing that would lead on to another one of monumental impact. Star footballer Ian Wright would join us and the whole town was astonished.

A year previously, in December, the club had been in a real crisis. Now, both on and off the field, it was not perfect but better. There had been some good days, including a tremendous cup win away at Derby, and right at the back end of December there had been a memorable home win against Oxford United. Before that, Ray Ingleby announced that the club was prepared to spend more than it earned in order to make money available for the manager on the grounds that we have got to get out of this division. And Ray Ingleby was now adding that it was his attempted takeover of the club that opened the door for Barry Kilby. He had plans to make money for Burnley through Burnley-branded credit cards, insurance and mortgages. Meanwhile, there was a loss of £1.8m.

Chairman Barry had a loss as well when his horse William O'Dee, leading at Cheltenham, fell at the third-to-last fence. Frank Teasdale had not fallen; he was still on the board. And after beating Bristol Rovers, we were fifth in the division and Barry Kilby was busy putting together a prospectus to persuade investors to put more money into the club. I sometimes sat back and thought, 'Is this the same club any more?' There was so much that was good.

Mind you, I well remember Barry once saying to me, 'Oh boy, you certainly introduced me to something that loses money quicker than horse racing.' The money he put in did not stop people shouting at him to get his cheque book out; something that his wife, Sonya, took great exception to, and she gave someone a real dressing-down on one occasion.

But how good was the final game of the century, a Christmas win; in attendance was chairman Barry's magnificent shaggy brown overcoat, an Andy Payton hat-trick, a game pulled out of the fire, the parade of the 1959/60 champions, the parade of the 1968 youth-team champions, the renaming of the Bee Hole End as 'The Jimmy McIlroy Stand', and presentations to Margaret Potts and Hilda Lord. It was a day that had everything. Jimmy's little speech was a masterpiece. He said he was speechless, but Jimmy was never speechless, and said the stand should not be named after him but should be called 'The Champions Stand', in honour of all his teammates. 'Next year you will all be supporting a First Division team,' he told the crowd.

The game itself was a classic. Within minutes Burnley were a goal down. Payton equalised with a penalty and we sat back to await the next Burnley goals. But out of nowhere Oxford got a second and again we were losing. It seemed ridiculous that we might lose. Frustration crept in and the crowd grew restless. Stan Ternent piled on the attacking subs. It worked. Weller passed and Payton scored. And then another Payton goal, a predator's goal, and Burnley had won.

At Christmas we would always invite all the staff into the boardroom for a drink after a game once the visitors had left. Bear in mind we had already had one set of drinks with the guests and now there were more drinks with the staff. After such a great win, bottles were opened with speed and enthusiasm. Alas, I was far from well with the beginnings of what turned out to be cancer. Still here, though, today. Lucky me.

The saddest moment of the season concerned the tragic death of Sam Ellis's son. We were on the way to an away match when the news was received. All of us were in shock and Sam immediately left us to return home. All of us wanted the game to be called off and, with me as the director on duty, it fell on me at incredibly short notice to contact the Football League. I knew immediately that this was unlikely to be granted, and so it proved, despite all my arguments and entreaties. The answer was a flat no, you must play. Players and management were dumbfounded and I am fairly sure I got as much blame as the Football League for the instruction to carry on. As it turned out, we got a draw, with Ian Wright scoring in the 86th minute. His reactions and celebration were magical.

All self-respecting Burnley fans will know how this season ended with four consecutive wins, and the scenes at Scunthorpe, where promotion was clinched on the very last day, were unforgettable. That game has been written about often enough but the game that stunned us was the home defeat to Gillingham immediately before those four wins. It was so unexpected and knocked us for six.

The celebratory bus tour of the town afterwards was a far cry from all the unpleasantness and acrimony that directors had experienced years earlier and it was astonishing to think just how far we had come since the days when we really believed that the club was about to fold.

Ian Wright! How on earth had he ended up at Burnley? What strings had Stan pulled to get him here? And what a part he had played in the promotion. He had scored key goals and brought life and energy to the team. He hadn't played in every game but his influence was there for all to see. It was a real coup and the question was: would he stay? He didn't, but though his stay at the club was short, the memories he created will stay for a long time.

Life works in funny ways; I'd worked so damned hard for the club since joining the board 13 years earlier, had all those battles with other directors. Got those two stands built, battled with Teasdale to get more investors and seen all the progress. But bowel cancer knocked me for six. It meant I missed the triumphant game at Scunthorpe and the bus tour afterwards. Instead, I was at Gisburn Park Hospital. Sod's Law. On the Saturday morning of the game, I was transferred to the high-dependency unit at Burnley General Hospital. Things were in such a bad way that there was a discussion amongst the staff as to whether I should be allowed to listen to the broadcast of the game on the radio. To my great relief I was allowed to listen. But not to be there on this day of days, how ironic was that.

After a lot of persuasion, my wife Sylvia did go. Despite wanting to stay with me, she went to the game with friends. It's been written about already but after the game they all ended up at Stan's local, The Kettledrum – players, fans, directors and wives. Stan knew where

I was and made a point of looking after her. I missed the bus tour around the town as well, but Sylvia told me how Ian Wright sat downstairs in the bus for part of the time, rather than standing up on the open top. She asked him why he was sitting down below. The player who had arrived so unassumingly at the club, with a few belongings and boots in a cardboard box, gave her a simple reply. He had only been a bit-part player, he explained. The day belonged to all the others, not him. Looking back, I wonder now if he sat there because he was feeling a bit wistful. His wonderful football career was now over, the best of days had ended. Player after player will tell you, there is no replacing the feelings that playing gives you – joy, elation, friendships, fitness, moments of fame, and all of the adrenalin. He could have stayed another year if he had wanted, but chose not to. Is that why he sat there lost in his own thoughts?

Meanwhile, for the moment, I sat in my hospital bed with my own thoughts. The game away at Oxford was memorable for the two last-minute goals we scored to win us the game. I'd driven with Barry Kilby to this game and remember telling him as we drove home that we would now get promotion. It was the second prediction I got right. The first had been after the Orient game when I said we'd get to Wembley the next year and indeed we did. Now we had won promotion with Stan. More memorable years would follow but we weren't to know that.

It was in March of 2000 that I made a life-changing decision. I wrote to Barry Kilby regarding the bowel cancer illness.

> Dear Barry,
> I would like to advise you of my personal position over the next few months. The diagnosis looks reasonable with a full recovery possible. I expect to have four sessions of radiotherapy next week, with the operation planned for around 11 April. I will be working normally up to this operation. After the operation I am likely to be out of action for a short period of around 3 weeks before I can do too

much, then slowly returning to normal over the following 8/10 weeks.

I have decided to finally retire from my full-time employment and only carry out part-time assignments. The reason I have not done this before; I like to be busy; I hate to do nothing. This means I will have more time to help our football club, certainly I wish to continue my role of looking after the ground. I should also be able to assist in other areas if you consider appropriate.

There was much more in the letter. We were adding staff at an alarming rate; we needed to review staffing levels. I thought some of the financial projections for the fans' loyalty account we were trying to sell were pie in the sky. Ticket-office figures were not balancing. Was money going missing? Were the right people doing the right jobs? Were some people actually able to do their jobs?

My questions in the letter were a reflection of the kind of person I am: not a blue-sky thinker but a nuts-and-bolts man, a details man, who looks at costs, figures, and all the realities and minutiae of how things operate. Asking questions didn't always endear me to people. Fortunately, that never bothered me too much. But for now, there was this damned bowel cancer to fight against.

CHAPTER FOURTEEN

2000/01 and a Near Miss

PROBLEMS, PROBLEMS, always problems.

Now it was Ian Cox and that he might be asked to play for Trinidad and Tobago in the coming season. When he joined us, he had agreed not to play for them but now Trinidad and Tobago had World Cup qualifier games to play in July, August and September against Canada, Honduras and Mexico. The T&T Football Association confirmed that they would be speaking to us about his availability and we would be compelled to release him if selected. It was the last thing we wanted.

However, under FIFA rules we had to let him play if he was selected, otherwise he would be banned for the next match. And if selected, he would have to report to their training camp on the Sunday evening of the training week. With flights from the UK being an issue, we would find it very difficult to get him there in time if we played on a Saturday.

So, we needed to talk with Jack Warner, a name that could well be familiar today to all football fans, since he would one day face charges of corruption in connection with FIFA, and face a ban from football for life. But all that was yet to come. He was a politician, businessman and was vice-president of FIFA, and an MP in his home country. *The Guardian* had once headlined a piece about him with 'Cut Jack Warner and he probably bleeds brown envelopes'. Whilst a Yorkshireman might say 'how much?' on seeing the price of something, Warner might say 'how much?' if you asked him for something, or for help.

Hearing that Warner was in London, Stan Ternent asked me to go and see him to request that Ian would be allowed to join up with them on the Monday. He was staying at Claridge's, one of London's most expensive five-star hotels, and not just in a standard luxury room but in a large, full-size suite. One assumed immediately that he was there at FIFA's expense. I was granted an audience and, entering the rooms, was struck by the sheer opulence of our surroundings. Small talk done with, he told me that he felt that this was an occasion when his country had a real chance of making it to the World Cup finals and they wanted every player with connections to play for them. At this point he began to talk about the high cost of hotels, so I simply answered that there were much cheaper hotels in London and smiled. Years later and thinking about it, it was possible he was nudging me for a bribe. But to be fair to him, he did acknowledge that our request, that Ian arrived a day late, was a fair one and so Ian joined the long and distinguished list of Burnley internationals.

Of course, it's an honour to be capped by your country, but the club still has to pay the normal salary and if they come back injured, what does the club get out of it? As we write, Maxwel Cornet is away playing for his country, Ivory Coast, in the Africa Cup of Nations. He will be away for five weeks in Burnley's mid-season. What good is that to Burnley, especially with extra insurance to pay? For the club it is a real problem and if the player does not get their international fee, this was another problem we had to sort out. Maybe now it's the agents that do that, so at least they do something for their money.

This was the season that Frank Teasdale retired from the board. As chairman he had been the centre of everything and he clearly found it very hard being demoted, as it were, to a supporting role. When once his phone never stopped ringing and he was in control, now he was on the fringes. I can sympathise. When the Americans, ALK, wanted me off the board of directors, the days suddenly became very empty and quiet. Your focus goes. There are no tasks to perform. Living alone did not help Frank and the club was his world. I did not get on with him as chairman; we disagreed on many things.

Once he left, we got on far better and both of us still laughed about his dislike of Darlington FC. Their old ground was a ramshackle place where even directors had their view of the game obstructed by posts. Frank moaned and groaned every time we went there about the post that obstructed his view. When it rained, as a bonus, he got wet from the drips from the leaking roof. We sat on spring padded seats and when Frank once moved to avoid the raindrops from the roof a spring came through the seat into his backside. It was funny but extremely painful. Whilst he was in agony, we roared with laughter. He took the laughter in good stead but always after that, mention Darlington and he grimaced.

Stan Ternent had the opportunity to sign another goalkeeper, a Greek, Nik Michopoulos. It was an odd situation in that his agent 'owned' him, having bought up his contract from Greek club PAOK. So, Nik came on a month's trial. Now, do forgive me, I have no wish to upset the Greek community, but there were always worries about Greek clubs 'throwing one in', in the betting world. The Greek league at this time had a reputation for being slightly dodgy. We had no such worries with him and he turned out to be a fine goalkeeper and Stan paid him many a compliment. He was a very fine shot stopper but maybe a bit flappy at crosses. A joke did the rounds: one day Nik is walking home and comes across a house on fire. He races to the scene to see if he can help. At the bedroom window of the house is a woman crying with her baby in her arms. Nik calls up to her, 'Hey, throw me your baby. I am Nik Michopoulos, the Greek goalkeeper.' The woman looks at him in more horror and shouts back, 'Fuck off, you drop everything.'

In truth, he wasn't that bad at all.

You do get the weirdest injuries. Paul Smith fell down a broken manhole cover outside his home in Skipton, resulting in a really bad leg wound.

Stan was never happy about what he got out of the youth policy. Once upon a time Gawthorpe had produced a conveyor belt of superb talent. Now, it produced little. He argued it would be better to disband it, save the money and concentrate on finding young players from clubs like Manchester United who weren't quite up to United's standards. He presented a report with his recommendations. The great problem then was that we could only sign young players within an hour's travelling time around Burnley. And within an hour of us were so many top clubs scooping up all the young lads. On one side of the Pennines was Leeds United, on the other Manchester and Liverpool. What chance had we? All we could argue was that any young lad had a greater chance of progressing to the first team with us. Anyway, the idea was not taken up. The PR of disbanding the youth policy would have been so negative. But even today, you have to wonder if the investment at Gawthorpe, now Barnfield, will pay off in terms of players coming through. Whether we should upgrade to a full-blown academy was another discussion. We didn't. Alex Ferguson advised that a school of excellence would work just as well for us.

Money, as ever, was the issue, not just with aiming at academy status at Gawthorpe but in fitting out the empty spaces in the East Stand that lay unused, thereby wasting valuable potential income. Only £1m to fit them out into corporate areas, but we just didn't have spare change like this lying around. New directors were putting money in through their share purchases but all this did was pay existing costs and wages. Barry Kilby's money was helping to pay off the new stands and new players. Gareth Taylor came in on a one-month loan deal but even that was costing us £5,000 a week and £750 match appearance money. Good players, and he was one, don't come cheap.

We played at Fulham in September. Would we get to meet the illustrious Harrods boss, Mohamed Al-Fayed, we wondered. Fulham were flying high and aiming for the Premier League but Al-Fayed had yet to erect the statue of Michael Jackson at the club. But when he did, he was ridiculed, and the next owners didn't want it and neither did the National Football Museum. Quite where it is now, I have no idea.

The big question was, would we get to meet him at last? On previous visits we had not. He was always holed up in a separate room adjoining the directors' room in what we assumed was solitary and resplendent splendour. Guarding the door were two security guards in dark suits and they never failed to look threatening and ominous. This particularly annoyed Bernard Rothwell, who always liked to meet the chairmen of our opposing club and if they didn't show up, he would complain to their other directors. Well, bless me, at half-time we did get to meet him. This, I suspect, was because they were winning. This time, before the game started, Bernard said to the other directors that he hoped that we could meet the chairman. So, at half-time Al-Fayed comes in beaming and smiling but we certainly weren't. There were handshakes all round and Al-Fayed, of course, was still beaming even more at full time when they won. On one occasion we saw at first-hand how concerned his guards were for his safety. His room was off a staircase at the top and as we climbed up the stairs, a waitress behind us carrying a tin tray tripped and dropped it. There was nothing on the tray but it dropped with a hell of a clang and immediately Al-Fayed's two heavies appeared grim-faced and hands inside their jackets. We knew immediately why their hands were inside their jackets; they were ready to whip their guns out.

This might be a good time to tell a few more boardroom tales that I came across. When I first started, boardrooms at the lower-end clubs were always friendly places. There'd be a small buffet, tea and coffee and in most a small bar but not always. At Torquay we saw that the tiny bar was locked up. So, someone walked in, shook all our hands and Bernard Rothwell, who loved his whisky, piped up and said a drink would be nice. 'You can have one after the game,' said the guy, gruffly. He turned out to be the secretary, and promptly marched out.

Today, Premier League boardrooms are less friendly but the food, often fine dining, is usually outstanding. Derby one time was less than friendly when I was challenged to a fight early in our Championship days. It is the only time I have seen directors fighting amongst themselves. One of them challenged me and I told him not to be so daft. I heard later he had once been an army boxing champion, so my decision not to accept the challenge was a wise one.

Do you remember Delia Smith at half-time in one game at Norwich coming out and berating her supporters and yelling at them to get behind the team? 'Let's be 'avin you,' she was shouting at them. There were quite a few folks who wondered if she'd maybe had a few too many. At Norwich there is an area cordoned off in the main lounge and she herself has a private room. On this occasion we won the game 4-0 and she could not hide her anger at this scoreline and says to me in exactly the same manner, 'You should be smilin' then.' Their manager Nigel Worthington was sacked immediately afterwards.

At Barnsley, a wonderfully friendly lot where there were three good stands and one that was semi-derelict and in danger of a roof fall, the directors' lounge remained in this relic of the 1930s and we often used to wonder if it would collapse and bury us while we were in it. We would sit in this stand to watch the game and there was an old and ancient telephone just in front of us, just sat there gathering dust. We used to wonder what it was for, who last used it, how long it had been there. Maybe it was for the chairman in the 1950s to call the manager and tell him to buck things up a bit. Anyway, we cracked a joke about it one time, and the next visit, it was gone.

At Blackpool it was mostly the Oystons we used to meet and the fans were up in arms about them. We were there on the day the fans decided to throw tennis balls on the pitch to disrupt the game to show their anger. Clearly, the Oystons knew about it and turned up with tennis rackets. After the match, which did go ahead and was completed, we were all locked in the boardroom with the Oystons, directors and guests, whilst the fans pelted the windows with tomatoes and eggs. The police let them get on with it but I assume would have intervened if they'd been lobbing stones. But then, maybe not, who knows?

At Stoke, when it was an Icelandic consortium that owned the club, it was just weird. The Icelanders really kept themselves to themselves and their boardroom was split in two with the English in one half and the Icelanders in the other half. But to get to their half they had to walk through the English half and could only do this when a path had been cleared and then they all marched along in single file one behind the other. I always thought how funny it would have been if they had all marched in step.

Perhaps it is here that I could describe what I have always thought of as the Battles of the Ladies Room. Old Bob Lord was a stickler for the segregation of the men and ladies up in the hallowed areas of the director hospitality areas and it was his good wife, the formidable Hilda Lord, who made sure that all etiquette was observed and never a man or lady should meet in any room. Margaret Potts, Harry's feisty wife, did her best to challenge this but was given short shrift. In fact, she was roundly chastised one day for wearing a trouser suit, so any hope of integrating the men and ladies was never going to happen.

At Burnley it was a slow process to get rid of these ancient traditions and not until Sonya Kilby arrived with Barry was true integration achieved. In between the rigid Hilda and the more modern Sonya, I did attempt myself to introduce something. It led to a real battle with another director, who perhaps shall remain nameless to spare his possible embarrassment. But it did involve him one matchday rearranging the two rooms I had organised so that we could have a mixed guest lounge and a ladies' room as well. I had actually telephoned all the ladies involved to let them know, and believed that all was well. However, the director, who shall remain nameless, took it upon himself to move all the ladies who had chosen their own ladies' room back into the mixed guest room. To me this was real Basil Fawlty stuff. When I arrived after a call from staff,

I gave them the choice of either location. The ladies, all bar one, actually preferred their own private little room where they could natter away and the men would not hog all the sandwiches, and so moved back into their own little room. All bar one that is; and the one exception was the wife of the director who shall remain nameless, who remained in the mixed guest room. Basil Fawlty stuff it may have been, but it led to a real rift between myself and this particular director colleague.

Directors have always argued and used as their excuse, when criticised and accused of misogyny, that they need to be able to discuss things in private with other directors from other clubs, but it was Karren Brady that really set the cat among the pigeons in a bit of a set-to at Notts County one day. Karren at the time was a Birmingham director working for Sullivan and Gold, the owners, and Notts County were at home to Birmingham. So, she goes into the boardroom, which is for directors, and Derek Pavis, then the chairman of Notts County, asked her to leave on account of her being a woman. Well, Karren does not take things lying down and so stood her ground and there was the mother of all discussions. The press got hold of the story and gleefully ran it for days. I mention all this because Karren, Sullivan and Gold are a real friendly bunch and always tell me they love to come to Burnley since it is such a wonderful traditional club. Karren, Sullivan and Gold are now at West Ham, of course, and land their helicopter at Gawthorpe. Helicopters have never been our style at Burnley. Tradition, by the way, at Newcastle and Chelsea is hard to find in their directors' lounges, which look more like nightclubs.

This was the season that we finished seventh, missing the play-offs by just two points. You can look at any defeat and say that this was the game that cost us, but in this particular season it was the penultimate game and the defeat at Sheffield United that was the sickener. It was also the infamous game when Stan was livid at Neil Warnock, who sent someone down to the Burnley dressing-room door to eavesdrop on the half-time talk. I believe there was a punch-up at some stage between Stan and Warnock's assistant, with at least one Burnley player ready to help Stan do some serious sorting out. Had I been duty director it would have involved me, but, mercifully, I was not.

Before that we'd had a really good six-game run that had us within sight of the top six. We could also point to two games where we had conceded last-minute equalisers. To rub salt in the wound, Blackburn were promoted to the Premier League. We'd played them twice and lost both. Before the first one there were appeals for calm, meetings with the police, apprehension and worries about serious trouble. These would be the first meetings for 17 years. These could be great sporting occasions, we said, more in hope than expectation. Stan Ternent was philosophical about the first defeat – good to get it out of the way was the gist of his response. And trouble? Let's just say that the dismissal of Kevin Ball for sending David Dunn six feet into the air, and the large number of arrests in the town after the game, were the icing on the defeat. The return game at Ewood Park was lost 0-5 and of that we shall say little, other than the Blackburn directors swigging champagne afterwards. Years later we had the last laugh when we beat them 2-1 at Ewood on the way to promotion. In the boardroom afterwards we asked for champagne at the bar. This time there wasn't any. Funny that.

It was during this season that the idea to buy the neighbouring cricket ground continued. Years earlier Bob Lord had done his best but, in the process, simply alienated the club officials, especially the chairman, who was more than a match for Lord. Mind you, after we abandoned the idea, it would be resurrected sometime later by Brendan Flood and Paul Fletcher. But for now, it was almost dead. We were prepared to pay for them to move to nearby Fulledge, but local residents put up a fight, arguing that too many of their windows would be broken by flying cricket balls, and dog walkers would lose their strolling area. The whole scheme involved us buying a suitable location, building them a new clubhouse, laying a new pitch and 101 other things that would be part of the scheme. The bottom line was that the cricket club people really did not want to move. That, plus all the objections, brought things to an end, or so we thought.

Anyway, off we went to Portugal on a post-season bonding-cum-reward trip. Vilamoura, to be precise, on the south coast, along the Algarve. Stan always enjoyed these reward trips and even included the players that had been released, if they wanted to join in. Club policy at the time was that there would always be a duty director, and in this case it was my turn. There is a golden rule: what happens on a trip stays on the trip, unreported. And so, all I can say is that we had a grand time in a beautiful resort, with its harbour, marina, beaches, old ruins, golf clubs, nightclubs and varied entertainment. This, of course, was 20 years ago and since then the place has grown and developed hugely. But the cost? Was it justified? What was the point of it? The best you can say is that it was a great unwind. Old Bob Lord 30 years before this was much the same and always enjoyed an end-of-season holiday. But it's the pre-season tours that are important, when you can justify the cost.

CHAPTER FIFTEEN

2001/02 Stan Ternent and Me

LET ME say straight away that Stan Ternent was good for Burnley Football Club and that we owe him a huge debt for what he achieved, and that today we are the best of friends. Working with him, there was never a dull moment. We had rows and confrontations galore. I suppose you could say he was high-maintenance and I was the maintenance man. And I mean that in the nicest possible way. You never quite knew what mood you would encounter, or what problem he would set you, or what predicament we would experience.

There are enough Stan stories to write a book. Ah, come to think of it, there is one: Stan wrote one with Tony Livesey. Frank Teasdale did not come out of the book too well. I too got a few mentions and am pleased to say came out of it unscathed, even though they managed to unearth one story of my penny-pinching. Sometimes I wish I had been born a Yorkshireman and my first words would have been 'How much?'

The team were training on the pitch at Turf Moor one morning and when I saw Stan, I called out, 'You got a minute, Stan?' We were standing in front of the Cricket Field Stand and I pointed up to one of the advertising boards bolted to the front edge of the roof, 80ft above our heads.

'Who's the best shot you've got,' I asked. 'There's a board up there for Hansen Offset and it's hanging off. If you have someone who could whack a ball up there and knock it off, it would save the cost of a crane.'

Stan looked at me as if I was joking. I actually wasn't.

'Clive,' he said. 'Do you want him to hit the O or the T. Pay up. Get the crane. Andy McNab couldn't hit that with a fucking rifle.'

What happens on the coach stays on the coach was the golden rule. I always kept to it as I was a guest on these journeys while they lasted, until Steve Cotterill ended the practice. But when Tony Livesey mentioned a few of the things that happened on coach trips, that rule was broken. So, I can confirm that the tuna sandwich story is perfectly true. Stan was indeed furious when he discovered that all the tuna had been consumed and tuna was his favourite. Up the coach he stormed, demanding to know who had eaten all the tuna sandwiches. One of the newest directors was on the coach with me and it was his first experience of this.

'Is this normal?' he asked. All I could do was tell him the golden rule – 'Say nowt. Keep your head down. Whatever happens on the bus, stays on the bus. And yes, Stan loves his tuna.'

Looking back, it surprises me how often the name Scunthorpe crops up in my time as director. Of course, as we know there was the marvellous triumph at Scunthorpe when promotion was won. Some years prior to that, in the early 90s, we always seemed to be ordered to play our games there at the ridiculous time of 11am, by order of the police. I was so angry on one occasion I wrote an impassioned letter to them and the local paper that listed all the reasons why this was such a ridiculous kick-off time. It was a waste of pen, ink, time and paper. And then there was a memorable cup tie, when Stan was manager and I was duty director.

It was a January cup tie in 2001 and we'd drawn the first game 2-2 at Turf Moor. The replay was at Scunthorpe, managed then by former Burnley player Brian Laws. It was 1-1 at full time, 1-1 after extra time, and Stan was livid with the referee, adamant that Burnley should have had two penalties awarded. In truth, Burnley were played off the park for most of the game and, but for goalkeeper

Michopoulos, would have lost easily. After extra time Burnley went on to lose the game on penalties, 5-4. But Stan fumed about the penalties and stormed off down the corridor to confront the referee. He fumed about the fans too, when they booed as Payton was subbed and young Mullins came on. But on the night, it was the referee he was determined to collar and barged his way past a steward and accosted the ref in his changing room. As duty director it fell on me to try to get Stan away and on to the coach. I barged past the same steward and got into the referee's room.

Stan was livid with me, 'You can't effing come in here.'

The ref was livid with me. 'You can't come in here.'

So, there I was in the middle of them with both of them yelling at me to get out. Dear God, I thought, all I'm trying to do is keep the peace and stop a real situation from developing. By this time too, the police had arrived in the shape of the match commander. At this point we headed for the coach. But the coach was nowhere to be seen. The police had stopped it from getting to where Stan wanted it, so we had to scurry along the pavement between Scunthorpe fans on one side hurling abuse at us and Burnley fans on the other hurling abuse because they weren't best pleased at the performance. On the coach I just sat there wondering, 'Just what am I doing here?'

'I'll help you write out your resignation letter then,' I told him one time. Barry Kilby had gone away and left me to handle Stan and all his requests. Demands might be a better word. Barry was glad to get away for a break, glad to get away from all the phone calls he got from Stan. With Barry gone, it was me that got the calls, day after day, and all the demands. My ears were hurting after a week of it. When yet another call came and I'd said, no, we can't do that, he collared me face to face in the offices and said with emphatic fury he would resign if that was the case. OK, I thought, I've had enough of this.

'Fine, Stan, follow me, we'll go into the secretary's office and I'll help you write out your resignation letter.' I headed towards the secretary's office, got there and turned round. Stan had gone, nowhere to be seen. I didn't see him for two days.

Stan was also a great one for managing to get games postponed. One such was against Bradford City one year when we were wanting to sign Bradford player Robbie Blake. This might well have been the occasion of our biggest row, when we were due to play Bradford City in the Christmas period when we might have expected a really good gate and a bumper payday. On the day in question the undersoil heating was on but there was a covering of heavy frost making the pitch look dodgy. The grass leaf had held all the frost and, when cold, the frost remains but is easy to clear. First you brush it and the heating will clear it if it is brushed in time. The referee agreed to inspect the pitch with us at 11am on the day of the game. Stan, however, had met with the referee at 10am, unbeknownst to me, and the game had been called off. So, there was me at 11am looking for the referee and Stan and they were nowhere to be seen.

Contrast this with a game in the early 90s, away at Halifax in the days of John Deary and Roger Eli, when the snow was so bad the mounds of it that had been cleared off the pitch were 4ft high. Fans still remember it, had some great snowball fights, and many of them in a convoy of buses parked up, and watched from the top decks of the buses.

Anyway, for the Bradford game, we had various players injured and Bradford had this little player called Robbie Blake playing for them who was a bit of a handful. Plus, we were wanting to sign him. I suspected immediately that this was why Stan wanted the game off. I was livid and we had the mother of all rows, with me telling him that the pitch was fine and we had missed a chance of a bumper income; we were well short of money and just couldn't afford to miss out. With supreme irony, the day of the rearranged game it was called off again at the last minute after a day of rain. When at last the game was played, we had Paul Gascoigne in our side by then (and that's another story) and we had signed Robbie Blake, who went on to become a great success. The game was a draw, with Gazza making a rather undistinguished debut, although to my delight there was at last a huge crowd and a bumper payday.

The bowel cancer was a nuisance, to put it mildly. I missed board meetings at the beginning of the season, there was another operation and more recovery time. I'd already had three. Truth is, it had knocked me out and I needed some quiet recovery time, but you still can't switch off. There were building operations to get sorted regarding the club shop and offices. There was a players' strike on the horizon. The players felt that they were not getting enough of the TV money so that 99 per cent of them voted to strike. That is to say, 99 per cent of the 90 per cent that voted, an exceptionally high turnout. It was an unprecedented level of support. Peter Ridsdale of Leeds United said if it went ahead, it would be the end of football as we know it. Common sense prevailed in the end.

Even though it was a forlorn hope, we still wanted to work with the cricket club and get them a new ground. The old Lucas Sports Ground at Reedley was a possibility, but it came to nothing. The cricket club weren't keen. Michelin were leaving Burnley and wondered if we would like their sports ground for the cricket club. It was too small. We looked at Fulledge and Burnley Wood. We talked with them about becoming a joint company. They resurrected the idea of moving to nearby Fulledge but politics became involved when we realised it would become an election item in May.

There were plans to possibly expand the Bob Lord Stand. It would have been reasonably straightforward, by retaining the old stand but taking off the roof and then extending upwards and backwards. Plans were drawn up and discussed but it was a simple decision not to extend; we couldn't fill the existing stand, let alone double it in size.

For tactical reasons, manager Stan wanted to reduce the pitch to a size that is now the minimum required for Premier League games. Given the choice, Sean Dyche would have made it even smaller to curtail the footballing sides like Manchester City and deny them the space they use so well. On the occasion one season that it was reduced below the required Premier League minimum, we were fined £40,000. The following season he wanted to keep it at the less-than-required size, but had we done that it is certain we would have been fined again, and possibly had points deducted. The board overruled him.

Discussions on whether to ditch the youth programme at Gawthorpe continued but I did get the go-ahead to begin the redevelopment and improvements to the training area. It would be a long, slow road and took years to get to where it is now with its array of pitches and indoor areas that eventually cost nearly £10m. The press said there was money available for signings. This was rubbish and Stan was not best pleased.

So, there's me recovering from bowel cancer and all the operations and all the recuperation and I'm still running round like a wild thing. Sylvia insisted we went away to get away from all this, so we took a cruise around the Caribbean. But you still don't switch off as you churn over all the things that you need doing and that are constant worries.

Punch Taverns wanted to know if we were interested in buying the Park View Inn across the road from the ground. We didn't buy it, but what an opportunity this would have been to develop it commercially, linked to the club, matchdays especially. A Claret Restaurant, social centre, shop maybe, museum area – the possibilities were endless, but there was no money. Years later it lay empty and derelict and thoughts of buying it were resurrected, renaming it after Barry Kilby, who by then was involved in his prostate cancer campaign. Those thoughts, too, came to nothing.

And then towards the end of the season Gazza arrived. Stan had pulled off a masterstroke getting him to sign and his plan was to put him up at his house with his mate, minder, friend, Jimmy Five Bellies, on Friday nights before any game. Stan's wife, Kath, put her foot down and said no. Whereas Ian Wright was a huge success and will always be welcome back at Burnley, this was – is – not the case with Gazza. Other than the memorable free kicks in the final game at home to Coventry, he did little to write home about. If just one of them had gone in, we would have been in the play-offs and he would have been a hero.

As it was, the Coventry keeper pulled off two magnificent saves from Gazza's two free kicks. In the boardroom, disappointment would be an understatement. It was the final game of the season and, in truth, it marked the end of any real hope of getting to the Premier League for us and Stan; it was all downhill after that. The Paul Weller book will tell you more about Gazza's time at Burnley. Sadly, he was less than complimentary about his time at Burnley and in his book that came out later he was largely ungracious. The players certainly enjoyed his company, and on the training ground raved about his skills, but these were rarely seen on the pitch when he played for us. Stan thought he could be just as inspirational as Wrighty had been, but it never happened.

At one point during the season, we had been seven points clear at the top, were playing some great football, and you could have been forgiven for thinking this was going to be the season that Stan got us to the Premier League. But following a 5-1 defeat at Manchester City, results after that were patchy to say the least, with some horrible defeats at places like Grimsby.

If, after the Coventry game, the trajectory was downwards, there was a huge reason for that, namely the ITV Digital fiasco. This was the season it reared its ugly head. ITV Digital, an ITV subsidiary, had cut a deal with Football League clubs for television rights. The deal put £1m a year into Burnley Football Club, so we spent it and budgets were based on that for the next three years. In March 2002 ITV Digital went into administration and for various reasons left all Football League clubs well and truly let down. Some clubs suffered financially more than others, and we were one because the contract was far from watertight. Football League solicitors had been very lax and had poorly advised the member clubs. Any thoughts about suing the solicitors came to naught. In suing the Football League, we would be suing ourselves, as it were. So, there we were, badly let down, a substantial chunk of income gone; it had funded new players and future wages. Our budgets were up in smoke. We sat for long hours considering the implications and how we ourselves had jumped the gun in the sense that we had done things that needed the future income from the contract, and that income had now vanished. The impact would be enormous.

We had signed Dimitri Papadopoulos, for example, for £500,000 on a three-year contract. He looked a really good signing – quick, sharp, athletic – but unfortunately we hardly saw him. Under FIFA rules he was always on call for the Greek under-23 side and they seemed to play every week nearly. He was probably back in Greece as much as Burnley.

Arthur Gnohere was another one who came in, a centre-half, a superb African player, built like a tank, powerful, muscular and skilful. He had the talent to have become a bedrock of the side for the next ten years, but that never happened. He eventually faded from the team, driving Stan and the coaches mad. One of his problems was a lack of understanding of money, or, shall we say, handling his money. He never understood hire-purchase arrangements and ended up with four or five cars and I wonder if he understood that the deposit wasn't the end of it, and that you then had to continue paying for the car. Anyway, they were eventually all collected on behalf of the finance company. It was a waste of a great talent and he was offloaded to QPR.

CHAPTER SIXTEEN

2002/03 Juggling with Finances

I REMEMBER the flight to Norwich this season with the players that we organised. I say 'we' but I had nothing to do with it. The memories of a flight I organised to Brighton some years earlier were still painfully imprinted on my brain. The trick was to get fans on to the plane to subsidise the costs. But in the case of the flight to Brighton that was only the half of it. This was in December 1992 on Boxing Day with Jimmy Mullen at the old Goldstone Ground. If I remember rightly there were protests at the ground that day about someone wanting to buy the ground and build houses and a DIY store. Whether these building plans ever happened is beyond the realms of my memory.

With it being a Boxing Day game and the Football League in its wisdom making this a long-distance journey, there was no way we wanted to travel on Christmas Day, meaning that the players and all of us, for that matter, would miss the day with our families. So, the flight was from Manchester to Gatwick on a daily scheduled flight, and then coach to Brighton. But the cost. This was the problem. Do fans have any idea of the lengths that we directors go to to get things done?

It involved me contacting British Airways to see if I could get a deal for the team and what we may call VIP supporters – in other words, those that could stump up the cash. BA were happy to cooperate in order to fill the plane. So, we booked two flights, actually cheaper than booking a hotel for all of us Christmas Day in the evening, the one down in the morning and one back at night. Unfortunately, nobody had told me that Jimmy was terrified of flying. He was less than happy with the arrangements when he found out what was happening. We got him to the airport and it was then that the problems began when he was clearly reluctant to board the aircraft. To get him on, we had to get the captain out of his seat, talk Jimmy on to the plane and sit him in the cockpit next to the pilot in the jump seat. The captain promised to talk to him all the way down to Gatwick. So that was how we got Jimmy to Brighton. There was none of the security back then that you see today when nobody is allowed in the cockpit and the door is locked. Indeed, in those days, if a plane was overbooked, one passenger sometimes sat in the jump seat.

So, we got to Gatwick and as ever my wife was with me. Players and directors got on the team coach but the wives had to travel on the supporters' coach. What we did not know was that many of the Burnley fans had been given miniature spirits bottles by the stewardess, so by the time we got to Brighton we had a lot of very tipsy fans. Lunch in Brighton was then at two different hotels – one for players and directors and staff, and the other for fans and wives. Ours went splendidly but at the other hotel the meal wasn't ready and more drink was taken. This by the way was at quite a posh hotel on the seafront. With minutes to spare, the meal arrived, was eaten quickly and by now it was half an hour to kick-off. All of them rushed out but in so doing, one fan fell over and crashed into a table of the best china. Much of it was broken when it landed on the floor.

So, on to the coach and even then the daftness continued when the fans, or some of them, kept opening the emergency exit at the back. My wife was furious when she finally arrived and refused point-blank to go back after the game on the fans' coach. To cap it all we lost the game.

Back to Gatwick but Frank Teasdale insisted the wives went on the fans' coach. Impasse. So, taxis were booked. At Gatwick we all met up in the BA Lounge. The fans, meanwhile, or some of them, were now causing mayhem riding round on luggage trolleys and having races down the concourse. The police threatened to remove them from the airport; I was summoned and had to tell them all to behave or they would have to make their own way home. That, I am relieved to say, hit home and all calmed down. On the plane, at last, was when I vowed never again to organise any flight to a game. On the flight to Norwich in 2002/03, I sat back, enjoyed the sausage breakfast, let commercial director Anthony Fairclough take the strain, and laughed like mad when at the airport someone shouted as we exited the plane, 'Hey, this is just like being in Europe.' We lost this game 2-0 on a roasting-hot day.

And whilst on the Norwich subject, it reminds me of a meeting between Barry Kilby and Delia Smith. This was at Turf Moor and there they were chatting away amiably with Barry convinced she was called Celia. She did nothing to correct him and so the conversation went on with all of us within earshot willing him to remember her proper name. It was his wife, Sonya, who decided something had to be done. Up she went behind him and gently tried to tell him he was talking to Delia not Celia.

'Barry … Barry … she's called Delia.' But Barry was having none of it.

'Sshhh,' he said to Sonya,'"Don't interrupt while I'm talking to Celia.'

The season 2002/03, was memorable for ridiculous scorelines, most of them with Burnley on the wrong end. Despite scores of seven and six and five by the opposition in this head-scratching season, it is in fact a 2-2 draw at Bradford that sticks in the memory. Bradford, just across the Pennines, a derby game almost and no love lost between the two clubs.

We had this young Greek player called Papadopoulos and in the few games he played he showed he was more than capable of emulating Burnley legend Harry Potts for winning free kicks and possible penalties. Papa managed to fall over – or, to use an unfortunate word these days, dive – so that at Bradford he was close to causing a riot. It was early in the season and in a game where the opposition has two players sent off, you do expect to win, especially in this game when we were leading 2-1 with just minutes to go. With Burnley showboating in their own half, they lost the ball and nine-man Bradford promptly equalised. Burnley fans were incensed by their own team; Bradford fans thought they had just won the Champions League.

Burnley were already thoroughly disliked in this part of the world, remembered as a physical, ugly and dirty team from the previous season. Brutal was the word used by the local press. Bradford manager Nicky Law (now employed at Burnley) said they had been warned by their scouts that Papa was a diver and that nobody should go near him. Some players are prone to falling over, gravity seems to exert an extra pull, mysterious forces help them keel over on to the floor. Papa naturally fell into that category.

In this 2-2 game, one Bradford player was duly sent off after an incident with Papadopoulos. He was in fine form with his reactions to tackles and going down. Bradford fans were ready to lynch him after this continued so that Stan eventually took him off for his own protection. Another player was sent off for giving Dean West a fat lip, but it was West who should have gone according to the furious Bradford fans. Once we took a 2-1 lead the abuse and derision that was hurled at us was appalling, including us in the directors' box and I really feared for our safety.

A third goal for us would have killed the game but three gift points were spurned. We were labelled cheats and nasty. At Burnley we still talk about the Orient game; at Bradford they talk about the day they drew 2-2 with horrible Burnley.

The season had begun with four defeats in a row, there were serious cash-flow problems thanks to the ITV mess-up, directors were asked to loan the club money; this was serious stuff. Two of us put in £250,000 each; others £150,000. There were discussions about the need to sell players. In simple terms, we were spending more than we had coming in. It looked like the budget would need to be halved; we calculated that over the next two years we would be over £4m short and just where do you find that kind of money? Cut the budget by 50 per cent and we wondered if Stan would see this as constructive dismissal. The Papadopoulos antics at Bradford were trivia compared to all this. Our CEO Andrew Watson was tasked with talking to Stan – 'Better you than me,' I thought. Within 12 months we reckoned to be over £1.5m short. Nobody was interested in buying players; all clubs were in the same boat.

Paul Gascoigne, who had now left the club, was claiming we had not paid him his one month's notice money. An agreement with the PFA was to do with employment law so when a player finishes a contract and is not offered another one, he is offered another month's pay in lieu of notice. Without this a player can bring an unfair dismissal action, or at least could do back then. When we signed him, he had agreed not to expect this payment and signed a waiver in front of myself and the chairman. I had been given the exact wording to be used, by the Football League. Unfortunately, we got the wording slightly wrong, so Paul – or his agent, more likely – spotted a loophole, claimed the month's money, even though he knew he had signed the waiver.

Yet another set-to with Stan: we had a trust fund for the improvement of Gawthorpe training area and out of this fund I paid £8,000 for drainage to two of the pitches, which up to that point had none. Stan argued that this was general maintenance and not improvements. Seeing as there was no drainage to start with, it could hardly be maintenance, I argued. It was an improvement as far as I was concerned. The board went along with Stan to keep him happy and the £8,000 was put back into the trust fund. Don't forget at this point we were struggling for money all round. I just shook my head with exasperation.

Stan was the instigator of yet another fiery board meeting and we'd just lost 5-2 at home to Reading. Let me say straight away that Stan was no different to any other manager, and if I was a manager,

I'm sure I'd be the same. A manager will ask for money without hesitation, be it for players, better pitches, and in this case a training trip to Portugal. However, I was not a manager and sat on the other side of the fence, responsible for money and budgets. The trip would be before an FA Cup match against Fulham and would cost around £10,000. Sparks flew, with me against the trip, as I went through the budget and cash-flow issues. Did I say that we hadn't got a pot to piss in and Stan wants £10,000 for a trip to Portugal? Maybe not those words but that was the essence of it. The board voted six to one in favour. Guess who the odd one out was? Of course, Stan thanked the board and then said he hoped that it would not affect the end-of-season trip to Portugal. I was speechless.

Here was I, coming across as public enemy number one, when at the next board meeting I refused to sign the paperwork that resulted from a plan to financially restructure the club and would have included spending money that we just did not have. I held out for a week and said if we went ahead with this, the bank could well call in its guarantees and foreclose on the outstanding loans. Administration would follow.

Loans from directors brought in nearly £850,000 and a loan from the PFA a further £1.1m. There was some salvation from a lengthy undefeated league run so that attendances rose slightly and a superb win over Spurs in the League Cup had seen a big crowd and takings plus the £100,000 TV fee. It led to another full-house game against Manchester United. More money in the coffers, but not enough. The word administration went on the back burner, but trust me, it had been close.

The PFA loan, however, came back to bite us on the proverbial bottom. A new ruling arrived that said a club that had taken out a PFA loan would be subject to an embargo on buying new players until it was paid off. We knew full well that this was going to be a difficult loan to pay back quickly. There were other creditors that we owed money to and it would have been unfair to tell them they had gone to the back of the queue when they had already agreed to wait longer for their money. What a balancing act it is finance-wise running a football club; you walk a tightrope, you borrow from Peter to pay Paul, you take out loans and struggle to pay them back. And all the time you have a manager wanting more money, not that I blame him, that's his job, it's inevitable – if you don't ask, you don't get.

It was at this point, sometime in March of 2003, that the idea was mooted of a sale of the ground and Gawthorpe, clear all the debts, and then pay rent to continue using them. Food for thought. The idea was not dismissed. The wheels inside Barry Kilby's head were in motion, I suspect, at this point.

A welcome diversion about something much simpler was how to publish the attendances at each game. It's a football thing, but how many of us out of interest always look at the attendance at the games on a results page. What did we do? Should we give the actual attendance, as in the number of people on seats, or that plus all the tickets sold, when people didn't turn up. Sometimes that could be as many as a thousand. We went with the former, solely the people who attended. Even during lockdown and games behind closed doors, out of sheer habit how many of us looked for the attendance?

Having beaten Fulham in the FA Cup, the quarter-finals beckoned. It would be an away game at Watford, a winnable game and we were definitely hopeful of, if not a win, then at least a draw and a money-spinning replay at Turf Moor. There would be money from TV for the away game and a sum not to be sneezed at, £400,000 if I remember rightly. And then more if there was a replay. Suddenly things were a little rosier.

What followed was one of the biggest let-downs of all time, with an abysmal performance from Burnley so that Watford cantered home 2-0. It was a dire display and a dreadful result, with the door now shut to the semi-finals and a real payday and the solution to much of our financial worry. In the event we shared the prize money with Watford, so it did help. Supporters who were there still remember the poverty of the performance. An appearance in the semi-finals was thrown away, with questions asked about the team that Stan selected.

At this point the name Brendan Flood comes into the Burnley story and yet again the subject of the cricket ground crops up. For those who have forgotten, we should perhaps explain that the cricket ground and the football ground are back-to-back. Today, the cricket club makes a tidy penny out of parking on matchdays and the pavilion bulges with home and away supporters eating and drinking. It is, of course, one reason why the cricket club is probably perfectly happy not to relocate, thanks to the income from football fans.

It was suggested that we should buy the cricket club for £5m via Modus, the Brendan Flood company, and that somehow, out of this, with commercial development, there was a £3m profit to be made. But the local Burnley Council held a covenant on the land that said, after they had originally sold the land to the cricket club many years earlier, that they had to be notified of any change of use. So, even if by some miracle we were able to buy the club, it wasn't just a simple matter of finding them somewhere else and then building a shopping centre and a hotel, for example. Burnley Council had the option of vetoing any new planning proposals. Modus, at this point, had a retailer in place to develop the site. It was agreed that for the moment all this should be highly confidential and hush-hush. Nothing should be leaked and the name Modus should be kept well out of it for the time being. Brendan Flood wanted to meet up with the cricket club, our MP Peter Pike and local residents.

But one big question was a simple one: would Burnley Council approve any idea to have another retail centre when they were trying to improve and upgrade the town centre and existing shops? I was sceptical but was in the minority. Nothing new there then. How Brendan first came to hear of this is a moot point; I'd already been discussing possible development of the site with various Manchester developers but Brendan wasn't one of them. Anyway, Brendan got involved and pushed for an exclusive deal, agreeing that Modus would pay the ensuing approximate £5,000 legal costs, whether it all succeeded or not. When it all fell through after some private talks – it never got into the public arena – it was three years before this money was covered by Modus. In truth, Brendan, who would eventually join the board, and I never really got on, and maybe this was the start of our irritation with each other.

I am not privy to the plans of the American owners and chairman Alan Pace, but if they include the purchase of the cricket club, they will face all the problems that we did. Burnley Council will not take kindly to any change of use and this is something I have pointed out to him. It would make a huge and lucrative matchday car park, as well as offer all kinds of fan-zone possibilities. I suspect the idea of the football club taking over the cricket field land has little chance of success.

And so, the season ended with seven directors: Barry Kilby, Ray Ingleby, myself, Bob Blakeborough, Chris Duckworth, Martin Hobbs and John Turkington. Barry had done well to recruit the latter three who had all invested sizeable sums.

Stan and the team went off on the second jolly to Portugal. This time I was not with them. There were three consecutive defeats to round off the fixtures and the final position was 16th. The financial position was poor, more cuts were needed, the prognosis was depressing. The squad would be down to the bare bones and to maintain the place in the Championship would be a tall order. Stan was understandably hugely concerned about his budget, the number of players he could possibly have and the level of wages he could pay them. There were players that he knew he wanted. What he was brilliant at was wheeling and dealing. He would need all his skills and more for us to survive. It was as bad as that. He wasn't to know that the coming season would be his last and he would be heartbroken.

CHAPTER SEVENTEEN

2003/04 and 2004/05
Goodbye Stan, Hello Steve and Financial Woes

TWO SEASONS of major change; two seasons of financial struggles. Occasional moments of light relief, one of them being the time that Sonya Kilby, Barry's wife, became so fed up of the constant phone calls from the manager to Barry that she threw the phone in the swimming pool whilst they were on holiday. I had this image of Stan holding the phone to his ear whilst all he could hear was the plop and then the soft gurgling sound, as the phone slowly sank to the bottom of the pool.

In the summer of 2003, the financial report was not good and sorting all that out was the number one priority. There was a loss of £1.2m and within a year we could see a cash hole of £2m without the windfalls you prayed for in cup runs. The chairman suggested that he was prepared to buy the gym/leisure centre for £1m and lease back to the club with a return of 8 per cent a year. I was never happy with this since it had actually been run at a small profit and now it was being loaded with rental costs and those rental costs would undermine any plans to invest a little money to provide more activities, that would perhaps in turn make a little more profit. In my view, the rent payable to the new owner, that is to say the chairman, was just a little too generous. Typical me – see the downside and say so at the risk again of being the awkward one. But it was never a case of being deliberately awkward or negative; I simply saw the difficulties of any situation that the club faced. Faces dropped even more when I threatened to bring it up at the next AGM publicly. So, a number of changes were made to the agreement.

There were hopes of further new faces on the board with their share purchases, so there was optimism that we could cope. John Wilkinson joined as an associate director and that was another £100,000. A loan of £330,000 was received from the Football Foundation but had to be paid back within two years and this we figured we could do with future TV money. What is that golden rule? Don't budget money that you don't have and rely on it coming in later.

I was about to say goodbye to £35,000 when we needed new emergency batteries for the emergency lighting. Rather more expensive than a box of AAA for your torch. Manchester United came to the rescue. They were getting new ones and we could have their old ones for free, if we collected them. I wasted no time in saying yes.

My confrontation with manager Stan while Barry had been on holiday came back to bite me on the backside. You may remember I had got fed up with his regular moans and groans and offered to take him into the secretary's office where we could type out a resignation letter, whereupon he had walked away. Barry brought this up at the board meeting in August and gently explained what a mistake I had made. Had Stan actually followed me in and signed any letter, his solicitors could most certainly have accused me of constructive dismissal as I had encouraged him to leave. One of Stan's arguments was that with the size of his budget, the squad was simply not good enough to stay in the division. We offered him a bonus if we stayed up and that resolved the matter. He forecast we would have 60 points by the end of the season; in the event it was 53 but it was only two wins in the last four games that ensured that. There were some tense weekends.

The subject of testimonials came up and we felt, through no fault of our own, that these things were not always lucrative for the player concerned. The reasons were simple enough. For it to be tax-free to the player, the club had to charge for facilities. Testimonials normally run over a 12-month period under the umbrella of a testimonial committee. No officer of the club can be a member of this committee. You'd normally have a dinner, golf day and a football match but the club had to charge for use of the ground and all that this entails. Stewarding, floodlights, corporate facilities, food, staff, all have to be charged for, otherwise the proceeds would not be tax-free. Don't ask me why this is so; ask HMRC. It goes without saying it is hugely expensive to stage a football match at Turf Moor and this, if the committee gets it wrong, will lose them money. An attendance of, for example, 5,000, using all the facilities may well lose money, and this has actually happened. When the time came for Brian Jensen to qualify for a testimonial year, there were problems, in the main because his committee seemed not to understand that we had to make charges. It was upsetting all round because Brian deserved something. The failure to get this off the ground was the last thing any directors wanted, because he had played his part over the years and been a splendid servant to the club. He'd had some memorable games over the years, been part of the Owen Coyle success story, probably his best-ever season. Who will ever forget his penalty saves in the League Cup at Chelsea on that glorious night when we won? There were times when he was magnificent.

And still discussions about the cricket field continued. The council would not entertain a supermarket on the site so that was Modus scuppered but the government at this time was planning to relax the rules on casinos. So, we turned our attention to proposing a new leisure centre on the site that could incorporate a casino. We had a presentation from an American company called Isle of Capri whose speciality this was. It looked a real possibility, with the council wondering if they could move their Thompson Leisure Centre to the site. These in fact were exciting possibilities but as usual came to nothing with no suitable proposals for a new cricket ground.

But it was in December of 2003 that the board discussed something that would have caused huge ripples around the town if it had ever gone ahead. The details of the discussions have never been released until now. It was agreed to have a pre-administration report completed by Kroll at a cost of £10,000. Kroll had previous experience of dealing with football clubs and administration, namely Bradford City and Notts County. The simple position was that we had ongoing costs of £5m and an income of £4m. In addition to that were existing debts. It was clear that if we decided to follow the administration route, we would need to do this before season tickets went on sale for the next season, and the Football League implemented its decision to administer a ten-point deduction to teams going into administration. By the end of February, the club would need £522,000 to cover costs of salaries. It was clear that things were on a knife edge.

The timetable for Kroll to complete their report would be 22 January 2004, roughly midway through the season; a season, by the way, when results were patchy and inconsistent to say the least. To add to the pot, Stan was wanting a new contract but he was told that talks on this could not begin for the moment. The aim was then to be out of administration by the end of March.

A manager budget, by the way, is always an issue. Some chairmen are happy to give a manager a known budget; others were not – for example, Frank Teasdale and more recently Mike Garlick. I could never see the problem with giving a manager an identified budget. At the end of the day, it is the club that signs the cheques so it can be kept under control or amended if things were going badly wrong. Giving a manager a budget also solves the endless problem of a manager continually asking, 'What is my budget?'

Kroll were back after the first meeting and spent several days at the club. Then they attended the board meeting of 15 January, at which they provided answers to our questions. Then they left so that we, along with manager Stan Ternent and CEO Dave Edmundson, could discuss the best way forward. The manager reminded the board that if players were asked to help by deferring or reducing wages, then the PFA must be involved. Barry Kilby was adamant that we could not continue as we were. Things were critical; time was running out but all of us asked, did we really want to go into administration? However, it was also agreed that the team must remain competitive and avoid relegation. The latter would bring its own problems of falling gates and reduced income. It was reluctantly decided that administration might well be the answer.

Kroll were asked to rejoin the meeting and were advised that BFC did indeed want to apply for voluntary administration. The mandate would be that BFC wished to enter into a period of a holiday from payments and then to pay off all debts in full over a period of time, if we could get the major creditors to agree. Kroll would be given the task of talking to them and getting the best deals possible. A sub-committee was set up that would include me and this sub-committee set to work at a pace that would have left an Olympic sprinter standing.

Fans see the team on the pitch, they see the newspaper reports and other media items, but they can never have any real notion of what goes on behind the scenes and how directors have sleepless nights keeping things running. Regarding these problems, there were endless meetings, innumerable phone calls, constant pressure and worrying, and don't forget all bar me were still running businesses. This was a period of needing real mental stamina and making your time available to devote to the club. And all the while, time was running out.

By 6 March, we had not entered into voluntary administration but the volume of work we had undertaken meant that Singer Friedlander, our most difficult creditor, would accept deferred payments that would be finished by 2009. Girlings accepted a two-year deferment. Our own bank agreed to stop taking repayments until 2006. Thwaites Brewery agreed to renegotiate the money we owed them, £224,000. The PFA would do all they could to help and support if we needed to speak to players. Everybody's favourite, the Inland Revenue, would defer the £420,000 we owed them for six months, and a VAT payment of £180,000 for ten months.

We also decided to look further into the sale and leaseback of the ground and Gawthorpe idea. CEO Dave Edmundson would begin what he would call his '500 miles' campaign to raise money from the fans. And Stan Ternent was given his budget, just £2.9m all inclusive, and at this point he was fully aware of the state the club was in.

By the time of the board meeting of 15 March, just nine days later, all agreement bar one had been made. In nine days, we had achieved the near-impossible. If you made a film or a TV series, that's what you would call it: NINE DAYS IN MARCH. The word exhausting was inadequate. Only Singer Friedlander were being difficult and had gone to the Football League for discussions with them. But at last, they too were happy with the arrangements; or at least, if not happy, satisfied they would get their money back. Today I look at the sums of money that we were dealing with back then, and then sit back in amazement at the debts the club is currently dealing with. It is not rocket science – debts and loans bring eventual trouble and problems, unless you have an assured income that will cover them; and if loans and debts are geared to being in the Premier League, but relegation happens, then you can find yourself in serious difficulties. The latter, probably the understatement of the year.

All the directors agreed to act as guarantors for the bank loans and paid for our own legal fees that this entailed. Director Martin Hobbs via his business interests in China came up with possible links to a Chinese club Shenzhen FC in the China Premier League. Barry Kilby and Ray Ingleby wondered if there would be any value in Alastair Campbell joining the board. And discussions continued with the manager, still unhappy about his budget, and a bonus package at the end of the season.

With 24 teams in the league, the safety mark was around 50 points, which we had not yet reached so these were nervous times. Redundancy discussions were taking place with club staff and this certainly lowered morale and did not go down well in the town. Two sets of cash flows were produced, one with sale and leaseback, and one without. Directors were asked to loan more money to the club.

A degree of salvation arrived with a new sponsors deal with Hunters Estate Agency, and a new director, John Sullivan, with a wide range of business contacts.

Let me mention one game and it was the strange affair of the goalposts at Hull City on Saturday, 15 October 2022 that reminded me. The Hull goalposts were deemed to be too tall and had to be taken down and sawed shorter before the game could commence. On Tuesday, 28 November 2004, Cardiff chairman Sam Hammam came to Burnley for the game that night and our groundsman telephoned me in the morning to say that Sam had arrived at the ground early and was walking around the pitch, commenting about the size and alignment of the goals.

Let's just say that Sam was one of the great characters of the game. 'Is he mad?' the groundsman asked me. Anyway, the call came to me from the club to say that Sam was wandering round the pitch at 10am. I was not happy. Why was he allowed in in the first place? Groundstaff should have advised him to come back at something like six o'clock. I get another call from the groundsman. Now Sam is complaining about the goals, would I come down and see Sam myself?

I arrive at the ground around 11am. From Sam I get an earful about the goals. All I can do is tell Sam to go away and come back in the evening and if he has a problem with the goals to complain to the referee. I have to tell him to leave the ground and hope that this will be the end of the matter. Er, no …

I'm now sitting in the directors' lounge on the evening of the game before it starts and I receive a call from the police match commander, who is under pressure to open the gates to the general public but will not do so until Sam is off the pitch either in the lounge or the dressing room; would I go and see him please? At the same time, I am informed that Sam likes to sit in the dugout during a game. Under the rules, only nominated people can sit in the dugout and as he has been registered as a coach he can therefore sit in the dugout. The police are unhappy and instruct me to tell him it is OK to sit in the dugout but if he comes out of it, they will have a policeman next to the dugout and he will be arrested.

By now I am thinking I am in fantasy land. This cannot be happening; it is so unreal. What kind of a mad football world am I in? The police are aware that there has been trouble at other games when he has walked round the pitch and are concerned that if his face shows outside the dugout, our fans will have a go at him.

Now I have to go out onto the pitch again and ask him to come off so that we can open the gates and that this is a police instruction. The referee has already told him there is nothing wrong with the goals. My message to him to get off the pitch goes down like a lead balloon and I get another earful from Sam. Nevertheless, he leaves for the dressing room and during the match stays inside the dugout. Just another average day for Clive Holt then.

Next, to muddy the waters came problems with the community department. This has always been separately run and it was not part of Burnley FC. But by mere association people believe that it is run by Burnley FC. It is not. The head of community persuaded the board that they could run the leisure centre and gym better than we could, at nil cost to the club. My belief was that it could have been built on if the club ran it with its various facilities, rooms, computer area and Café Claret. The problem was that the community department ran on grants and if the grants ran out, they had minimal money. It was a real bone of contention on the occasions the club had to bail them out. At this point they were awarding over-the-odds wage increases and taking on company cars. So, whilst the club was paring things down, the community section was ramping things up. I was asked to become a trustee but declined knowing full well the direction things were heading.

If I have made all this sound to be a real tale of woe, then this is exactly what it was at this time. And, believe it or not, sometimes Friday night arrived and I would remember, oh Lord, we have a game tomorrow. An actual game was a welcome distraction. On the football field itself there had been one or two memorable events; the

5-3 defeat at Preston when Stan in the dressing room afterwards, I do believe, was close to walloping Brian Jensen and Barry had to go over to the dressing room to calm him down. 'Stan quits,' said Sky within minutes. But he didn't. Fake news.

Rotherham was the watershed for his time at Turf Moor. Exactly when Barry decided that Stan had to go, I can't say, but I received a call from Stan in between the final two games, Rotherham and Sunderland, to tell me that his contract would not be renewed and was there anything I could do. I did telephone Barry but the answer was no when I put forward a case for giving him one more year. My feeling is that it was not just the Rotherham result, and this was certainly a bad day at the office, but maybe Barry had simply had enough of Stan's demands during what had been a massively difficult financial year. We had reached 53 points and were safe, so that in itself might have been good grounds for retaining him. But no.

Reactions were mixed, of course. The news came as a shock, whether you were in favour or not. There were those who agreed with the decision and those that didn't. That was inevitable. I'd certainly had a love-hate relationship with him and was not alone in that. He had certainly pulled the club out of the doldrums into the Championship and against all the odds had kept it there. He loved the club with a passion and I thank him here for what he did at Turf Moor.

The task in hand now was to replace him and the eventual choice was Steve Cotterill, a young and up-and-coming manager who was certainly different. He inherited the same problems as Stan, however – a lack of money. But at Cheltenham he had learned his trade and how to deal with that. What he also inherited was a threadbare squad because some players had left, Glen Little being one. We could only offer him £4,000 a week, a big reduction on his previous wage. He joined Reading. Several players were out of contract and it was felt that it was the new manager's job to decide did he want to renew them. He didn't and brought in his own players. What he also badly wanted was a decent training pitch and surface at Gawthorpe instead of the well-established mudbaths. It reminded me of the time that we had said to Stan and his staff when they first arrived that we were sorry the pitch was so poor and that we would aim to provide a better pitch for him. 'Don't worry about that,' said one of his coaches, Sam Ellis. 'We play with the ball in the air, not on the ground.' He was joking, of course, I think.

Sometimes nice things do happen in this job. One of the legacies of Stan's tenancy as manager had been the cancellation of the Supporters' Awards Night at Turf Moor and the presentation of trophies that some players had won from the different groups. Basically, it was to do with the standoff between Stan and CEO Dave Edmundson, who wanted a much more polished presentation evening. Anyway, as a consequence, one of the players that had not received his trophy was Robbie Blake. In August we were due to play at West Ham, so the London Clarets group got in touch with the club to ask could their representatives meet up with the team at our Docklands Hotel. As luck would have it, I was the director on duty accompanying the team.

If memory serves, three of the London-based Clarets arrived at the hotel and, as they arrived, several of the team were in the foyer and directed them to Steve Cotterill and his assistants. Eventually the whole squad settled down to watch Amir Khan and his Olympic semi-final bout. The players couldn't have made them more welcome. It was clear that our three guests were impressed by Steve Cotterill and they spent a fair while chatting with him. Eventually everyone moved to a private side room for their meal and the three fans came in. They were clearly overawed as they stood at the front ready to make the presentation. It needed the manager to establish a bit of quietness. He introduced the threesome and the trophy was presented to Robbie Blake to loud applause and an embarrassed and surprised Robbie, who muttered the immortal words, 'Cheers and thanks,' in response to the chants of 'speech, speech'. I'd been entrusted with a digital camera to record the event and this I managed with something of a struggle. A very pleasant evening and the three amigos vanished into the night to 'find the nearest pub' they said.

A word or two about Robbie Blake, who in Stan's final season had found his feet and scored 19 league goals. Without him we may well have been relegated, such was the importance of his contributions. His start at the club had been poor but that was misleading since he needed a hernia operation. Back to full fitness, he was a magical little player, with wonderfully quick feet and a stunning shot that he put to good use at free kicks. He was the nearest thing to Jimmy McIlroy that the fans could see, with a backside that was put to good use shielding the ball and runs along the goal line that were almost a copy of the great man. The club were lucky to have him, but upset was just around the corner as we were soon to learn.

With Stan gone and, in connection with Steve's appointment to the job, the first mention I heard of his name came on the car phone when I was driving along the M65 sometime in May of 2004. It was a phone call from 'Harry'.

'Harry who?' I answered.

'Harry Redknapp,' said the now recognisable voice. He was ringing to support Steve in his application for the job and spoke of him very highly. Steve's CV was a very detailed and impressive booklet. He was duly appointed and it was me that drew up his contract, very quickly, to get him signed up.

Finance dominated the next board meetings, cash flow, whether or not to go ahead with the sale and leaseback plan, and what we could afford to pay the players. We could manage a core of 18 players on just £1,850 a week. But again, salvation was nearby in the shape of local man Ray Griffiths, who was willing to invest £250,000 and become a director. It was only when Bob Blakeborough resigned that this could happen. What does that ASDA jingle say? Every little helps. Regarding the permissible £1,850 per player we could afford, we already had three players on £4,000 a week and three-year contracts.

By this time, it really was clear that any plans to take over the cricket field were dead in the water, but somehow we were saddled with a Modus bill of nearly £5,000, and they appeared to be ignoring my emails. Brendan Flood of Modus would eventually join the board and this would cause problems between us when he arrived. You might say that our relationship was doomed from the very start.

Steve, in the meantime, was starting discussions with Robbie Blake about extending his contract, but trouble was brewing. We'd just had a brilliant win against Aston Villa in the League Cup, morale was high, Steve was doing well. He'd come to one board meeting and asked immediately could we talk about football, not budgets. We looked at each other almost in surprise. This made a pleasant change from the previous manager, whose talk was mainly about budgets and what more could he have.

Unfortunately, Steve had to report to us that Blake was now unsettled by attention from Wigan Athletic and manager Paul Jewell. As always, you wondered just how much stirring up was the agent doing. We refused offers of £500,000 and then £600,000, but all the while Blake was more and more unsettled at the very time that Steve was trying to extend his contract. It was infuriating to both directors and supporters. The agent next informed Barry, the chairman, that Blake was now really upset and would not sign a new contract at Burnley. Steve decided to leave him out of the team for the December game against Wigan, which we duly won 1-0, to our great satisfaction. Paul Jewell received the Burnley crowd's finest selection of abuse and insults. Sometimes you just have to love your supporters. The manager dugouts are right in front of and below the front-row seats of the Bob Lord Stand. I doubt there is more than a couple of feet separating them so that no manager (including our own many times, I have to say) can escape the invective and vitriol. Jewell got what he deserved was the general consensus. Our player had been targeted and unsettled by all the reports that he was a wanted man, that Wigan were heading to the Premier League and that Robbie would get a better deal and more money. He would indeed leave us, but ironically not to Wigan, which gave us huge satisfaction.

A 1-0 win over Liverpool in the FA Cup at Turf Moor was one of those special occasions when we had to wait until the Liverpool directors had left the boardroom before we could let our hair down and celebrate. There is this unwritten boardroom etiquette that says you don't show any real celebration in front of your guests. Our joy was not just to do with the result but also the size of the payday and who we might play next. When it turned out to be Blackburn Rovers, our joy was unconfined. We lost the replay but this was a tie that provided two splendid paydays.

Sale and leaseback of the stadium and training-ground discussions continued. Cash-flow projections indicated that this would give us a working surplus of £1.3m. We were happy about this as long as the chairman was the majority shareholder. The balance would be bought by John Sullivan and his property company, after Magenta, a finance company, had dropped out. The main feature was the agreement that the club could buy the ground back after seven years from the date of sale. All of this was approved at the next AGM. We still laughed at what had happened at the previous AGM when director Chris Duckworth forgot all about it. There were urgent telephone calls that revealed he was standing in a wetsuit, in the middle of a very large fish tank the size of a small swimming pool, cleaning it out.

Robbie Blake had played his last game for us (in this spell) in December, but the manager now reported that young Chaplow was unsettled and Steve wanted to let him go to West Brom for £1m, thinking that all of this sum would be made available to him. Chaplow duly went to West Brom. The season ended with us on 60 points and we were well pleased with the conduct of the manager and the way he had handled things. But the sale and leaseback agreement caused some consternation among supporters worried by the fact that the club no longer owned the iconic stadium or Gawthorpe. Concerns were best summed up in the statement issued by the newly formed Clarets Trust.

> The Clarets Trust board have read with interest the proposal from the chairman, Mr Barry Kilby for paying off the debts of Burnley Football Club. However, the Trust board will not be backing the proposal or recommending that their members do so until further information and guarantees

have been provided. The Trust board wish it to be known that they do not doubt Mr Kilby's integrity or loyalty as a Burnley supporter and believe he is acting, as always, in what he sees as the best interests of Burnley Football Club.

Mr Sullivan, having only recently joined the board, is less well known to the Trust board although he is said to be a Burnley fan. It would be wrong however, to accept the deal on merit without raising certain concerns which we would hope have already been raised by members of the club board, who have already accepted the proposal.

A report commissioned by Supporters Direct in 2002 and produced by the Football Governance Research Centre at Birkbeck University, heavily criticised the use of 'sale and leaseback' arrangements by clubs who sell their ground to a third party and lease it back.

The report said: a number of football clubs in parlous financial positions have opted for the sale and leaseback, of the ground, as an alternative to mortgaging the property, and in order to alleviate long-term debt. Whilst this may be an appropriate strategy for certain businesses to adopt, it is hazardous for football clubs for a number of reasons. Firstly, while the sale of the freehold may assist in alleviating short-term financial pressures and also secure the football club's continued use of the ground, in the medium term, such an agreement can place the club in a vulnerable position. The value of a stadium in a sale and leaseback is likely to be less than the total cost of buying the freehold and stadium construction. It is impossible for the football club to realise the full value of the ground to the club in a sale and leaseback arrangement. In the case of a football club, ownership and security of the ground is essential to the long-term health and this may be jeopardised by moves to sell the ground.

In conclusion, if a football club is to survive the increasingly uncertain future, then maintaining the ownership of the ground will play a crucial role. Ownership of the ground and freehold remains a symbol of long-term financial health. Club ownership of the ground also allows the football club to maximise the use of the stadium as a strategic commercial asset. Clubs should avoid transferring the primary asset to either holding companies or to other third parties in exchange for short-term alleviating financial gain. The hazards associated with loss of control may be irreversible.

The Clarets Trust went on to ask if there are instances of the holding company concept being detrimental to the club. Extremely few, in fact. But has it ever been beneficial?

The football club board has gone against all recommendations, so why will it work at Burnley when it has failed so many times elsewhere. Have other avenues failed? What are the long-term plans of Longside Properties? What is there to stop a third party taking over control and evicting the football club? Have the board of the club taken independent financial advice? How does the £320,000 a year rent equate to the interest on existing debts?

The Clarets Trust weren't the only ones asking all these questions, and more. In the end, way down the line, all would be well, but to buy the ground back, the story became complex and at one stage extremely fraught.

Back to simpler matters. My trips by coach on away days with the team were coming to an end. Steve did not exactly ban directors from travelling with the team but asked the chairman, who never himself went on the team bus, to request that his directors did not do this. His reasons were that he had a bigger management team than Stan, and seats had been removed to give the players more legroom.

It left me with a problem. How to get to all the away games with Sylvia?

CHAPTER EIGHTEEN

2005/06 and 2006/07
Getting the Motorhome

HOW TO get to away games? The problem set by Steve Cotterill just about coincided with my wife Sylvia developing an even greater interest in Burnley Football Club. That, plus we had a dog. The decision we made was to buy a motorhome. It was rather bigger than average I must admit – leaning towards a Winnebago – that could tow behind it a small car. It was a Niesmann and Bischoff model called a Flair. Somehow the idea of driving into a directors' car park at an away game in a 30-foot Winnebago, be it Chelsea or Hartlepool, didn't really appeal, hence the small car. Having said that, had I done so at the Emirates, for example, the effect and reactions would have been quite spectacular. So, we'd find a nice campsite and then use the small car to the ground. The dog was quite happy to be left guarding its mobile luxury kennel. This purchase also coincided with the end of the custom of having a duty director, whose role it was to pay the bills, staying at any hotel with the team. Our general rule was that for any game further than Birmingham we would use the van, with its bedroom at the rear that could be screened off, kitchen and fridge, heating system, Sky TV via a satellite dish, generator, a shower and toilet. Double insulated, it was like being inside a toaster sometimes.

It was ordered from Germany in 2006. Not cheap either – £100,000. We ordered a small VW car that we were assured could be towed and got that in writing. Good job we did; we towed it on its first journey after collection, but because of excessive clutch-plate friction, the car set on fire. To put it mildly, it was somewhat disconcerting to see smoke billowing from it behind us. It needed the fire brigade to put it out. This was the car that the garage had assured us would be towable. Because I'd got that in writing from them, they replaced it without question.

The van's football debut I am fairly sure was for the game at Crystal Palace on 26 August 2006, a 2-2 draw with goals from Alan Mahon and Kyle Lafferty. We stayed in Greenwich, near the Thames. Sounds nice but it was in fact quite a rough area. The Woolwich area was nearby, where Arsenal first started, before they moved to North London. The campsite itself was a good one and we had long walks along the Thames into central London with Jasper, the cocker spaniel. It was the first of many, many trips in this vehicle that still sits in my drive. It has served us well, travelling all over Europe, including to the World Cup in Germany.

Steve Cotterill was keen to sign Leroy Lita from Bristol City and we came close to that in what was a novel but permissible way at that time. Steve suggested that a director might sponsor the transfer fee, plus the agent's fee, and then when the player was sold would retain any fee from the sale. The club would then just pay the wages and bonuses. Today this is not allowed. The chairman made enquiries at Bristol City but the fee they wanted was too high, so that was the end of that.

Midway through the season, the sale and leaseback deal was at last agreed between the club and the purchasers, Longside Properties Ltd, Barry Kilby and John Sullivan. The funding was finally in place and it was all completed a week later. It had been over a year since first mooted. The club would still be responsible for upkeep and maintenance. Make no mistake, this was a major step to get the finances under control.

From the routine to the ridiculous. Two youngsters, Kyle Lafferty and Chris McCann, had signed professional contracts, Kyle on £260 a week and Chris on £300, plus £91 each towards accommodation costs. Compare those salaries to what a couple of 18-year-olds might be earning today at Arsenal or Manchester United. Today they are paid thousands even at this early age. They moved into a rented house together but it was the club that had to sort out their rubbish problems. What did they think happened to household rubbish? Well, most people realise it is collected by the council after you have put it in the bin, and back then this was every week. Alas, our two young footballers simply let it all pile up in the garden until irate neighbours contacted the club. Secretary Cath Pickup went down to investigate and had them piling up the bags in the road for proper collection. Two young footballers learned one of life's lessons: that there is no magic fairy that comes to collect your rubbish. Footballers, eh? Bless.

No one could say that this had been a successful season, but Barry was pleased to have Steve sign a new three-year contract. His problems were just the same that Stan Ternent had experienced: a shortage of money. Results had certainly not been helped by the sale of Ade Akinbiyi to Sheffield United but the offer was too good: £1.5m plus a further million in July. And there were add-ons if Sheffield were promoted to the Premier League. This was serious money. When he left, we were tenth. By the end of the season, we finished 17th. At the board meeting when Steve was asked to comment on recent poor form, he was quick to point out that the sale of his top striker had been critical and had he not been sold, then results would for sure have been better. Spread over February and March there had been a run of six consecutive losses but then a home win against Norwich City had ended the depressing sequence.

The 2-0 win was in front of the Sky cameras and a huge relief for everyone. As someone once wrote: sometimes you have to go without something for a long time to appreciate it when it finally arrives again. Sometimes you forget what a goal feels like, what a win feels like. The gap between Burnley and the bottom three grew a little bit wider. The relief was enormous. Sometimes you can only wonder why a team will lose six games one after the other when they are not really that bad.

The mundane behind-the-scenes stuff continued. Should we sell naming rights for the stadium? But how could we dispense with the iconic, nationally known name of Turf Moor? We couldn't. You could only do this by calling it, for example, The Turf Moor Endsleigh Stadium. In the event, nothing has ever been done along those lines. Possible corporate rooms in the Bee Hole Stand remained empty. To develop them would need money, and there wasn't any available. The number of directors was approaching double figures; it made board meetings lengthy and unwieldy. There was the danger of cliques and factions developing. The thorny subject of the cricket club reared its contentious head again. We talked about a new ploy, buying shares in the club and trying to take control that way. Our information was that something like 5,000 shares existed and we had 250 of them. But only a third of shareholders were traceable. Major shareholders, if we could have found them, might have cooperated. We knew who they were from the shareholder list lodged at Companies House. But it was how to approach them and all the upset it might cause that was the problem, so the idea was abandoned.

Two names entered the picture as possible new directors. We already knew about Brendan Flood via our dealings with him and Modus and the possible development of the cricket field. But a new name was that of Mike Garlick. This would have meant the board would be comprised of 11 members. Both were Burnley men, born and bred, with Mike having been born just 200 yards away from the club. Both would go on to play huge roles in the story of the club. The one, property developer Brendan Flood, with his Modus money funding progress towards the memorable Wembley play-off final and the Premier League. And the other, Mike Garlick, eventually becoming sole chairman and selling the club to an American group in 2020.

Another new season loomed, 2006/07, and the October board meeting confirmed their appointment as directors. It cannot be said enough that these two would affect the club in their own different ways quite monumentally. Mike initially bought 1,500 shares. Steve Cotterill did not attend this meeting but the message was that he wanted another two players to strengthen the squad. I have to smile at this for, having read the diaries of former director Derek Gill, I noted that he, many years earlier, had noticed that all managers seem to suffer from an annual illness called 'strengthening the squad'. We did chuckle, however, at Steve's assertion that he needed a better goalkeeper than Danny Coyne. He informed us that Michael Duff was a better goalkeeper, but Michael was actually a centre-half.

We were in trouble with the Central League for at the last minute deciding to resign from the league. Well, at least Steve Cotterill decided. We were fined £5,000 and embarrassingly I was a member of the Central League Committee from which I had to resign. The board supported Steve in his view, but I was just about the sole voice of opposition. Perhaps I had too many memories of how useful it was, how it aided player development, how it could be used to showcase players we wanted to sell, and if it was to be ended, just where would younger players get competitive match experience? I actually did a two-page memo to list the disadvantages of not having a reserve team. The jump from youth games to first-team games became enormous. It was a backwards step. The PR would be poor. We'd sold season tickets on the promise of free entry to reserve games. Some fans would be far from pleased. Even Accrington had a reserve team. How could we attract loan players?

Chief executive Dave Edmundson insisted it had been done for good reasons, none to do with cost-cutting, and that it was all to do with avoiding the risk of burnout to Burnley's young apprentices. It was allegedly after consultations between the manager and his coaching staff, so as to ease the workload being placed on the young players. It was felt there was risk to their development and yet in the previous season there had been only 18 reserve-team fixtures. But with youth-team games as well, some of them had been playing twice a week towards the end of the season.

My personal view is that it was just nonsense. These were young, fit lads, eager to play, and all keen as mustard. They wanted to be professional footballers and were now being told that playing twice a week, not every week, was not good for them. Ah well, who was I, a mere director, to have an opinion on such matters? Perhaps Brian Clough and Len Shackleton were right. What did I know? My suspicion, wrongly or rightly, was that Steve Cotterill just did not want to use Turf Moor and its pitch for anything other than first-team games. It was not in the best condition and over-use was a problem. That suspicion was strengthened when we later applied to rejoin the Pontins League again but would find somewhere other than Turf Moor to play the games.

Brendan Flood, now on the board, bought more shares and offered to loan the club something near £6m. It was clear he was developing a bigger profile within the club and with the supporters, and he was made joint operational director with Barry, the chairman. This gave him considerable scope and leeway to develop initiatives, sometimes without keeping the board informed. All this new money made a huge difference and made things far different from the years of scraping by and living hand to mouth. I never disliked Brendan, but we were chalk and cheese. He had the best motives for the club and wanted it to succeed. Nobody could argue with that. But even though he had introduced so much new money to the club, the little matter of the unpaid bill for legal costs that Modus had promised to pay in connection with the cricket-club takeover still niggled. In the end there was a compromise and he bought another £5,000 of shares.

Our backgrounds were different. Mine was in engineering, where precision and exact costs were paramount, knowing where every penny went, watertight contracts and sticking to plans. Brendan was an entrepreneur, in property and shopping malls. He might not agree, but in my eyes, he was a risk-taker. Opening shopping malls involved razzmatazz and a degree of showmanship and this is what Brendan wanted to bring to Burnley. When I put this to him, he argued that it was his money to do with as he wished. But the loans he made would one day have to be paid back. None of this should detract from the drive he brought to the club and the pathway he opened up to the Premier League.

Despite all this new money, 2006/07 was the season marred or marked, whichever you prefer, by the run of 19 games without a win. During this time Steve was never in danger of being sacked; the chairman was never one for knee-jerk reactions and both he and Brendan still had great faith in him. Whether supporters did is a different matter. The longer the run went on, the poorer gates became, with the attendant loss in income. Another £2m from Brendan helped, but this was part of a deal the directors initiated that set up a promotion-fighting fund. The deal was that for every £1 invested by a director into this fund, they would get £2 back if we were promoted. If not, they could either be repaid or convert into shares.

But on and on the poor run went. The penultimate game away at Southend was a horrible 0-1 defeat that had fans who were there fuming. They were right. The Southend goal was in the 92nd minute, when a Burnley mistake gifted them the ball. The goal was slammed home. They said thank you very much and we faced a long journey home in abject misery, wondering just where do we go from here. I have it on good authority that the dressing room was like a morgue afterwards. Steve was never short of a reason for a defeat and this time it was because the team had run out of players, for one reason or another, and there was no proper right-back, from which position they scored their goal. There were still two more games to come before we ended this awful run of poor results.

One of the most magical Cotterill games had been away at Luton Town. Ade Akinbiyi scored a stunning hat-trick. Brian Jensen was sent off, so midfielder John Spicer went in goal, but we hung on for an amazing 3-2 win. It was simply one of those games that you never forget, not just for that result but also for the ground itself. To get to the turnstiles you had to pass almost through someone's front room and the boardroom was so small there was hardly room for us all. In the middle of the floor lay a huge dog, usually fast asleep. It was the only boardroom where you had to step over a dog the size of a small pony to get to the drinks cabinet. It was also a room that used to get so hot that they would open the door, but right alongside that was the road, so the traffic noise drowned out all conversations.

Sadly, in April, a great servant of the club passed away aged only 70. I'd come to know Brian Miller over the years in his different capacities at the club and not for nothing was he known as Mr Burnley. From one of the great players of the title team of 1959/60 he had stayed at the club and filled every role there was. He was manager of the side that won promotion in 1981/82 and then, after an interval away from the club, returned to guide it through the Orient season, when the club so very nearly exited the Football League. I shall never forget the part he played that day and the reward was a trip to Wembley the very next season. It shocked us all that such a mountain of a man should pass away aged just 70.

It was during this season that Leeds United went into administration and had ten points deducted. I got to know two of the characters involved with the club quite well over the years. Ken Bates was one of them, and I sat next to him for a whole day at a Football League meeting and one of the things discussed was a Department for Education initiative that was looking at the role that football clubs could play in the education of difficult pupils. It was in fact a great idea and we all agreed on this, until Ken pointed out that it would be the clubs footing the bill. That was true enough when we started just such a scheme at Burnley but had to pay for all the costs involved.

Peter Ridsdale was the other high-profile character involved at Leeds and it did seem that he copped much of the blame for the predicament that Leeds found themselves in, thanks to huge overspending on just about everything, from players to wages to the fish tanks that adorned the offices over there. Presumably they were very expensive fish.

Meanwhile, back to tales of the motorhome. We did a memorable trip to Cardiff, not sure of the actual season, and stayed at Newport in the Tredegar House Country Park. This was, of course, a beautiful place with an ancient house, run and maintained by the National Trust. We arrived one Thursday evening, had a meal in the van and then set about exploring the locality the next day. The only problem was, when we opened the van door, we were in the middle of a snowstorm and deep snow. Anyway, off we went and somehow managed to get back to the van later in the afternoon. The next thing we learned was that the match the next day was off. When we finally left, it took us three hours to dig our way out of the campsite to get to the main road. The M5 was pretty much at a standstill and we pulled off at a service station only to find when we wanted to leave it, everything was stuck on the icy, sloping exit road. Somehow, we got up this slope and eight hours later crawled along the road to our house, which also has a sloping access drive. The drive had to be cleared and it was the following day, Sunday, when we finally got the van and car parked up by the house. So, in terms of getting to away games and back again, I can trade stories with the best of any Burnley supporter. Let no one think that directors, because they are directors, have it easy. And, let me tell you, a motorhome tyre blowout doing 60 on a motorway is not a happy moment. Twice that has happened – once on the way to QPR and once to Brighton. I'm not sure what made me prouder: controlling the van as it careered down the inside lane, or managing to sit through both games.

CHAPTER NINETEEN

2007/08 A Season of Huge Change

WE KNEW that many fans were restless and unhappy with the manager, the style of football, the results and the lack of any prospect of improvement. A run of 19 games without a win does not look good, even though the previous season had ended with some decent wins. Nevertheless, there was no talk yet of replacing Steve Cotterill, at least not at board meetings. But with a board of ten, there might well have been small groups that were thinking his day was done.

The season began with a pre-season trip to Austria with two games to play – coach to Luton and then a flight to Austria, with me the only director. We were based in a sports camp run by David Moyes's brother, somewhere near Salzburg, a beautiful location in a beautiful country. The first game had a backdrop of rolling meadows and small chalets on one side and mountain scenery on the other. It was a stunning location on the outskirts of a small village called Abtenau.

Here, we played a team called Prefab from Romania and John Harley contrived to score a spectacular own goal within minutes. We lost 2-1 in front of at least 200 Burnley fans who had made the long journey. Our manager ignored them all and strode off the pitch without any kind of thank you or acknowledgement. I suspect he might have been happier if no one had been there. A small act of appreciation would have been good PR. Anyway, the highlight of the game was provided by a Burnley fan who had brought a Klaxon and just as a Prefab player was about to take a throw-in right in front of him, he gave the klaxon an almighty burst. The poor lad jumped three feet in the air and must have thought World War Three had arrived.

The second game was at Bad Goisern on a misty, murky day and again the manager ignored the Burnley fans after the game, even though we won this game 4-0, and these were fans that had probably spent a month's wages to follow us out here. This time we had played a Greek team from Limassol and their goalkeeper coach was none other than our very own Nik Michopoulos. The season before, we had, if you remember, beaten Liverpool 1-0 in the cup and this was big news all around the football globe, even as far away as Greece. I chatted with the Greek directors and all of them wanted to know how we had beaten them and what sort of money had we paid to bribe them. At that time, bribery was not uncommon in Greece, so it was simply assumed that we had bribed Liverpool to lose. When I said that no we had not and this sort of thing did not happen in England, they refused to believe me. Stan Ternent used to worry that whilst at Burnley, Nik, being Greek, might just throw one in, if you get my meaning.

Anyway, without bribery, we beat them 4-0 in a feisty game and young Kyle Lafferty was sent off, and this in a friendly. Many of the Burnley fans were by now treating this as an Austrian beer festival and were well lubricated, shall we say. How Kyle and Chris McCann got there was interesting enough. There just happened to be two spare places on the tour, so the youth-team coach was asked which were his best players who might benefit and they could come along. Good job they did, as they were so helpful to me after an accident that I had. The training camp had bicycles and we had the use of these whenever we fancied a bit of exercise in this most beautiful of countries. But on the day that I go for a ride, I had an accident when applying the brakes on a downhill stretch and I went straight over the handlebars into the bushes. My shoulder was agony but I managed to push the bike all the way back to the camp and went to see the physio. He seemed far from sympathetic. He took a quick look, assured me that all was well, told me that I'd be OK, and that was my treatment. However, for the rest of the trip I could hardly use my arm and it was Kyle and Chris who were of great help carrying all my luggage.

As director in charge (this practice of having a director in charge would soon be stopped), it fell to me to be the usual party pooper when it was brought to my attention, by a local chap, what the team-bonding exercise was. Next to the training camp was a river and at one place it was spanned by a bridge from which the players were jumping from some great height into the water below. The local chap was quite aghast because he knew that if the river was too shallow on some days when there had been no rain, anyone jumping from the bridge could be seriously injured. Some players of course jumped in quite happily, but some, and rightly so, were quite apprehensive but were nevertheless pressured into taking part. You might actually say bullied. But the culture was one of macho bravery and the key word was, of course, bonding. If it's bonding, then it's OK. But it wasn't and I had to be the one to say to Steve Cotterill that this is dangerous and that I was far from happy about it. It was stopped. Some players were more than happy with this; management I suspect probably thought, 'Oh, it's 'im again.' But the thought of someone with a broken neck meant it had to stop.

On the final night, I have no idea what the players did, but management and myself went to a nightclub in Salzburg, surely one of the most beautiful cities in Europe. Alas, we did not distinguish ourselves very well and were asked to leave when we began to sing songs from *The Sound of Music* rather too exuberantly. The locals, we learned, actually think that the film is a load of rubbish. Anyway, back we came to Burnley and, apart from the shoulder, this trip was a real treat and a great experience.

The shoulder turned out to be broken, by the way.

I'm sure I've used the expression 'the minutiae of running a football club' before, but this is what takes up so much of the time. Barry Kilby and Brendan Flood put more money into the club under the heading of Project Premiership. Directors put a total of £5.86m into the club during the season, including £1.5m from Barry and £2.7m from Brendan.

The Jimmy McIlroy Stand was at last being fitted out so that there were rooms available for hire, community, business and matchday hospitality. But the signs were there that the community arm of the club was losing money again and we had already bailed them out once already. It can't be said too often that this was separate from the club but when things went wrong, the club, by association, was tarred with the community brush.

Billy Bingham, the former player and Irish manager, was due to be appointed as scout in Northern Ireland. I was never sure how that would work as he lived in Southport.

But how complicated did we make things? The board were very keen to erect a big screen at a cost of £225,000. Modus would pay, and we would then lease the screen via an arrangement with the Royal Bank of Scotland and repay Modus.

We had bought back Robbie Blake for £250,000 and he was raring to go after a poor time at Leeds United. He had been vilified by Burnley fans whilst at Leeds but was now welcomed back as the prodigal son, as if nothing had ever happened. Such is football.

Meanwhile, we were assured that all was well with the preparations for the new ground developments. Brendan had stressed to the authorities that this was an 'all or nothing' plan, rather than doing things piecemeal. But where would the money come from? – new investors, half from borrowing from banks, and then the rest from a combination of grants and money from Longside Properties. John Sullivan was contacting various sources in China and Russia but nothing would be heard of that for a few more years.

In October Brendan brought in ex-player and great favourite Paul Fletcher to assist with the ground redevelopment plans. Fletch had great experience of stadium building and development and was what one might call a blue-sky thinker. Lucky is the board that has someone like this, but luckier still is the board who has someone like this and can also see round corners and what the problems and obstacles and costs might be. Perhaps we made a good unintentional partnership – Paul had the ideas and it was me who could see round corners and all the cost and problems. Brendan's original plans were forecast at £20m but soon went up to £30m when Paul came aboard. Don't get me wrong, there were some great plans, but they were doomed to fail when the world of finance went pear-shaped.

The season began so well with a really good 2-1 win at home against West Brom. Even more gratifying was the attendance of over 15,000. Lafferty and Akinbiyi were outstanding and the second-half performance was eye-catching. Before the game there were jazz bands and even free programmes whilst the sun shone down with August warmth. Alas, the big talking point was running out of peas to go with the pies in the James Hargreaves Stand before the game had started. The subject of pies and peas is always paramount at Burnley Football Club, at both AGMs and board meetings.

West Brom were well fancied to do well so to beat them was seen as an important yardstick and, in fact, within a few weeks we were in the heady position of sixth. But it was not to last and the calls from supporters to replace Steve were growing. Many were right behind him in the Bob Lord Stand and made their feelings known loudly. They are getting 'fidgety' he acknowledged. At this time, too, we had a goalkeeper called Gabor Kiraly, a Hungarian, I think, famed for playing in tracksuit bottoms that looked more like one half of a pair of grubby winter pyjamas. The manager had a love-hate relationship with keeper Brian Jensen, the Great Dane, so he was always on the lookout for someone to replace him. But Brian always managed to reclaim his place.

Shortly after the win over West Brom came a piece of business that must rank as one of the best ever. You may remember the name Wayne Thomas, whom we had signed not too long earlier. He had featured in the game against West Brom but it would be his last for Burnley. There were divided opinions amongst rank and file, and the board for that matter. On the one hand, he was deemed worthy of a place in the side, but on the other hand always close to an error or a sending off. So, when Southampton came along and offered over £1m, our eyes popped wide open. We immediately sanctioned the transfer before Southampton changed their mind. Then when Steve Cotterill went out and signed a replacement for just £200,000, Clarke Carlisle, it was clear proof that Steve had an eye for a deal, and if he had made a mistake with Wayne Thomas, he signed an absolute gem in Clarke Carlisle. None of us had a crystal ball and none of us would have predicted that Clarke would be man of the match at Wembley in 2009. One by one he was gathering the players that would take us to promotion. It was just such a pity that by the end he was unable to get the best out of them.

Crunch time came in November after an abject defeat at home to Hull City and what was coming through the grapevine was that several of the team were far from happy with the manager and that it looked like he had 'lost' the dressing room. When that happens, a club has problems. Following a meeting with Brendan at his home and supper, it was agreed that Steve should leave. In working on this book, I found a very kind letter from Steve thanking me for my help and support during his time at the club. He had clearly forgiven me for stopping them all jumping in the river in Austria. All I can say is, he had a very good eye for a player, especially on the low budgets he had to work with. His downside in my opinion was his rigid approach with the players with defined roles that they should not stray from. Flair was in short supply, shall we say.

I was involved in arranging the press conference to announce his departure and went into the club on the day, arriving in the Bob Lord Stand, then to walk around the pitch to get to the pressroom. To my astonishment, who should I see but Steve. Gathering my wits, my first question was, 'Steve, what are you doing here?' 'I was told I could come by Brendan,' he replied. The next person I meet is Barry Kilby who looks at me and asks, 'What is Steve doing here?' I could only answer that he had been told he could come by Brendan. And so, Steve sat in on his own parting-of-the-manager meeting.

Steve Davis took the team to Leicester and oversaw a 1-0 win. It did his case no harm, but I was not sure about appointing him, wondering if he had enough confidence to be the new frontman.

We appointed a Scots guy, Owen Coyle – well, a Scots guy with Irish roots. A quite unknown quantity. It was a surprise to many; certainly Peter Reid, who was convinced the job was his, from what I read afterwards. His impact was immediate. You could tell that the players were being allowed more freedom and were under one simple instruction – attack and use the wings. There was a real transformation, but results were inconsistent between his appointment and the end of the season. There were definite questions as to whether we had appointed the right man, but when I say 'we', the appointment was down to Brendan and Barry, with a little help from a journalist called Alan Nixon, and Phil Gartside the chairman of Bolton Wanderers. We shall hear more of him later and none of it will be complimentary. Whilst Stan Ternent had signed Ian Wright, Owen signed Andy Cole, another great goalscorer, and his hat-trick at QPR was one of those memorable events that you don't forget.

If Owen's appointment was of huge significance, something else happened that was hugely significant to me. There were issues regarding the company secretary. In a nutshell, we hadn't got one, which affected board meetings. Not having a company secretary was something that could not continue, so I was asked would I take the job on temporarily. Yes, I said, if it's only temporary. I'm not sure you'd describe eight years as being temporary. It was in fact an onerous, unpaid and thankless job, and certainly time-consuming. It consisted of being responsible for board meetings, agendas, and taking the minutes, and it certainly entailed knowing just about everything that was going on at the club, be it legal or financial. It probably put me in a position where nobody knew more about what was going on than I did. And that included the chairman. The company secretary had to run a clean ship, as it were – everything above board and recorded correctly, and making sure the company was solvent. The draft minutes were sent to the chairman to be signed off and then had to be accepted and passed by the board members at the next meeting as being a correct record. Oh, but the complications when I recorded something that someone had said that they couldn't remember, or now objected to, or didn't like, or hadn't wanted to be recorded in the first place. Then there was the matter of money. Our accountant Ken Stout sometimes had the unenviable job of going round directors at the end of some months to ask for money to cover the wages, via loans. He hated doing this and rightly so. In the end it was yours truly that did the job of going round with the begging bowl when it was needed.

So for eight years, until 2016, I was involved in most aspects of the running of the club simply by being company secretary. I therefore knew an awful lot. Some might have thought that I knew too much. The time came when I was asked to relinquish the role, I suspect, because of that very fact: I knew too much.

The season ended with a 5-0 defeat away at Crystal Palace. The London Clarets group, there in force with it being a London game, applied their three-goal rule and left, heading for the pubs to cheer themselves up. We, the directors, were obliged to be made of sterner stuff, and, alas, had to stay to the very end.

CHAPTER TWENTY

2008/2009 and Wembley

THIS WOULD be a season to remember. A stunning season, in fact, so that today, many years later, fans look back on it and say it was one of the best ever. But behind the scenes it was financially traumatic, with endless problems and money shortages. If this chapter does one thing, it will show supporters that all that glistens is not gold and that the nearer that we got to the Wembley final, the nearer we also got to a financial meltdown. In some ways I want this book to be educational, so that people can see just what work goes on behind the closed doors of the boardroom and the accountant's office.

If you want to read in some detail of the great games against Chelsea, Arsenal and Spurs in the cup games and then all the dramatic league games as we edged our way to the final, then you need two books: *Entertainment, Heroes and Villains* by Dave Thomas and *From Orient to the Emirates* by Tim Quelch.

We began with some doubts about Owen Coyle, and was it the right appointment, but this was to be the season that emphatically demonstrated that he had been the right choice. We had ended the previous season with that crushing 5-0 defeat away at Crystal Palace. I confess to spending much of the summer worrying about the club's prospects. On top of that I was now the company secretary, which entailed a huge amount of work and all the aggravation that went with it.

A new member of the team, however, was former player Paul Fletcher, who came in as chief executive following the departure of

Dave Edmundson. Paul was very much Brendan Flood's appointment and his salary was in fact paid by Brendan's company, Modus. So, what could go wrong? I welcomed Paul's appointment. He had a good pedigree as well as being a very popular player in that lovely Adamson team of the early 70s. His overhead goal in the 4-1 defeat of Leeds United at Elland Road was still talked about, although it was a little before my time as a Burnley supporter.

He had worked on stadium projects at Huddersfield, Bolton and Coventry, and had then moved on to the new Wembley project with Ken Bates. All of this is in his book *Magical*, in which he writes that he could not wait to get away from London and return to the sunshine of Rawtenstall. I saw him as someone with knowledge and experience of all the workings and complexities of stadiums and along with this he had his StadiArena visions, which might well have been developed at Turf Moor but for the economic crash that was imminent. He was a man with energy and ever-present cheerfulness with commendable social skills. But we would eventually clash; me, the dogged pragmatist and Paul, the blue-sky thinker. That too is reflected in his book, with some comments that had me pondering on the nature of libel and defamation. But then I thought, 'Can I be bothered to take it further?' He actually began Chapter 17 of his book with the opening line, 'There was one director at Burnley who I have to say I did not get on with.' And then named me. Nothing wrong with that; he is perfectly entitled to say it.

Just one example of the way we came to see things from differing perspectives was the case of the expensive fountain pens. Paul had sourced some fine pens that really were impressive. So, his idea was to buy a supply of them so that new players could sign their new contracts with the new pens, which would then be presented to them as a memento. The problem was they were so damned expensive that my mouth dropped wide open when I saw the invoice for payment. They were £60 each. Of course, a Chelsea, an Arsenal or a Manchester United could have bought them by the barrowload without raising an eyebrow, but we were just Burnley, scrimping and scraping along, even when we reached the Premier League and all its money. That money was soon swallowed up. They were indeed a classy pen but as company secretary I knew where every penny went, and I knew what was essential and what was not. The story is that Chris Eagles used one and left the room saying that it was something that he would show his grandchildren. Apparently, we gave one to HRH Prince Charles when he visited.

Anyway, according to Paul I tore up the cheques that were due to be sent to the pen maker, a guy who I'm told made them in his workshop. When he rang Paul to ask where his payments were, Paul came to me bridling, whereupon back in his office we had the mother of all rows.

My account is simply this. The first I knew of this habit of giving expensive pens away was in connection with signing cheques for payment, and when I received one for several hundred pounds, I just looked at it in astonishment. We had Ken Stout coming regularly to us warning us of cash-flow problems and here we were, the directors, having to loan money to the club, and here was Fletch dishing out fancy pens to people who would probably just shove them in a drawer and forget all about them. What was the point? What did they achieve? In our penniless state they were just frivolous. So, in fact I signed the cheque. It wasn't the bloke who made them that was at fault. So he was paid. But yes, we did have a row, Paul kicked up a fuss, and the practice was stopped. The irony is, to this day, I have still not seen one.

Pre-season we had been to the USA and I had been there as director. Cary Railhawks was in Carolina and a member of one of the leagues there. Football was hugely popular in colleges and universities but had not yet really taken off in any big way, but Brendan had links out there and was convinced that there was a vast reservoir of talent we could tap into. Cary actually beat us 2-1, so they were no slouches. The idea of a partnership was sound; one 17-year-old came over and was hugely talented, but work permits were the problem. A formal partnership was actually agreed with the Cary club and they would be renamed Cary Clarets, and Burnley would provide full support, share training methods and help generally. Alas, it all came to nothing.

My own company had a factory in Springfield, North Carolina, so I was happy to go and share a little local knowledge. But pre-season trips and me were fated to be accident-prone. In Austria I had fallen off a bicycle, and for this one I fell down the stairs at home and thought I had simply twisted my foot. So, off I limped on this marathon journey, gritting my teeth, battling on, and then when I returned home found it was broken.

Prior to the first game we were given an area to train in at a local college that had a wonderful wildlife area and ponds in the middle. Coaching staff and managers are all very much alike in wanting to know that every last ball has been returned after training. Unfortunately, two of the balls had been booted into the wildlife area, so everyone went in to look for them only to be shouted at loudly to get out fast as this was full of dangerous snakes. I have never seen 20 grown men run out of long grass so fast. On my limping ankle, it was a relief that I had not been in there with them.

And so the season began, and not very well, it has to be said. New players came. Kevin McDonald was an outstanding prospect, a joy to watch, but never really fulfilled it at Burnley. Motivation or attitude, you could never really put your finger on it and when he left the ground at half-time after a mauling at home to Manchester City, it was a serious offence. Christian Kalvenes was a classy full-back, short on pace maybe, but scored the goal at Blackpool on a foul night of gales and torrential rain that set the club back on the promotion trail after a blip. Martin Paterson was a huge success.

But what was not a success was the parachute display at the first home game. Some things have gone down in Burnley history as comedy moments: the Smartie Pants Dog troupe, the streaker that was upended by mascot Bertie Bee. And then the parachutist who took a wrong turn and landed on the stand roof. Initially, Brendan wanted to get a helicopter in to land with the ball. As the ground-safety certificate was in my name, I got that idea stopped without too much trouble. Open corners between the stands made the possibility of strong air currents and movements affecting the helicopter stability. OK, so next it was, we'll have parachutists, the Red Devils, and Modus would pay for it. In some ways I felt more comfortable with this as I knew they would be fully safety conscious and have all their own checks and safeguards.

The plans were meticulous … or were they? The first thing I noticed was an officer up on top of the roof with a flare to guide them in. But how had he got up there? Before anyone goes up there, they have to sign in and fix a safety harness which clips to the safety wires. But there he was, up there with no harness. In comes the first parachutist and they all land well, except for the last one unable to control his direction. What did I say about air movements and currents? I was standing next to Brendan to watch it all and, to my horror, saw the last one land on the roof. I had to turn to Brendan and say I wish you'd listened to me earlier. It was the last stunt he ever suggested.

Luckily the guy that landed did so on one of the steel beams that supported the roof. Had he landed in between two of the beams he would have gone straight through. As it turned out he suffered just a cut leg. The police, of course, wanted to call off the game. Would they ever think of anything else? But we persuaded them to let us carry on, once he was down, and this involved the local fire brigade and a big turntable ladder. It all took an age to sort and in fact he was still up there when the game started. Perhaps the police hadn't noticed. It made headline news all round the world.

The world's finance crash was on the horizon. That would affect us badly 12 months down the line, but, meanwhile, Paul Fletcher was keen to develop his StadiArena design at the Cricket Field End. I had no qualms about this as an idea and as a potentially exciting development, but naturally, as ever, I was suspicious about the costings. Yes, I thought, Burnley could well support a venture and facility of this kind and, in a perfect world with perfect finances, with a thriving Brendan Flood Modus company behind it, this would have put Burnley well and truly on the map. Mini-concerts, exhibitions, Asian weddings – the potential for commercial success was there. But mention the word concerts and you'd have a real job persuading local residents to accept and back the idea. That, plus car parking problems were just two of the issues. Looking back, it was never going to happen on finance grounds alone. What did Brendan write in his book? Something about the winds of financial change were beginning to sweep through the world. And soon it would be a tsunami.

But Fletcher soldiered on and his first problem was to persuade the cricket club to sell us a substantial strip of land behind the stand. The cricket club, those words again. How often have they cropped up since the days of old Bob Lord wanting more land from them. How often had we already contacted them about moving them and financing that move. I sat back and let him get on with it, being fairly sure that not even Paul's persuasive patter would get the land. He advised us that the cricket club had been offered £12,500 for a strip that was just five metres by 75 metres. The answer was no, but frustratingly their chairman would not come up with a figure that he might have accepted. The project slowly died and, in a way, it was a great shame and we never saw a full and detailed feasibility study or an itemised business plan.

We, the directors, are on the inside of a club, battling daily with cash-flow issues, finding wages, paying bills, supporting the manager as best we can. Supporters are on the outside. They see the team, the matches, read the newspapers, talk in the pubs and clubs. But what supporters are basically concerned with is results, where we are in the table – can we be successful? Can we win games and have we been entertained? Did they know that we had continual warnings from our finance director, Ken Stout, that there might not be enough money in the kitty, that we were over £1m short to see us through the season? Even as early as November of what was to be this stunning season, there was a shortfall of half a million.

While Owen and the team were doing the job on the field, our job was to keep the club afloat. Brendan emailed us all asking for more loans. We worried about a big fine for our poor disciplinary record – 37 yellows and four reds even before Christmas. Owen was asked to talk to the team about it.

It was put to the board that only members who could give financial input should stay. Brendan was insistent that everyone had to pull their weight money-wise. Again, as early as November he insisted that all directors support his efforts. I'm not sure at that point if we were fully aware of his own business problems. Two directors declined to put more money in and we needed a revised business plan, budget and cash-flow projections.

Meanwhile, the team was doing well. Games were entertaining, exciting; there were some key wins. Owen Coyle had the knack of persuading his players that they were better than they really were. Not that they were ever poor, far from it, but it was Clarke Carlisle who later said that he had the skill of making good players feel that they were very good, and very good players that they were excellent. It made a winning mentality and this was an attack-minded team. The blip came in December and on into January in the league, although cup wins continued. The cup wins were inspirational and brought us to the attention of the media in a big way. How was it possible that a small-town club like Championship Burnley could beat the mighty Chelsea on their own ground in the League Cup? Some of the football was dazzling one-touch stuff that had the pundits purring. Inevitably, I suppose, Owen wanted a better salary, on the grounds that he was one of the lowest paid in the division.

The cup runs had been stunning but everyone at the club was devastated when we lost so cruelly in extra time to Spurs in the semi-final of the League Cup. The home game was one of those wonderful nights under the lights with a full house and a three-goal deficit to overcome. We did just that and then just did not have the legs to hold on in extra time. In its wisdom, the Football League decreed that away goals did not count double, so that, in effect, that was what scuppered us. Players were in tears at the end and they weren't the only ones. Come April we had picked up in the league after the mid-season slump and with three games to go it wasn't certain, but it looked like we would be in the play-offs. We crossed more than just our fingers hoping to get to the final and then who knows what might happen.

By now fans knew that financially things were not good at all, with a transfer embargo made public because of our failure to complete payments for Chris Eagles. What they did not know was that we had more money to find for wages, VAT payments and payments to HMRC. In total, over £1m. Quite frankly it was touch and go and Lloyds Bank sent us word that no football clubs were to be allowed new overdrafts. The types of loans that some directors were prepared to make caused some tension and differences. Finance director Ken Stout was frantic with his warnings of what was needed. Yes, new investors and directors were needed but only if their investments were big enough. Leaving directors would want their loans repaying if new directors joined. In the end, nobody new arrived and it was four existing directors who saved the day with more loans to the club to tide it over to the play-off final. Brendan Flood, with Modus business problems, was unfortunately in no position to be one of them.

By May, and some miracle, the remaining games and the play-offs were all won. Not one goal was conceded. The final home league game was a goal procession and a 4-0 defeat of Bristol City. It was almost celebration, samba football. Reading were beaten twice, 1-0 and 2-0. The two goals away at Reading were wonder goals and Paterson's run from just inside his own half and then a 30-yard strike that went in like an arrow will live in my memory for a long time. Thompson's goal was a fabulous dipping strike as well from the edge of the box. John Madejski was very gracious in defeat. I got back to the motorhome after the Reading game and was receiving phone calls until well after midnight from friends, supporters and business customers.

But next up was the scramble for tickets and the truth is we had an antiquated ticket system; just a small ticket office and a small staff. Elaine Clare worked miracles. Next up was the problem of all directors wanting Wembley tickets for themselves and wives and families if that was possible. I grit my teeth as some directors who had barely been to an away game all season joined the scramble, whereas I had been to just about every away game possible, in the motorhome when necessary. It occurred to me I was the only director in the country who had bought a motorhome specifically for this purpose. Priority was given to the chairman and vice-chairman, and then it was in order of who had been on the board longest. And that was me. I was assured of a decent seat. In fact, we all had a table each for our families and I took my brother, his wife and two daughters.

How time flies. It was only a few years ago that my two nieces were Burnley mascots, dressed in their Burnley shirts for a game at Dartford against Maidstone. Today, Megan is a headmistress at a primary school with two young daughters of her own. Jennifer, the eldest, is still a Claret and works for the Red Bull F1 racing team as an aeronautical engineer. She played a big part in Red Bull 2022 successes via the air-flow control over the current car.

The win has been recorded enough times, the sea of claret and blue, the Wade Elliott wonder goal, the two penalties that might have been given against us by Mike Dean, the man-of-the-match display by Clarke Carlisle. And all the joy and celebrations afterwards. Going on the pitch afterwards with other directors and the players, the view from the pitch of the dancing fans and the empty Sheffield seats. Many journalists wrote wonderful things about us. Little Burnley had done it. The Promised Land. No more cash-flow discussions, loans could be repaid. Ken Stout smiled. He wasn't the only one.

But, going down to the dressing-room area – he didn't see me – but there was Owen Coyle on his mobile phone. To this day I remember my reaction to hearing the snippets of conversation, and me wondering if he was being tapped up with the game not ten minutes over. It was only later that I wondered if this may well have been Celtic making the first overtures to him. At the end of May we had a meeting to discuss the manager's position. Barry Kilby had spent the morning with Owen and the approach from Celtic had been rejected in no uncertain terms. I couldn't help thinking, was it Celtic that phoned him immediately after Wembley?

In the evening the players were at one hotel and we all met at the Stafford down in the basement restaurant area of the hotel to let our hair down and relive the whole day. There was a huge screen showing a replay of the game. The Stafford is known (or maybe not) for the tunnel that goes to St James's Palace, presumably so that various members of the royal family could get there and back undetected. I wonder why? A bit of hanky-panky I wouldn't wonder. The evening contrasted wonderfully with the miserable journey down we had the day before. In pouring rain, we had a puncture on the motorway; fortunately in the car, not the Motorhome. Changing a tyre on the hard shoulder is not an experience to be recommended. 'An omen of a disastrous weekend to come?' I wondered as we set off again. Thankfully not. We parked up on the outskirts of London and got the tube in. I never did see the bill for the Stafford Hotel. I never did see the bill for the players at the Grosvenor Hotel. For once I was not too bothered. But before the game, of course, we were still concerned about money issues, so every director paid their own expenses for travel and hotel.

For me it was an opportunity to think how far I and the club had come since I had first joined in 1986 and experienced the horrors of the Orient game and the old Fourth Division for seven years. And now here we were, all these years later, with so much having happened in between. No one could have forecast this back in 1987. From penury to this. For the first time I could remember we would have a positive bank statement. And in the Premier League. The word astonishing did not do it justice.

CHAPTER TWENTY-ONE

2009/10 The Promised Land and Exit Owen Coyle

SO HERE we were, the land of milk and honey and all our problems solved with that one magical Wembley goal. Games to come against all the top teams in the land, Premier League money filling the bank account, TV coverage, media spotlights, packed attendances and a bit of glamour shining on little Burnley with its cobbled streets, terraced rows, still a few mill chimneys here and there, chip shops and back alleyways. Or at least that was the stereotype view. Now the world would see us, from South America to China. They would catch a glimpse of us for real in Los Angeles and Portland. A great pre-season in prospect until LA Galaxy cancelled a game with us so they could play Barcelona. It cost us £50,000. Then a five-hour stopover on the way home and the next day a game at Accrington. Who says this is a glamorous life?

If only it were simple. If only it was going to be so simple. But in my experience, life – and certainly not football – is never simple. Complications, pitfalls and obstacles lurk around every corner. On every committee or in every boardroom in the land there always needs to be someone who can see round those corners, or make some sort of prediction of what might happen, what might go wrong, if indeed anything could possibly go wrong. Some people live in their own little worlds, where everything will be alright on the day and the sky is always blue. I was usually reasonably good at seeing around those difficult corners or being able to see where trouble might lie ahead. But not even I could have foretold or even imagined the upset that was to come in December and the new year. Our special season would be special alright, but for all the wrong reasons.

From the outside, I suppose everything looked marvellous as the new season approached, but in the boardroom, there were decisions galore for directors to make. But some of them had personal financial pressures to solve – three of them in fact – and another one, Ray Griffiths, was extremely ill.

Once upon a time, only the most dedicated directors wanted tickets for the away games to places like Hartlepool and Stockport. The seven years in the old Fourth Division were a test of resolve and determination. Trips to the dentist were far more pleasant than some of the places the hardy few went to. But now it was the Premier League and everybody wanted places in the directors' box. And there just weren't enough. The usual arrangement was 24 tickets, of which ten were for the boardroom. Extras could go into a guest lounge. Prior to this, demand had been low. Sometimes only two directors would attend an away game. Sometimes directors asked for tickets and then gave back word at the last minute. As you can imagine, this now became unacceptable. In previous years I had been to over 90 per cent of all the away games and was also the senior director and company secretary. Paul Fletcher had to tell us that ticket staff were occasionally coming to him in tears because of the pressure they were under to satisfy insistent directors. On occasions a director would ask for a ticket for his wife and then bring someone else. A supporter buys his season ticket and is assured of a seat without fuss. You may argue that a director is assured of one of the best seats in the house. At home games, yes, but at away games would you now actually get a ticket without fuss? It was requested that directors should be fair and considerate towards their fellow directors.

Next, Owen Coyle came into a board meeting very unhappy in pre-season. An article in a daily newspaper contrasting the lifestyles of Chris Eagles and Michael Duff had caused some fallout. Not so much in the dressing room between the players, but their reaction to how a *Sun* journalist had got into the training ground. For years at Burnley the nearest thing to a chic car was an ageing saloon that might have had a stripe down the side for effect. Chris Eagles then stunned everyone by turning up for pre-season training in a £150,000 Lamborghini. As an ex-Manchester United lad, he was not short of a penny or two and here at Burnley he was one of the top earners. It was a car that stood out amongst the Clarets humble offerings. It contrasted hugely with Michael Duff's mode of transport, his wife's Ford Focus. *The Mail* reported Chris to be on about £15,000 a week.

What a different story it is today, however, as one of them went on to play at the top level until he retired, and the other drifted around the leagues and clubs, finally ending up at Oldham Athletic for a short period. Whilst Chris Eagles's career in its later stages slowly faded and he is no longer in football, Michael Duff has gone on to become a successful manager with all his coaching badges. Whilst Chris is now a recovering alcoholic, Michael Duff took Cheltenham to promotion and is now Barnsley manager. All that glistens is not gold, as the saying goes. At his best, manager Brian Laws said that Chris was superb, in magnificent form after he scored five goals in just four games. At Bolton he excelled and in one season he was their top scorer. The University of Bolton awarded him an honorary degree for his services to sport. But somewhere, it all began to go wrong and his time at Oldham at the end was after a year out of the game. In 2021 he was arrested when police found him inebriated in his stationary car. In total he played 423 games for all his various clubs, scoring 62 goals, so no one can say that his career was a failure. Far from it. We will remember him fondly at Burnley. Michael Duff will not mind me saying he did not have Chris Eagles's skill levels, but Michael was a defender, tough and uncompromising. He ended his playing career with distinction, as a newly promoted Premier League player. Even though he was out injured for a year, he made over 640 appearances and played for Northern Ireland. If one had a

Lamborghini and one had a Ford Focus, it simply shows that money does not buy a long-term future and a continued career in the game.

At the first game of the season, away at Stoke, I was reminded of their curious boardroom again. At one point they were in the hands of an Icelandic consortium, which appeared to be half Icelandic and half British. This was supported by the Banking Group in Iceland until all the banks over there went bust. The boardroom was split into two – one side for the Icelanders and they entered the boardroom using the same door as the rest of us, but then marched in single file across the room to their half. Monty Python came to mind. It was so funny. We lost that first game quite tamely.

The Chelsea boardroom was very much like a glitzy nightclub. Until I visited their boardroom, I could never understand how Roman Abramovich could sit outside in shirt sleeves in most weathers. I soon found out. Above his head were radiant heaters. Bob Lord's heated stand ran up such a huge oil bill after one game, the heating was never used again. Taking it out years later was a devil of a job; it was so enormous. But he was far-sighted so that he did use this heating system to initiate undersoil heating, but it was never finished. Eventually we did get heated seats in our directors' area. A heated seat for me and a sheepskin jacket – just the job.

There was the chairman's pledge to honour. This was the deal whereby Barry Kilby had pledged the previous season that everyone who bought a season ticket would get a free season ticket for this one if we won promotion. That sounds simple and worthy enough but when it was decided to offer to give shares in Burnley Football Club, instead of the free season ticket, it was me that shouldered the huge workload. I silently cursed the chairman's pledge. The paperwork was mountainous. Then, when one disgruntled supporter in the 100 Club wanted a completely free place there, when it was a price three times that of a season ticket, the paperwork and legal responses to his demands fell on me, of course. It was a truly messy situation and took a lot of sorting over many weeks. The pledge looked so simple and straightforward but, by golly, it wasn't.

There were endless things to do to get the stadium ready and up to scratch to meet Premier League requirements. The last one was completed on the day that Manchester United were due to play our first home game and involved alterations to make the away dressing room meet requirements. It is true to say that the fresh paint on the walls was still drying as their coach rolled up. Somehow, we got everything done, but it used up a lot of the new money. Never mind, we won this first game at home in the Premier League, on what was as good as a gala night, with a sumptuous Robbie Blake goal. The football world was in awe of the story of David beating Goliath.

In August of 2009, we held a minute's silence at the board meeting to remember Ray Griffiths who had passed away. He was a great loss with a gruff and blunt homespun wisdom. He was one of the four that put more money into the club as we worked to get into the play-offs to enable us to meet our commitments. Without people like Ray, you do wonder where the club would be and how they would have paid the bills. He was no mean footballer himself and was once on Bradford City's books. It was Barry Kilby that invited him to join the board after he had sold his business, Target Express. He knew finances and the value of a pound inside out. Sadly, he did not get to Wembley to see the wonderful win. He was in hospital. He served the club and asked for nothing in return. If players see how many games and goals they have scored in programmes and lists, maybe directors should have a mention somewhere for how much money they have put into a club.

We talked long and hard about a possible foreign investor who had materialised. There were whispers of someone offering to buy 50 per cent of the club for £25m. And they would provide another £10m of working capital. I never did find out who these mystery people were, but it did lead to discussions about overseas buyers having the real interest of the club and community at heart. Project Ping Pong, named by Paul Fletcher, was another wild goose chase. The gist of it was that Chinese investors would buy 51 per cent of the club for just over £20m. It was never clear quite who we were dealing with and nobody was that keen on handing over 51 per cent of the club. All this via Chinese banks. And were the Chinese government involved. Without proof of funds, it all vanished like so many others and Project Ping Pong became Project Gone Pong.

By November results had seen us in a safe position in the table. Away form was poor but wins at home had made us secure. The one that will never be forgotten is the 1-0 win against Manchester United. Enough has been written about that incredible evening already. The manager was already suggesting, however, that things could well tail off so that loan signings would be needed in January. Director loans had been repaid and with administrators recouping over £5m of Modus money from the club, by Christmas we were in the old position of needing more director loans to aid cash flow. Premier League money comes in two main tranches, with smaller amounts each month. By the time the second tranche comes, needs become not quite desperate but almost, as the first payment is swallowed up.

What a strange atmosphere there was at the home game against Bolton on Boxing Day of 2009. I always loved Boxing Day games, be they home or away. The festive spirit remained in full swing, a feeling of good cheer to all men and all's well with the world. But not at this game. You couldn't quite put your finger on it. Maybe it was the Bolton fans chanting for Owen Coyle. The Bolton party in the directors' box knew something was going on. You could sense it. What was all that about? It soon came to light via a phone call to Brendan from Phil Gartside, asking for Owen's phone number. Brendan gave it to him, unsuspecting of any subterfuge. But what a mistake it was giving him that number, which I suspect anyway, and always will, that Phil Gartside already had. Enough has already been written about this saga, so I'll be brief.

The next game was at MK Dons on 2 January and we won 2-1 in the FA Cup. By this time the story that Bolton were interested in Owen had reached the press, so I went to listen to the press conference after the game. Owen was nowhere in sight and speaking was Sandy Stewart his assistant who told the press they were going nowhere.

A very early memory of the tension of the 1987 Orient game. (Burnley Express)

1990 and the squad and directors gather for a team picture. I'm in there somewhere. (Clive Lawrence)

1994, chairman Frank Teasdale with whom I had many a tussle. (Steve Lockyer)

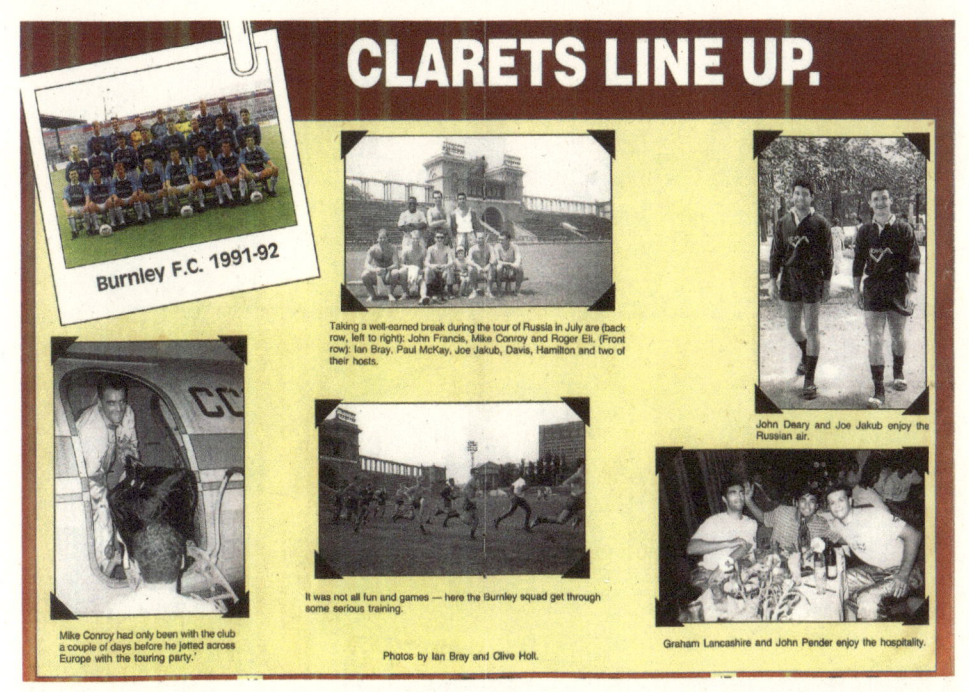

Our trip to Russia. On late arrival in Stavropol, all the players wanted to do was get back home. In the sunshine, the next day, they changed their minds. (Ian Bray and Clive Holt)

1993 Wembley play-off win. (Burnley Express)

Rebuilding begins. The Longside is demolished. (Clive Holt)

And up goes the new. (Clive Holt)

Demolition of the Beehole End. (Clive Holt)

The finished product on completion. How I had to fight to get the stands built, on time and within budget. Not forgetting the arguments that I had to have proper facilities, not just benches bolted on to the concrete terraces. I'm proud of them, my biggest contribution to Burnley Football Club. (Clive Holt)

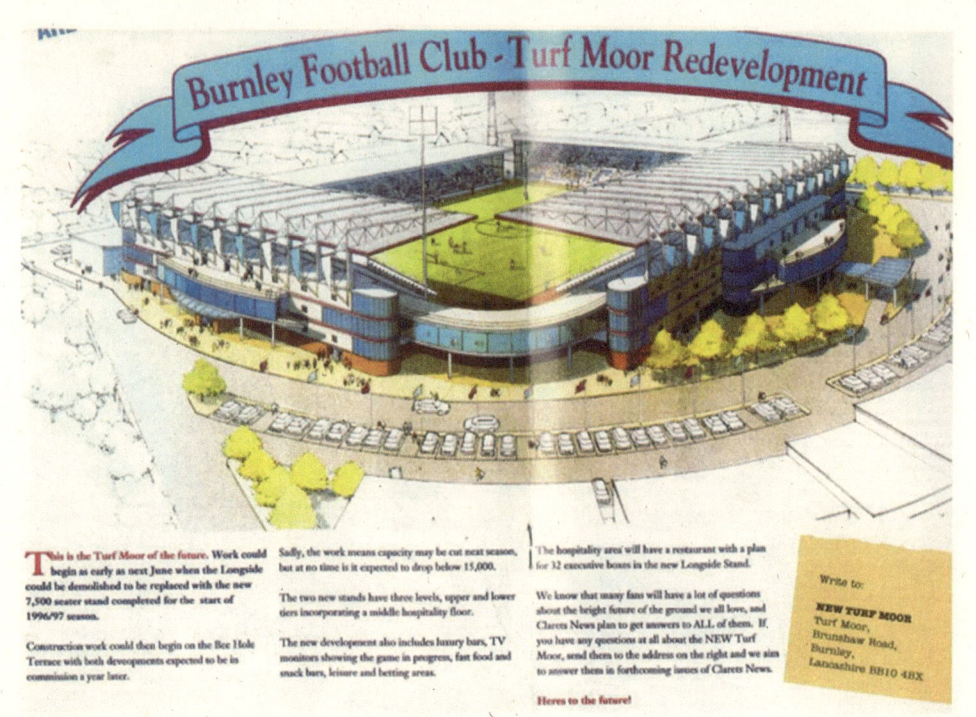

Burnley Football Club - Turf Moor Redevelopment

This is the Turf Moor of the future. Work could begin as early as next June when the Longside could be demolished to be replaced with the new 7,500 seater stand completed for the start of 1996/97 season.

Construction work could then begin on the Bee Hole Terrace with both deveopments expected to be in commision a year laster.

Sadly, the work means capacity may be cut next season, but at no time is it expected to drop below 15,000.

The two new stands have three levels, upper and lower tiers incorporating a middle hospitaliy floor.

The new development also includes luxury bars, TV monitors showing the game in progress, fast food and snack bars, leisure and betting areas.

The hospitality area will have a restaurant with a plan for 32 executive boxes in the new Longside Stand.

We know that many fans will have a lot of questions about the bright future of the ground we all love, and Clarets News plan to get answers to ALL of them. If you have any questions at all about the NEW Turf Moor, send them to the address on the right and we aim to answer them in forthcoming issues of Clarets News.

Heres to the future!

Write to:
NEW TURF MOOR
Turf Moor,
Brunshaw Road,
Burnley,
Lancashire BB10 4BX

2002 projected improvements came to naught.

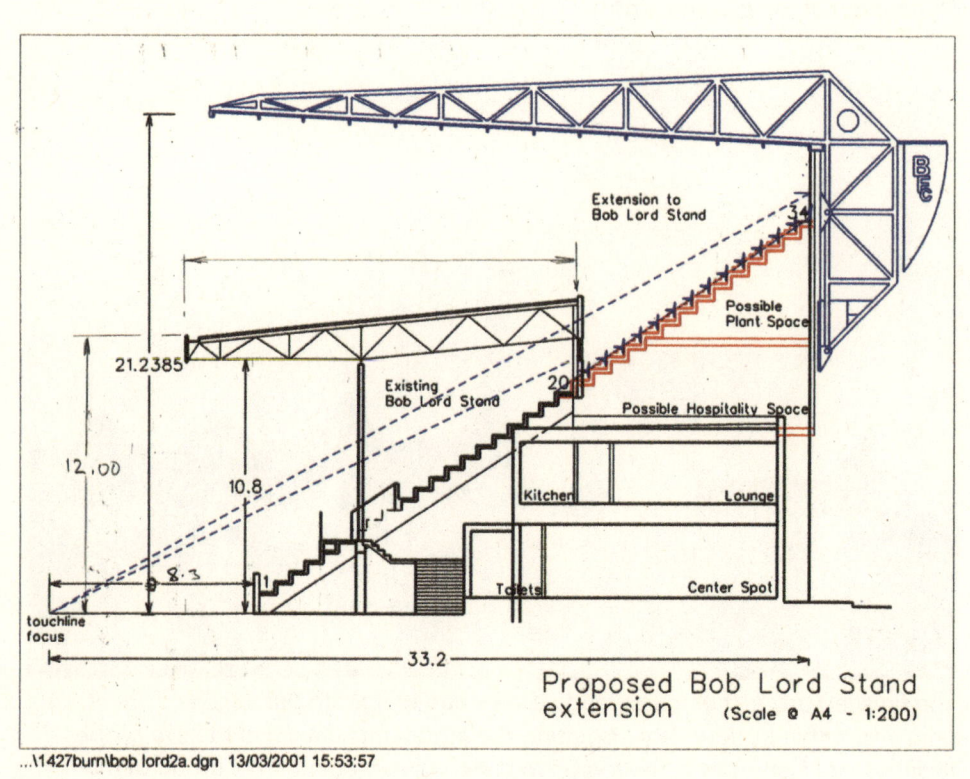

How the Bob Lord might be extended. (From the Clive Holt collection)

Playing on waterlogged pitches was not unusual. (Steve Lockyer)

Jimmy Mullen and the team celebrate promotion at York. (Clive Lawrence)

2002 – opulent living in the Trophy Room. (Steve Lockyer).

2002. Stan Ternent manager and Barry Kilby chairman. (Burnley Football Club)

In less than a week they had gone, along with most of the backroom staff. Owen made his famous comment that one reason for his move was that Bolton were ten years ahead of Burnley. A ruthless Gartside replaced Owen after Bolton were relegated and I wonder to this day how Owen would summarise his career since he left Burnley. Does he regret the move? Would he do it again knowing what he knows now?

Director Brendan Flood and chairman Barry Kilby worked quickly to appoint Brian Laws, an appointment that I had no involvement with, and Laws arrived just three days before the next game at Manchester United. Things were not so rapid for me, tasked with the job of battling with Bolton Wanderers for compensation. It took eight months to resolve and the file of paperwork I still have is six inches thick. Under the rules of the Premier league, Football League and the English FA, it is generally understood that clubs do not sue each other via the courts here in the UK but use arbitration services, which is provided for. It works in a similar way to a court of law, with solicitors, barristers and expert witnesses. In our case, the expert witness was Graham Taylor of Watford and England, a thoroughly nice and straight man, full of football tales and stories on the occasions that we met.

In the compensation struggle that followed, the Gartside defence was that Brendan had given him his permission to speak to Owen by giving him his phone number. This was, of course, nonsense as no official permission had ever been given. What I needed to do was to find evidence that Owen had been approached before this alleged permission. Owen had a club mobile phone, but had he taken or made calls to Gartside using it? He also had his own personal mobile phone, to which I had no access to records.

Bolton did their best to avoid a fair settlement for the staff who had left with Coyle, so one had to prepare a full case just as you would do in a court of law. A huge amount of paperwork and statements, a colossal amount of time, weeks and weeks of it. At last, the thing got to the Court of Arbitration and at this point Gartside realised he was going to lose. So, up he came with a reasonable compensation sum and costs, the exact amount of which is still subject to a non-disclosure clause, but we received something around £1m for the manager. That was reasonably straightforward, but for the others it was around three quarters of a million. It was the claim for the latter group that dragged things on for months. So, to cut a long story short, we got the Coyle settlement sorted and then pursued the rest.

Come the next time we played Bolton Wanderers at Turf Moor, I think it was a League Cup game perhaps and, if memory serves, a Bolton fan had walked to Turf Moor for charity. Before the game, Phil Gartside walked out on to the pitch (the brass cheek) to meet the fan and receive the charity cheque. Well, I never – someone on the ground staff at this exact moment turned on the sprinklers and dear Mr Gartside got very, very wet. I can only apologise to the chap who had done the walking if he got splashed as well. Gartside was furious and of course accused us of stage-managing the whole thing, but in all honest truth the directors knew nothing about this beforehand. We never did find out exactly who had turned them on, but maybe if we had, we might have given him a bonus that week. The very large crowd were delighted and showed it.

Poor old Brian Laws. Looking back, it is easy to see how much was stacked against him; not the least of which were the players. He had the unenviable task of preparing the team for his first game – at Old Trafford. We lost.

However, it was a real glamour game that all the directors and most of the wives wanted to attend. What a contrast to a horrible game at Scarborough, years earlier, at their ramshackle ground and their tiny boardroom with the rain teeming down, and an awful defeat that finally finished off Frank Casper as manager. Nobody wanted to go there, but I couldn't anyway; I was in Singapore on business.

Anyway, the ladies were not too pleased to be in an outer guest area at Old Trafford. We were met by that great former player Bobby Charlton, who I got to know reasonably well over the years. On one visit we made, there was a tap on my shoulder and a Scottish voice bid us welcome, and to my delight it was Sir Alex. From the boardroom down to, eventually, the dressing rooms was a staircase, with presumably other rooms in between. On the occasion we won there, the boardroom quickly emptied as they all trooped out and down the stairs.

Very quickly, with that irony and coincidence that football brings so often, we were soon away at Bolton Wanderers. There could probably not have been a worse fixture so soon, with Coyle in situ at Bolton and poor old Brian carrying the hopes of us all that we might just stuff him and them. It was not to be, in an appalling game that we lost 1-0. On scoring their decidedly scruffy goal – was it actually over the line? There was no VAR back then – Coyle's staff behind him celebrated wildly, having scored against the team where they had been employed just weeks earlier. We all trooped into their boardroom afterwards, a huge room, and kept well away from their directors. To the best of my knowledge, Gartside was not there. However, one of our directors did decide to go and chat with the Bolton lot, whereupon Sonya Kilby gave him short shrift.

And still the cricket field saga went on. Perhaps it merits a book of its own. Fletcher was still in discussions with their chairman, John Stubbs, and there was talk of getting a valuation for the land, but who would pay for that valuation? But in any case, the StadiArena idea was waning, although not quite dead, because it was proposed that it could be used for a football university, and therefore the need for the cricket field land remained. But with money problems in the finance world, the lack of progress with the cricket club, what emerged in its place was the plan for a football university but using rooms in the existing stadium as the campus, and the idea was not dismissed. Student accommodation would be built in the refurbished old industrial Weavers Triangle area of the town. It was another of Brendan Flood's ideas and is now well established although not at Burnley, from where it did originate but moved on. It eventually became the University College of Football Business and initially used the rooms in the Jimmy McIlroy Stand. Would the club invest in this project? It was decided no. But individual directors did invest and the rooms in that stand were rented from the club so that the club had a new income stream. Its completion, of course, was a fair way down the line.

It was the Weavers Triangle and its future as a tourist attraction that interested Prince Charles – now King Charles, of course – on his visit to Burnley when he also visited the football club, and thus has grown the notion that he is a Burnley supporter. Of course, it was a feather in our cap that he visited the club and somewhere there is a picture of him signing the visitors' book in the reception area. Of further interest in the picture is one of the special Fletcher pens that was presented to him as a memento. For all I know, he may well still be using it. If the history of the club was ever written in the form of 100 objects, the pen might be a worthy inclusion.

As all good Burnley fans know, the club was relegated at the end of the 2010 season. Brian Laws reached the objective of 30 points that he had been set by Barry and Brendan but it was not enough for safety. Quite why this figure was ever set still baffles me, since 30 points was never going to be a secure figure. West Ham, the club above, were safe on 35. At the board meeting in early May there was a long discussion as to whether he should stay or not. All of us had our doubts, but it was left to Barry to make the final decision and Barry decided to stick with him and let him start afresh with what we felt was a bunch of players good enough to get us back up, with one or two new faces.

A trip to Singapore was in the offing and a new name was about to enter the fray, John Banaszkiewicz, and you will forgive me if we now refer to him as John B.

CHAPTER TWENTY-TWO

2010/11 Exit Brian Laws

PRE-SEASON WAS to Singapore, an idea mooted by our new contact and soon to be director, John B, who had extensive business interests out there. He wanted to expand the Clarets' footprint in Asia as it was dominated by Manchester United, Liverpool and Arsenal. He was tired of arriving in Singapore only to be met by taxi drivers who asked, 'OK, who is Burnley FC?'

The problem with these faraway overseas jaunts is that they do cost money and it was imperative that we covered the costs. I accompanied Brendan on the trip as I too had business contacts out there and paid my own way. I loved to travel, whether it be on holiday, business or with the club, and one business trip to Romania had seen me locked in a Romanian jail. Somehow, on a free day, with my interpreter, we had strayed into forbidden territory up in the mountains and the car broke down. We found the local police station for help and when they found where the car was, they put us both in their cells. These cells were like those in a Wild West sheriff's office in the corner of the room, and there we sat, watching a black-and-white edition of *Bonanza* with Romanian subtitles in the other corner of the room. Anyway, it was all cleared up, but I look back on this as one of the most surreal events of my life.

Paul Fletcher was sent out to scout training areas but none of them was deemed suitable and we ended up training at a golf club on their putting area. Chris Eagles was mobbed wherever we went because of his Manchester United connections, for which he was mercilessly ribbed by the rest of the group. But with his film-star looks and immaculate coiffure he was a natural target for the hero-worshippers. The heat and humidity were unbearable. We had to play one game on an artificial pitch that footballers generally hate, but John B had done a great job of organising it all and the hospitality was superb. Ten goals were rattled in at the first two games and the third against a national XI was a 1-0 win. We were well pleased.

Seven thousand one hundred fans attended one friendly at the Jalan Besar Stadium. Players also got involved in local charity work which helped boost the team's local connection and profile. The 'big' teams tended to jet in, play the game and return home promptly, so our efforts to 'mix' went down well.

And so we began the new season with Brian Laws and we could only hope that he had more success than the previous season when we did acknowledge that he was on a hiding to nothing. Clarke Carlisle makes an interesting observation in his book *A Footballer's Life* that there was far more power in the dressing room than in Brian Laws's hands. Some of these players were released, but, alas, for him, not all of them, and then Robbie Blake decided not to stay.

The season and the games trundled on in no real outstanding way other than being in sixth place briefly, and then there was the 1-0 win over Bolton and Owen Coyle in the League Cup that gave us all huge satisfaction.

At the time, I do believe it was referred to as the Night of the Long Knives, when the board was reduced from nine members to five. In truth there was nothing sinister or Machiavellian about it. With his own problems to deal with, Ray Ingleby left the board and this made way for John B to join. I think we were all agreed that nine was too many and, as far as I remember, it was Brendan that suggested that to qualify you should have 4,000 shares. Five of us would have to leave and I certainly didn't want to, so I bought more shares from the departing Martin Hobbs. Four of them duly decided to leave: Chris Duckworth, Martin Hobbs, John Sullivan and John

Turkington. So that left five of us: myself, Barry Kilby, Brendan Flood, John B and Mike Garlick. Much more comfortable, much more efficient and certainly more workable.

But again, what tangled webs we weave, what complications we make. It was all to do with how much I had paid for my new shares – £50 over the odds if memory serves – so I wanted an arrangement that if ever I was removed from the board I would get my money back: £200 a share, plus interest. It was when three directors – Mike Garlick, John B and Brendan Flood – wanted to sell to the Americans, ALK, in 2020 that these complications surfaced. But that was to come, and when it was mooted that we should have 4,000 shares I was determined to keep my place on the board. Let's just say it was something that I could not give up easily. It had been part of life for the last 20 years nearly. Never mind the aggravation, frustrations, the messes I had occasionally cleaned up, various confrontations and arguments; and more than that, the sheer thanklessness of it. What we do behind the scenes goes unseen, and fans are quick to moan at directors when things go wrong.

At this point, let me talk a little about a very good player, Chris McCann. He had come from Ireland along with Kyle Lafferty as a young lad, was given his debut by Stan Ternent, and went on to have a very good career at Burnley. In the Owen Coyle promotion season, he played a staggering 59 games and it was his lay-off to Wade Elliott that enabled Wade to score the deciding goal. As a member of that team, he has earned his place in the Burnley history books.

Skilful and athletic, the mystery was why he never went on to have a regular international career with Ireland. Perhaps this was to do with something he did when he was selected for the Ireland under-21s but was only on the bench and not in the side that played. He declared it was a waste of time him being there and opted out of the squad entirely. Don Givens, the manager, was taken aback. Despite patching things up with Givens, he was not selected again. Maybe it was this that was held against him, when he was certainly good enough to play for the full international side in later years. In one of the pre-season games in Singapore he was injured. This was when Brian Laws was manager and I do wonder if that injury, that restricted him to just four games that season, was one reason why Laws had such a poor time. A fit and fully firing Chris McCann would have been a regular in the Laws side, I would have thought. Would he have made a big difference? Who can say, but this is one of the fascinations of football. If Chris had been fit, what might have been? He was back for the Eddie Howe period and was a permanent fixture before moving to Wigan, by then managed by none other than Owen Coyle. As far as I know, he went to Shamrock Rovers after a couple of spells in the USA. He amassed a career total of nearly 500 games.

I shall not forget the consideration Chris showed to me when I came off the bike in Austria and struggled with mobility that week and the journey home. Chris was the one that was a huge help carting my luggage around. You don't forget little things like that.

Results in the Brian Laws Championship period were inconsistent. But you always sensed there were undercurrents in the dressing room, although you could never put your finger on them or identify who the ringleaders were. There were some strong characters in there; in fact, probably too many of them to ensure a stable dressing room under Brian. Owen Coyle had the knack of handling them but then, of course, players are much easier to handle when the team is winning and Owen created a triumphant, winning team. From the minute Brian came in, I always thought it was going to be downhill for him in the Premier League. Add to that the fact that so many of those players felt like a deflated balloon when Owen left. Some were on the floor with dismay. Brian was unable to lift them.

You don't need me to tell you that money, cash flow and wages continued as an issue, but Brendan came up with an idea that would be a money-maker if we supported it and got it off the ground at Turf Moor. This was the University College of Football Business (UCFB). But it would need funding and we as a club decided that the club just did not have the funds to develop it. Yes, we had rooms that could be made available and these could be rented to the UCFB. We were sure it was a good project but it would need outside or director investment, not BFC money that we did not have. Paul Fletcher eventually came to be working more or less full-time on this project, which led to problems later as to who exactly should be paying his wages.

The UCFB was indeed established in connection with Buckingham University and as soon as a CEO was appointed it got underway. Two directors underwrote it under their own steam, not the club – Brendan Flood and John B. It is now well established nationally with a campus at both Manchester City and Wembley. It was, I suppose, a brilliant idea, where students could learn all the fundamentals of football business from journalism to finance. It is no longer based at Turf Moor but it began in Burnley, a little feather in our cap I suppose.

If it was Mike Garlick and Sean Dyche that eventually got the Gawthorpe training area massively upgraded, developed to a Premier League and academy standard, it was back in 2010 that plans were first drawn up for vastly improved facilities and new pitches. Buildings were to be extended and there would be a new indoor pitch. We anticipated completion for July 2011. The full plans never happened at that time; there was not enough money. It needed not far short of £2m. Ironically, we could barely afford the running costs as it was, with those net costs having risen from £97,000 in 2006 to over half a million in 2010. It was simply unsustainable on Championship revenues. Upgrading Gawthorpe was put on hold.

Full planning approval for the new plans was in fact received from the council, almost unanimously with just one objection – I never did bother to find out who that was. But the restrictions and caveats were interesting. This was an important wildlife area, particularly birdlife. Snipe, in particular, were mentioned. Floodlighting for the pitches would interfere with the bats that frequented the area. It was an area that was also part of the River Calder floodplain – what would we do to protect new facilities from that? There were access difficulties for the heavy machinery and construction traffic to sort. We had a right of way but the council had just paid for resurfacing. A local farmer had a skip business at the end of this lane and used to buzz Turf Moor with his light aeroplane.

Paul Fletcher had to bring to an end his StadiArena visions, the plan to demolish the Cricket Field Stand and rebuild. Alas, the old stand is still there today. Brendan Flood and Modus certainly could not provide the funding for the development, and with the possibility of a double-dip recession, the plans were put on hold. The Americans who now own the club, I understand, would certainly like to resurrect plans for a new stand there, but they too face the problem of finding the finance. I always suspected that fans were quite relieved that this StadiArena project was shelved. And if there was to be a priority then Gawthorpe would be the first choice. At the AGM it was Brendan that explained that other key decision-makers at the club were far from convinced by the project anyway. Was I to assume he meant me? No, what I was unconvinced by were the costings. And then on top of all that was the need to get the cricket club onside, and we all knew how unlikely that would be. Perhaps one day this stand will be replaced; perhaps one day it will have to be, as it reaches the end of its lifespan.

But then, lo and behold, the cricket club did agree to relocate to the Towneley area of Burnley, where a school was due to be demolished. Towneley Park was a huge area of outstanding beauty. This, however, was not in connection with the new stand project that had been shelved but in connection with the new UCFB expansion. Basically, the club would cover all costs but it was agreed that for the long-term future of the club this would be a worthy investment. You don't need me to tell you what the eventual outcome was of the cricket club move to Towneley. Nothing. It never happened. There were many objections, although only one councillor on the planning committee voted against approval of our plans, all of which we had to satisfy and were added to planning approval. The workload was immense, but it was all for nothing. A huge opportunity so tantalisingly close but lost.

Today you will still hear the thwack of bat on ball as a four is dispatched to the boundary behind the Cricket Field Stand when the football and cricket seasons overlap. And the cricket club on matchdays has an assured healthy income from allowing car parking, and the clubhouse is open for both home and away fans. Dare I say it, why would they want to move?

In amongst all this, the actual football team was not doing too well, or at least not as well as we had hoped or even expected with what in effect was a good squad of players by Championship standards. And well paid, with a wage bill of £12m a year that was too high to be sustained. One of them was Chris Eagles, still with us and having a good season, so much so that I rather hoped a bigger club like Everton might pay us something decent for him. I remember a conversation with Ron Greenwood, born in Burnley, former West Ham and England manager, about his ability. I must have said something on the lines of he was a decent player on his day.

'Ah, but is he a tanner footballer?' asked Ron, to which I replied a bit puzzled, and asked what he meant.

'Can he turn on a sixpence and not lose the ball?' was Ron's answer. On his day, he certainly could.

Brian Laws by December had still not managed to win two consecutive games and all of us were well aware of how we had thrown away two-goal leads and lost points. Nevertheless, we flirted with the top six but it was all so unconvincing. I had not been involved in his appointment, this being above my pay grade, as the saying goes. But when there were early moves to replace him I, along with the chairman, argued that he should be extended more time; that we were so close to the top six. But not even I or Barry could save him after the home defeat by Scunthorpe United. Barry wasn't there but I was and have never felt such disappointment at the sorry display. The fans made their feelings absolutely clear. There was the feeling that they had never taken to him in the first place and were baffled when he wasn't sacked after we were relegated. Directors always have one thought in the back of their heads: if the fans start to vote with their feet, that is money we are losing. It was Brendan who phoned Barry in New York and that, I am afraid, was the end for Brian Laws. One fan who used to write a column for one of the supporter websites described Brian as a sort of human punchbag. Cruel indeed.

And so it began, the task of finding the next manager and the first choice was Paul Lambert, then at Norwich. Delia had already given us short shrift when Owen Coyle left and we had made an approach. John B thought it worth another effort. The snag being it would trigger a £750,000 release clause in his contract, and we would have to find another £400,000 to compensate Brian Laws. Lambert, meanwhile, had, via his agent, let it be known he would be interested in talking to us. So, John B and I met him off a train from Norwich at London's Liverpool Street Station. For an hour and a half, we talked to him in a nearby hotel. We left thinking that it had been a very successful meeting and it was agreed that I would write to Norwich and ask official permission to speak to him again. Next thing I know is a very angry phone call from Delia telling me he was only using us to get a better contract at Norwich.

Next up was Eddie Howe of Bournemouth, after stories that Sam Allardyce was interested. Eddie was duly appointed and I remember thinking, 'Good Lord, he is so very young.' Only 33, looks even younger, was very good-looking and as such could have been mistaken for a member of a boy band. But as far as Barry and Brendan were concerned, he ticked all the boxes. Like all new managers, or at least the majority of them, he presented his shopping list and said we needed a new and far more mobile centre-half, a midfield ball-winner and a natural goalscorer. Eddie then told us he felt the biggest weakness at the club was a lack of fitness or, better still, athleticism. His stats expert told him that we were second-bottom in the league for how much distance our players covered in a game. Next up, Eddie was critical of the scouting system and told us that the first-team training pitch facilities were poor.

It was tempting to say, 'Ah, but, Eddie, apart from all this, everything else is OK?'

To be fair to him, he did identify areas where savings could be made and instead of a long-distance overseas pre-season training tour, why not stay in the UK and spend the savings on the training areas? Accordingly, we dropped plans to go to Switzerland and settled on the pleasures of the south coast.

As well we know, natural goalscorers are as rare as hens' teeth, but lurking at Swindon Town was Charlie Austin, whom we secured. Give Eddie credit, he could spot good young players and in time came Danny Ings, Kieran Trippier and Ben Mee, all outstanding players. Shackell was the centre-half we managed to get from Derby County and he too was a very good signing. The good news for Eddie was that Chris McCann was nearing fitness, but then Chris suffered a further setback when a growth was discovered in the back of his head. He needed an operation to relieve the pressure. I felt desperately sorry for him. The good news was that he did recover from this and went on to continue his career.

As ever, it fell to me to be the fly in the ointment when it came time to discuss new pitches at Gawthorpe. There was what they called the cabbage-patch area behind the dressing rooms that would cost £72,000 to restore. Two brand-new pitches across the bridge from the changing area would cost £300,000 per pitch. Add to that the cost of strengthening the bridge at another £60,000 for the ferrying of all raw materials across, and by now it was all becoming prohibitive.

Sometimes you can feel the vibes – 'Oh, what a miserable bugger Clive is, always finding problems.' But somebody had to be the one to ask 'HOW MUCH?'

Costs everywhere throughout the club were going up – policing, stewarding, matchday director hospitality that we offered to others, media department had more staff, commercial department had more staff, catering department had more staff, Eddie Howe's backroom staff was going up in numbers, staying overnight for away games, cleaning company costs – and how efficient were they? One supporter had a lovely story to tell that for a whole season he had himself cleaned the pigeon droppings off his seat in the James Hargreaves

Stand. And on the final day of one season, he had left the droppings there, only to find them still there at the beginning of the new season. If we couldn't keep his seat clean, he asked, could we not shoot the bloody things?

With the new manager in situ and the supporters happy with the appointment, on went the season, but there was no top-six place at the end. But here was the difference: Eddie was shown a degree of patience by supporters that was never shown to Brian Laws. Eddie was extremely personable and articulate and always came across so well in interviews and was able to show supporters that this was a rebuilding and transition period. Very much a case of 'out with the old and in with the new', so that players like Brian Jensen, Graham Alexander and Clarke Carlisle could see their time at the club was nearing its end.

And so, 2010/11 came to its conclusion with nothing really to shout about in terms of events on the field in the second half of the season under Eddie. What would the next season bring? A very big change actually.

CHAPTER TWENTY-THREE

2011/12 An Average Eddie Howe Season

IF EVER there was a season when I sat and thought, 'Just what am I doing here? Why do I do this? Why is it me that seems to be the one that cleans up the messes?', maybe this was the one. And being the person that cleaned up the messes and tidied up the problems, that was the thing that made me not exactly everybody's best friend. I never had any dislike for anybody at the football club, be it in the boardroom or anywhere else, but I knew that I was not exactly popular, if that is the right word, because I continually asked, 'Well, how are we going to do this? How are we going to pay for this? Can we have some accurate costings?'

It was down to the basic premise that every committee, every board has to have someone that does this. Nor at any time, I suspect, did anyone have any idea of the hours of work involved in being company secretary.

Three examples of all this during the season come to mind. One was the UCFB, which today John B says is valued at over £75m. One was the ground buyback scheme, and the other was the Eagles and Mears transfers. Just sometimes I had time to think about the football and Eddie Howe's progress. That, by the way, was labelled 'transition' by Eddie himself. Sadly, if there is one thing that turns fans off, it is when a manager says we are in a transition period. It came after an early game at Crystal Palace with a 2-0 defeat. He talked about building and long-term plans, getting new players, one of whom in fact would be Danny Ings. Things were progressing slower than he wanted.

Eddie's struggles were themselves an issue, because, as Brendan's protégé, he had Brendan's full support and Brendan was also the one person in the boardroom with whom Eddie had a close relationship. That was a Brendan skill, I have to say, being almost a confidant and counsellor to managers – Cotterill, Coyle and now Eddie. So, questioning Eddie's progress was something else that did not go down too well.

Buying back the ground was a complex business that began during this season, but you couldn't just phone Lionbridge, the new owners of Turf Moor and Gawthorpe, who had bought the shares from Longside Properties, and say we're sending you a cheque. And one reason was that lawyers had not quite been on the ball with registering key documents. That problem would soon emerge in the process.

But even in the most exasperating seasons there are always shafts of light and one such was in pre-season when a couple named their son after 14 members of the Burnley squad and then donated the money this raised to Burnley's youth-development fund. Fanatics Stephen and Amanda Preston really did hit the headlines when they named their baby son Jensen, after our goalkeeper. It wasn't so much that that hit the headlines; it was when they named him Jay Alexander Bikey Carlisle Duff Elliott Fox Iwelumo Marney Mears Paterson Thompson Wallace Preston. A national magazine paid for the story, and the money was donated to Burnley. A happy couple indeed. Did he keep all the names, I wonder? I do hope that today he is a Clarets fan. Who knows?

Somebody else happy was Eddie with the improvements at Gawthorpe. These were in fact part-funded by director John, who loaned the money to create a new pitch out of what was called the cabbage patch. The club was still dependent on loans and the repayments of them were always a bone of contention with supporters. The promotion of 2009 would not have happened without director loans but the criticism from supporters afterwards was directed at the interest or bonuses that came with the repayments. Not all directors claimed their bonuses but every director was fully entitled to them. It has to be said that the directors at Burnley never saw themselves as a charitable institution. Loans had to be repaid whenever it was possible. Bonuses were normal practice. Some directors claimed them and others, Ray Griffiths for example, did not, and left that money in the club. A director loan helped to buy Danny Ings. Another one had helped buy Kieran Trippier.

The primitive conditions at Gawthorpe had been a concern for some time. A football wonder when it was created in the 1950s, there were parts of it now that were barely fit for purpose. Players changed at Turf Moor, drove to Gawthorpe in their cars, trained and got plastered in mud and drove back to Turf Moor, often caked in the stuff and still in their boots in many cases, to shower and change. There were occasions when prospective new players were kept well away from Gawthorpe until they had signed. The changing and treatment rooms there were sparse, dank, uninviting and it was a three-mile drive to get back to Turf Moor in soaking-wet kit after a training session in the rain. The £300,000 facelift was badly needed. The existing building was updated and modernised with a canteen, lockers in new changing rooms, even carpets. There was a base now where players could change and eat after training. It saved on time. Driving back and forth to Turf Moor took an hour each day, sometimes more.

Goalkeeper Lee Grant joked that the players now had an extra hour in bed each day. The whole mood was lifted by having somewhere on site, as it were, to unwind after training. Grant had been at the club before the new alterations and knew full well how bad the old ones were, once the envy of the football world in the days of Jimmy McIlroy and Ray Pointer. But football moves on and even these new ones would be deemed inadequate another few years down the line. It's not rocket science really. Whatever job you are in, you need good working conditions, and the days when old manager Harry Potts said that Gawthorpe was better than being in Switzerland were long gone. Eddie added that the players could do extra work after lunch. That brought a wry smile. There would be some that would love it and others would rather be at the bookies.

A constant was the need to raise new money. So, for £100,000 you could be an associate director for five years, with a seat in the directors' box and lounge. That was just for one seat. Your partner would be an extra £5,000 a year.

Money-maker number two were the premier seats in the Jimmy McIlroy Stand. Splendid idea – 400 seats with corporate facilities, at £1,200 a time. But this meant moving 200 season-ticket holders who had been there for years. Forty refused. Others went to the press. As a PR exercise, it was a disaster. We used Chris Eagles in the sales brochure and then he was sold. The brochure didn't mention that when it rained heavily with the wind from the west, you received a soaking. We reckoned it would bring in another £80,000 a season. But this is a kick in the teeth for us rank-and-file fans was their consensus.

With the transfer of Chris Eagles and Tyrone Mears to Bolton Wanderers, the claims against Bolton Wanderers in relation to Owen Coyle and the mass move of all the coaching staff was finally put to bed, with the Mears fee increased by £750,000. It was a reminder of an episode in the club's history that still left a sour taste and that was the strange affair of the Boxing Day Christmas party that we'd held after we had played Bolton that day and Gartside had announced he was coming for Owen. All the families were there, including Owen's, in the lounge and there was just such a strange atmosphere. Owen made a big fuss of my wife, helping her in the food queue. 'How odd,' I thought. We met the staff families quite often, so it was easy to pick up the different vibes. Something was afoot. My wife and I talked about this all the way home and wondered if there had already been talks between Gartside and Owen. Another clue:

a big game was coming up at Manchester United and staff always let the ticket office know what tickets they would need. For this game, none of them asked for tickets. At a game at Wigan I'd chatted with Sam Allardyce, then the manager at Blackburn. He asked how our relationships were with Bolton and added that the whole of football knew that there had been meetings between Owen and Gartside long before it became public. A firm fact or just football gossip? Will we ever really know?

Should we invite Jimmy McIlroy to be club president? Would directors loan more money for more Gawthorpe improvements? Would the UCFB settle their bills with us? Would the stadium buyback scheme get off the ground? Would we get the wage bill down? Could we introduce Sunday markets along Harry Potts Way? Who should be the next CEO? Could we sign Sam Vokes? How could we cover the £1m cash shortfall in February and March? Player sales, what else? Were we about to be fined for late payments on the Charlie Austin instalments? Should we have a Brian Miller statue? Should we erect cabins on the club car park as UCFB student accommodation? How to cut costs? We talked long into the evening about who to sell. Lee Grant, Keith Treacy, Ross Wallace due to his high wages, Jay Rodriguez purely to balance the books, Martin Paterson because of his injury record, Zavon Hines hadn't lived up to expectations, Chris McCann's high wages.

A personal bombshell for me came when Brendan Flood challenged the honesty of the minutes that I took at board meetings. What was sent to all board members were the draft minutes and if there were items that were incorrect, they could be amended. Brendan had sent an email to everyone in which he felt that sometimes these minutes were my own personal views and were not a true record. The rest of the board agreed that Brendan's comment was incorrect and all that people had to do was let me know what they wanted changing before the minutes were up for approval. It was at this point that I did suggest that in view of his business problems, he should withdraw as a director until they were resolved. This would certainly come to a head later. Let us just say that at this point, Brendan and I were not best friends.

Was Paul Fletcher reaching the end of his tenure at the club? Could I be bothered to challenge him about some of the things he had inferred about me in his book? What I would like to think is that he reads this book and reconsiders his opinions.

The UCFB was in fact an ongoing problem, as they owed us money and our resident accountant was forever having to tell us they were somewhat tardy with payments. Again, the club was not a charity able to part-fund the university and it was not up to us to pay for gas and electricity, the season tickets we gave them, postage and cleaning, or the use of the gymnasium. Yes, they paid for catering, but could they have discount? And then there was Peter Ashton and Longside Properties that he owned via Lionbridge, our landlord, telling us we had no permission to change the use of the building to an education establishment. Ah, problems, problems and more problems. I look back and wonder how I ever got a good night's sleep.

Meanwhile, back to Chris Eagles asking where was the balance of his loyalty money following his transfer to Bolton, or at least his solicitor was asking. 'But you asked for a transfer,' we replied, 'so goodbye loyalty payment.' But he had never submitted a transfer request, we were told. Nonsense, we retaliated. In fact, he had, but by text message, not in actual writing, which was the correct procedure. It was annoying. Eagles went ahead with his claim. Two people in the club, who shall remain nameless, argued as to whose fault it was. We offered £50,000 but quietly decided to go up to £100,000. The former was turned down. Nobody wanted to go to a tribunal. On and on it dragged – paperwork, letters, solicitors, arguments; enough to fill a filing cabinet drawer. It eventually cost us £150,000.

The buyback: you may remember that chairman Barry Kilby and John Sullivan had once been our landlords via Longside Properties when the club was in desperate need of money and they bought the ground and Gawthorpe. They had then sold it to Peter Ashton, the Lionbridge owner. So, there we were paying £372,480 in rent per year and still responsible for upkeep and maintenance. To say it was dead money was an understatement. On top of this, for any improvements we made, or alterations, we paid an extra £5,000 to him. Had supporters known this at the time, I suspect they would have been outraged. He threatened action against us for using the ground for UCFB. We got round that by saying the ground had long been used for educational purposes via the community programme and Myerscough College, which was true enough. But then a bombshell came from the club landlord.

Yes, we had the option to buy Turf Moor and Gawthorpe back, we thought. But, er, no, we didn't have an option, because the lease was not registered within the allotted legal period. Quite simply the lawyers had 40 days to register the transfer but had not done so within those 40 days. This would mean renegotiation. This meant there was a possibility that the landlord would want more money above the originally agreed figure for which we could buy back. In fact, he was under no obligation now to sell it back to us at all, ever. The new figure would be £3.8m, as long as we could prove we had the option, and we would have to pay their solicitors' and administration fees. Their lengthy and formal email had come not from Peter Ashton but his CEO on behalf of Longside Properties.

Our immediate reaction was to seek legal advice and to see if our solicitors had or had not registered things correctly at thre Land Registry. If they had not done so, would we have a legal claim against them? Does the average football supporter have any idea how much time is spent on legal work at a football club? When it is caused by solicitors it is a double imposition. Directors Mike Garlick and John B agreed to meet with Peter Ashton in London. They were told the new price would be £4m, unless we could prove we had the option to buy back. Mike Garlick and John B offered £3.9m; a deal was possible if we could work out how to do it. Our own regular solicitors, Forbes, agreed that, because of the registration error by another solicitor, Ashton was right. We no longer had the agreed option to buy back.

More discussions with Peter Ashton, who came up with a new suggestion. He would lend us £1m and then we would buy back at £5m, spread over five years. There was an immediate no to this. We mulled over different ways of financing it but, for this season, there it ended. It would continue into the next.

But nice things do happen and the Queen was due to visit Turf Moor. Barry Kilby and I ran through the arrangements, which included lunch at Turf Moor. The lunch would be for 100 people and the guests would include 50 people invited by Lord Shuttleworth and 50 to be invited by the club. Nightmare. Just how do you choose the 50 people to invite? Who do you include? How many people would be offended by not being invited? Think of it as your wedding you are planning for and the time comes to sit down and organise the guest list. This was your worst nightmare. It was decided that each director should have six tickets – that would be 30. Ten would go to senior BFC staff and the balance of ten would go to commercial guests and long-serving staff. Every guest would be vetted by Special Branch.

Two of John B's children would present a posy to the Queen and a small gift to the Duke of Edinburgh. Trouble is he had four children, so which ones would he choose and how? His problem, not mine. Palace officials would have to approve of any gifts. While lunch was being served, children would dance on the pitch. Everything was planned to the last minute. The Queen and Duke would emerge to acknowledge the crowd and children, hundreds of them brought in on coaches and double-decker buses.

At this visit John B gave the Duke of Edinburgh a season ticket and suggested that if he couldn't make it, he should let Prince Charles have it, our number one fan.

Sadly, we were forbidden from taking photographs but what a memory it all left behind, sitting on the Queen's table, talking about racehorses, but only when she spoke to you first, and when it came time for the Bishop of Blackburn to say grace, the Duke of Edinburgh muttered, 'Not more bloody prayers.' Then there was the great hat affair. Ladies had been instructed to wear a hat or a fascinator. One lady did not get the message, she said. And who got the blame for that? Why me, of course. The kitchens did us proud with an all-English menu – lamb, wine from Kent, local goose, Lancashire cheese. And how precise the Queen's drink had to be: gin and Dubonnet, mixed to a precise amount and the level to a certain part of the glass. And, blessed relief, the weather was good.

The bad news was that the club would foot the bill for everything – stewards, parking, hiring barriers and the police needed inside the stadium grounds. Further bad news was Barry asking me to take over all the arrangements and work with Lord Shuttleworth and a subcommittee that consisted of 23 people. Can I use the word nightmare for a third time? Boy, did Barry know what he was doing when he did that. The work involved was enormous; everything organised to the last detail. From that to trying to get the UCFB to pay up their debts, by now over £40,000, which, if we could get it would cover the cost of the royal visit.

As we finished this book, we heard the news that the Queen had passed away. I spent some time thinking about her visit that day and her grace and charm. She was a truly remarkable lady. I have met the King twice, both occasions when he was Prince Charles. We like to think of him as a Burnley supporter.

And so the season finished with a draw at home to Bristol City, 1-1. It had been a mediocre season and there was no great enthusiasm for Eddie Howe, it has to be said, at supporter level. As it ended, we knew we also had to appoint a new chairman, since Barry Kilby, with health problems, had told us earlier that his resignation at the end of the season would be definite. Paul Fletcher was quick to suggest in the press that Brendan Flood would be a great replacement; the only candidate that made sense, he said. Barry would stay on the board and give a helping hand if needed.

The best thing is they make decisions with their heart not their head, Fletcher added. I looked at it askance. You make decisions with your head. Make them with your heart and that way insolvency lies. That was Barry's strength. Burnley was his great love, but his heart did not overrule his head. Fletcher really laid it on – Brendan was a visionary, the driving force behind the 2009 promotion, the risk-taker. All true enough, but the Wembley win had saved our bacon and along the way we had needed more loans.

The resignation was accepted with great sadness on our part and the fervent hope that he would solve his prostate cancer problems. He had chaired 147 board meetings and his chairmanship had overseen some splendid times, some marvellous games – especially the cup games in the Coyle season – and some great occasions, not the least of which were the promotion with Stan Ternent and then the promotion with Owen Coyle. He had provided a steady hand in some difficult times. In the times when the club was almost insolvent, he had found solutions to money shortages. He was excellent at finding new investors in the days of Stan Ternent and Steve Cotterill. He was calm and unruffled and not easily shocked. But I do remember one occasion when even the good-natured Barry was taken aback at the size of the bill for staff kit. It was an astonishing £50,000. It turned out that kit was finding its way onto eBay. But the eye-catcher was the bill for white socks. Steve Cotterill, it turned out, would only wear a pair once, whereupon they were disposed of. If I tell you that it was me that tackled him about it, you will not be surprised.

The offer of £6m for Jay Rodriguez from Southampton was gratefully received. Payable in three stages, the add-ons took it to nearly £7m. We immediately spent £1m on Jason Shackell, who would become a keystone of the team soon to win promotion.

All that remained was to choose the new chairman. Barry had privately approached John B, but he was reluctant, having four children and his huge business to run. At the board meeting, Barry then proposed a joint chairmanship of Mike Garlick and John B. I seconded this. Brendan stated that he was not happy with the arrangement and felt he had not been considered. 'Would Mike Garlick provide financial support?' he asked. Mike confirmed that, yes, he would put in £5m over the next few years and would put this in writing. Brendan would support this if a legal agreement was drawn up. He was also himself trying to find an investor who might well put in between £10m and £20m.

And so that was that. We had new chairmen. If directors could hibernate, they would do this in the summer. But, unfortunately, the work never stops. And the UCFB still owed us £30,000.

CHAPTER TWENTY-FOUR

2012/13 and Big Changes

ANY FEEL-GOOD factor was sadly missing, season tickets were not exactly flying out of the ticket office. Supporters asked where all the money had gone. Don't they always? It's the little things that add up – a stand roof that had 60 leak points would be £100,000 to repair, the Chris Eagles saga, the cost of the Queen's visit. I never did find out the precise costs for that. Running costs at Gawthorpe exceeded budget, pitch repairs over £50,000. There was the rent payable to Lionbridge and Peter Ashton. On and on these bills piled up. And still some players on high wages that we needed to shed. There was even a point when suppliers for our matchday needs threatened to withhold their business because we were slow in paying bills. Imagine our signature, famed meat-and-potato pie without the meat. The bare fact was that the club still needed loans and prop-ups from directors, in particular Mike Garlick and John B. Mike always preferred to convert his loans into shares. His Burnley shares were mounting, slowly but surely putting him in an increasingly strong position.

To be fair, supporters had been patient with Eddie Howe, but they were restless and you could sense it. He had 'the charisma of a blunt pencil', wrote one fan. The 'building for the future' mantra was wearing thin. The football was pedantic and predictable. The previous season had been neither entertaining nor exciting. The first game of the season was a 2-0 win over Bolton Wanderers and Owen Coyle. It went down well, of course. And later in the season Phil

Gartside would sack Coyle, proving that football is such a cruel game, filled with twists and turns, and the grass is not always greener on the other side.

I had a number of part-time consultancy posts that continued to take me around the world on business trips. First question: would I miss any games? Would I be able to spread the Burnley flag? The motorhome was in frequent use, towing the small car behind it. Any game south of Birmingham was the rule and we loaded up and set off a couple of days before. The dog, Tom, always came along, and was happy enough under a pub table, or residing in the mobile kennel that was his motorhome as much as ours. We tended to go regularly to familiar sites, which he came to sense as we neared them and he knew all the walks inside out. On the return home he knew within a couple of miles where we were and would get out of the basket and stand between us in the front seats, furiously wagging his tail. He had a superb memory. We miss him still. Only another dog lover will understand the feeling of loss when a treasured pet passes away.

Ipswich was a favourite destination and had a new chairman, Marcus Evans, who had invested a fair amount of cash. David Sheepshanks I remember well. But the one thing you remembered Ipswich for was the very good wine. The Cobbold family breweries were still involved at the club, so the drinks were freely available and the wine was always first-rate. Mr Cobbold was a real character, with a home that dated back centuries. It was once featured on *Antiques Roadshow*. I well remember him asking my wife what she thought of the wine he had just poured. Before she could answer, he decided it was poor stuff and told the server to change it at once and bring another bottle. I'm not sure why, but Doc Iven, president at Burnley FC, once told me that the Cobbolds and Bob Lord were great friends, although they couldn't stand each other.

How strange it felt at first with Barry not being chairman, but he was still there at meetings, despite his illness. The joint chairmanship seemed to work better than we perhaps expected. But there were certainly undercurrents between myself and Brendan.

They would come to a head when the headline of a *Lancashire Telegraph* article about Brendan proclaimed 'I WAS FORCED OUT'. In sub-headlines it said he was heartbroken to leave, the co-chairmen failed to support him and he would only return if there were changes in the boardroom. He cited myself and Mike Garlick as the catalysts for his departure and that it was us that had forced him off the board. 'I don't get on with them,' he said, and didn't understand our agenda.

That agenda, if that is what it was, was simple enough. With his business problems, Brendan had taken out an IVA to help settle his affairs. Football League rules were simple enough and if you had an IVA, you could not be a director of a football club. As company director it fell to me to telephone people at the Football League to inform of the situation and ask what we should do. Their reply was interesting. 'Oh, we wondered when you were going to advise us,' or words to that effect, and added they were about to write to us.

Brendan said he had continued as a director while he tried to get special permission from the Football League. But, he said, whilst John B and Barry Kilby supported his efforts to continue as a director, Mike and I did not.

All this had come to a head with other accompanying headlines that ex-director John Sullivan, who had various Russian business interests, was having or had held talks with Russian investors to get money into the club. John maintained he had contacts that were close associates of a certain Mr Vladimir Putin. Despite newspaper reports to the contrary, the football club had nothing to do with this officially. But since Brendan was involved, it then all came out into the open that Brendan, in any case, had been 'forced out' of the board. Oh dear, I was the bad guy again, but it all seemed clear enough to me that if you had an IVA, you were not allowed to be a football club director. I felt no personal animosity towards Brendan at all, either then or now, and in fact he returned to the board in 2014.

Igor Grymov was John Sullivan's contact in Moscow and you could be forgiven for thinking that all this had echoes of a Len

Deighton spy thriller. Brendan was happy for John Sullivan to represent himself, John B and Mike Garlick in any enquiries he made with his Russian contacts. Igor and John Sullivan had met in Moscow. Igor had emailed Brendan to introduce himself, knowing that Brendan was looking for investors. But when it hit the news, Mike Garlick made it clear that this was not an official Burnley approach.

Through his job – no mention of what that was – Igor said he knew a number of Russian businessmen and bureaucrats who might be interested in investing money that they had 'free' in a British venture. Being close to government decision-makers was a big plus. He mentioned Abramovich at Chelsea and that Russian businessmen would only be interested in a long-term investment. 'What benefits might a chap with a cheque obtain?' asked Igor. He wanted to know minimal amounts being sought, time span and interest rates.

Suffice it to say that Brendan's reply was a selling job making the club look as attractive as possible and also mentioning the UCFB. Let me say right now that there was nothing underhanded in any of Brendan's communications. Brendan's vision was for a global sports platform involving Burnley, Orlando in the USA and the UCFB. He suggested to Igor that the minimum investment would need to be £12.5m and more into the UCFB. There would be shares in both. Perhaps there might even be a larger investor, he added. Emails flew back and forth between Sullivan and Igor Grymov. There was never anything devious about any of this.

Of course, it all came to nothing, one reason quoted being Brendan leaving the board before anything concrete had been settled, plus there was a need to wait for the ground buyback to be completed. The press had a field day. John Sullivan was described as an international ambassador for the club; and the two chairmen were involved in the negotiations, which was of course nonsense. Fans should be assured that there was no takeover of the club planned, said the local paper. Since all this took place, I was recently told by John Sullivan that a loan of £14m at ten per cent interest – although he was trying to get this reduced to eight per cent – was on the table and would have been available. The Russians then called it off when they learned that Mike Garlick had made it clear that John Sullivan was not on any official visit.

The 'forcing out' of Brendan Flood divided fans into two camps. A fair-sized group remembered that it was Brendan that had driven the club towards Wembley and promotion and were sorry to see all this happen. But on the *No Nay Never* website, Brendan gave an interview that caused real aggravation and upset around the boardroom table. He was upset at the release of the statement involving him in the possible Russian investment and claimed not to be in regular contact with John Sullivan regarding any potential overseas investment. He felt that there was currently a lack of leadership at the club, but he himself had no wish to be chairman, and that there was lack of belief around the club. If he were to come back, there would need to be changes in the boardroom. It was clear that there were divisions between him and two other board members, myself and Mike Garlick. 'I don't want to work with them,' he said in the press. 'And I'm sure they'd say the same of me.'

What do you do? You step back and let it all settle, which it slowly did.

But at least we had got the ground buyback sorted. Terms were agreed, bondholders were signed up, the legal stuff sorted, the paperwork finished, and Football League approval was granted. I remember in the last stages being on the phone for an hour, in the car driving home from Manchester Airport, to Peter Ashton with last-minute details. But at last, the grounds and Gawthorpe were ours again. What a long, drawn-out process it was, ending with us successfully suing the solicitors that had neglected a key action and made the negotiations so difficult. The scheme was simple enough: bonds were for sale at £250,000 each and would pay a five per cent interest for seven years, during which time they would be repaid. The offer would be underwritten by the two chairmen. Nobody was more pleased to get this sorted than Barry Kilby.

If these were the major issues, then there were a whole host of other concerns. Players that we wished to move on were still at the club, Keith Treacy and Ross Wallace. Football works in funny ways. The latter would be a key part of a promotion that was yet to come. We were concerned at rising costs around all parts of the club. A new gang mower that we needed would cost £29,000. To raise money, we had a scheme to be a director for a day at £250. We were fed up of ex-directors not turning up on matchdays; if we knew in advance, we could sell the spaces. Over the full year we expected an operating loss of over £4m. The UCFB was always behind in its payments. Players would not agree to a new bonus system. Danny Ings was out with injury again. Settling the Chris Eagles dispute set us back over £150,000. The director for a day was not a great success. Marvin Bartley's girlfriend had returned south and he wanted to follow. You do not want an unhappy player. Totally Wicked, a smoking-aid company, sponsored the Bob Lord Stand for £40,000. It was now the Totally Wicked Bob Lord Stand and the signage looked ridiculous. Bob Lord would have turned in his grave. There were quarrels, if that is the right word, about payments for gas and electricity, with the UCFB.

And in October, there was a real and genuine crisis for Eddie Howe when his mother died unexpectedly. He was devastated and so were we on his behalf. She was the main carer of his handicapped brother. On top of all that, his wife with a young baby had not settled in the north. Results on the field had not been going terribly well and at this point Bournemouth dispensed with their manager. They were very keen to take Eddie back and paid us £859,375 in compensation so that Eddie and Jason Tindall left us in mid-October. Quite why it wasn't a rounded £860,000 I cannot remember. But Bournemouth were like us – every pound was invaluable. It was just one of those times when everything comes together to everybody's benefit and satisfaction. There was no acrimony, no complications and notwithstanding the tragic origins of the move, you were left thinking if only all moves were as amicable as this. Just one small snag; we were left with a team that was not performing at all well. That plus the need, of course, for a new manager when we had originally thought and hoped that Eddie would be the one to take us back to the top six at least.

When you are a director, you are always looking at opposition managers and making comparisons, of course, and we had played a game at Watford the previous season, then managed by someone we did not know well, Sean Dyche. We went into a 2-0 lead, but then Sean Dyche made changes and they scored three goals in the space of just 20 minutes and won 3-2. Losing two-goal leads was then a quaint but not endearing habit of ours. His name, of course, and the manner of the defeat stuck in our minds and it was clear that he was a good, young, up-and-coming manager. At the end of that season, the Pozzo family, owners of Watford, sacked him so as to be able to bring in Gianfranco Zola. If they too had a quaint habit, then sacking managers was the favourite one.

When the time came for us to replace Eddie, Sean Dyche was the eventual choice and the way Watford had beaten us a year earlier stood him in good stead. So, 30 October was the beginning of a great chapter in the Burnley story but we were not to know then just how good that chapter would be. He came as a spectator, a guest of the Cardiff manager to see us thumped 4-0 at Cardiff City. It was a poor result, a poor performance, but we did it in the motorhome so the walks with the dog and the pub meals did at least provide some consolation. It meant that when he arrived for the first day of training, he knew exactly what he was up against. He started on £275,000 a year. By the time he left, let us just say it was a damned sight more. He wanted an analysis room set up and better sport-science facilities. He elected to keep Ross Wallace. We all knew that Charlie Austin wanted to go, but we offered him a new contract so that fans would at least think we were making an effort.

John B remembers Sean's PowerPoint presentation and his declaration that if we continued with our strategy of letting in more goals than we scored, we were doomed. He wanted to build a wall, create an iron shield in the defence, just like Barcelona.

As is the custom with all new managers, he declared the players not fit enough and Gawthorpe not good enough. My idea was to hire an inflatable dome to cover a new indoor pitch. I enquired about prices, learned it would be £200,000 and the idea was dropped. Attendances were under 14,000; money was in short supply.

And then Sean began to ask us questions. What he did was a first for us. No manager had ever sat us down, albeit in a board meeting, and asked us to have a think about things. He had them under two broad headings. The first was our mid-to-long-term strategy. Yes, it was a first. Usually, its directors that ask the manager what their strategy is, not the other way round. The second heading was, what kind of a club are we?

Under the first heading he asked us, did we actually have a clear mid-to-long-term strategy? We were all businessmen and in our business lives, yes was the answer, and the club had year-by-year financial projections plans. But overall? Other than saying we were aiming at being in the top six or even promotion, did we really have a clear action plan? Did we just appoint a manager and hope it all turned out well? Next: were we aware of the challenges of cutting costs? That was a definite yes. But then he wanted to know, did he have a mandate within those challenges and cost cuts? A mandate for what? To make decisions without having to consult the board at every turn. How much of the decision-making process would actually be his? And were we all aligned, board and manager? It was a word he used a lot. Were we all singing from the same hymn sheet? Were we all giving out the same messages to the supporters and the press?

The second heading: what kind of club were we? Were we going to be just survivors in the football world or did we really want to develop? What was our place in the community? Of course, we had one but Sean brought in Neil Hart and the community programme rocketed. He had worked with him at Watford. Did we want to be promotion chasers? That might have seemed a daft question, as of course we said we did. But were we truly committed to that aim, truly enthusiastic or were we just simply content to say we were, as long as the bills were paid? Did we want to build the club? Develop the infrastructure, get Gawthorpe better equipped and aim for full academy status? Were we future thinkers? Could we envision the club in five years' time, ten years' time, were we up for that challenge or were we in a comfort zone? Were we building on sand or stone? Did what we do have real strong foundations for the future or was everything we did going to be just a quick fix? And the final question: DO WE KNOW WHO WE ARE, and clear, as a group?

I'm exhausted just reading through that list.

On a more practical, organisational, mundane level, he asked if we had a cheaper pre-season trip than going to Holland. Could he have the saved money for an analysis room and equipment? How could we say no?

CHAPTER TWENTY-FIVE

2013/14 Who Expected Promotion?

WE LOADED up the motorhome and set off for southern Ireland. Why? Because this was where Burnley had headed for their pre-season, with a game against Cork City. Behind it was the small car in tow and inside the van was the springer, Tom. The club trip was 10–16 July, but we headed over there a few days early, with the ferry journey from Holyhead to Dublin of around four hours. Customs was straightforward, passports were checked, including Tom's. He was a well-travelled dog and had been with us in the motorhome all over Europe, including the World Cup in Germany and the Under-21 Nations Cup in Sweden. Did Paul Fletcher really believe that all I was interested in were the perks of being a director, a glass of red wine, and a four-course meal? In truth, I can't ever remember having a four-course meal in any boardroom anywhere.

Our first stop was just south of Dublin, passing by, on the way, the main rugby stadium, Lansdowne; now named the Aviva, unless it has been changed again – sponsorship and naming money talks. It was next to Rathdrum, alongside the Avonmore River and by the Wicklow Mountains. From the campsite into Rathdrum was just a ten-minute walk and we had two nights there in a place lined with traditional pubs and shops, beneath good weather and sunshine. Two days and nights of eating and drinking, with walks for Tom by the river.

The plan was to travel across to the west coast and then move slowly down the coast towards Cork in the south-west. In the centre of Ireland, we stopped at Athlone, and camped in the middle of a forest that gave welcome shade in the very hot weather. We finally reached the west coast at a place overlooking the Aran Islands. The weather remained wonderful, but it struck me that this was no place to be in a bad winter. We took a boat trip across to Inishmore on the islands and as the boat waited to depart, we watched swimmers playing tag with the local dolphin. I've seen some special things in my time but this was a really special one.

We arrived at Inishmore in mid-morning and landed right next to the pub, but by now, I was suffering from what seemed to be a bit of gout, a type of arthritis that is extremely painful. Walking was difficult, so the pub garden in the sunshine seemed a far better prospect than walking the dog. The afternoon was most pleasant. Tom was thoroughly unhappy without a walk and spent the afternoon sulking. Inishmore was a place that seemed to specialise in wonderful woollen jumpers. The temptation to buy a pile of them was resisted. Half asleep after the beer and lunch, the boat took us back to the mainland, cruising down the coast to the Cliffs of Mohar.

Next job was to find a doctor to see if I could get anything for the gout. Apparently eating and drinking too much doesn't do it any good. He looked at my EU card and prescribed me some pills that most certainly did the trick. On returning to Burnley, I mentioned all this to Doc Iven and showed him the pills that had produced the miracle cure. On seeing the box and the label he was horrified. 'Good God,' he said. 'These are banned in the UK. They are classed as unsafe.' But they certainly cured me. One small victory for the EU, I suppose.

The next site was the best of the trip, right next to the beach and overlooking the sea at the Ring of Kerry and Rossleigh Beach. Tom was delighted, of course. The local restaurants had the most wonderful fresh seafood. The weather was still hot; perfect for a dip in the sea. So good, in fact, that we had three days here. Then it was down to business at Cork for the game. We tried to find the boardroom to say hello but couldn't find it. To be fair to them, we had just turned up unannounced at the ground. Mind you, the half-time cup of tea sitting in the lovely sunshine was possibly better than any boardroom. It was a nice little ground and the ticket office was quite charming. It was an old hen hut that had been spruced up and had wheels in each corner so it could be wheeled out on matchdays.

John B was over there on the trip and promised that, before the game, anyone who was wearing a Burnley shirt would be treated to a pint in the local pub. Much to his shock, nearly 300 people turned up, with one lady asking for three pints as she was wearing three shirts. Typical Burnley. She offered to show him all three shirts as proof but John was firm and bought just the one pint for her. Nice try. I never did ask him what his round of drinks had cost.

None of us had any idea what the new season would bring and with new players acquired on free transfers – Tom Heaton, Scott Arfield and David Jones – you could have been forgiven for thinking, 'Let's just aim for halfway this season.' The names discussed for possible transfers or loan deals at the June board meeting make for interesting reading. Patrick Bamford, who eventually came later and barely featured. Harry Kane, yes that one, then finding his way at Spurs. Jamie Vardy, possibly then at Fleetwood, can't remember – £1m would have bought him but we simply had no spare cash to speculate on him. And Dale Stephens, but not signed until later.

Martin Paterson left because, with Ings in such good form, Sean could not guarantee Martin the No. 9 slot and Chris McCann left for Wigan. We knew that Charlie Austin would be sold. The question was, how much could we get for him? We wanted £5m. Hull City offered £3.5m. Then they pulled out, possibly because of worries about Charlie's suspected injury weaknesses. Hull had been caught out with another player with similar problems, spent several millions, and so Charlie was rejected on medical grounds. Hull made this public, which made it difficult for us to sell him and get the price we wanted.

No club showed any interest other than Reading, and Charlie said he didn't want to go there. Until this money was in our bank, then we could not figure out how to fund the coming season. The two chairmen said they would put in a million each. We asked Peter Ashton for the loan of a million – yes, he of Lionbridge who once owned our ground. This, dear Burnley supporter, is how we funded the season and the promotion that came at the end of it – the wonderful, unexpected promotion; the Bisto Gravy Kids promotion; the little club that everyone thought would never see the Premier League again. We were the loan arrangers – an old joke, I know, but true enough.

The Bolton game would be televised, another £80,000 for the finances. Two directors put in an emergency £300,000 between them; between October and February of the season we would need another £3m. The Cricket Field Stand roof urgently needed repairs. Until Charlie Austin was sold, it would have to wait. We did sell him to QPR; £1.5m first payment, and a second in January of £1.4m. They had offered him £25,000 a week. How could we possibly compete with that? We had wanted £5m when we set out to sell him. We were £2m down. Could we get Billy Sharp as a replacement? No, we could not. He would have cost too much, plus his wages were too high.

Meanwhile, Gawthorpe training pitches were flooding. Dmitry Rybolovlev, a Russian, signalled an interest in Burnley. He owned AS Monaco and had just spent €150m on players. It came to nothing. We had enlisted the help of Eurofin, a company that brokered company sales deals – for a fee, of course. And it was them that introduced us to Rybolovlev. We had a huge list of names from them to look at but none came to anything. Their services were dispensed with.

Politics was rearing its ugly head at Gawthorpe with some of the youth-development staff who were resistant to some of the changes being initiated by Jason Blake. I had no involvement with this and had no comments to make about whether those staff were right or wrong. It was left to Sean to sort. But one thing was for sure: all was not well with youth development.

Sean Dyche, in his manager's report, was happy with the progress of the team. He had taken Michael Kightly on loan. Other clubs were after him as well but, in view of the fact that Michael would score the second goal in the win against Wigan that secured our promotion at the end of the season, this was a key signing. Another name came into our discussions – Ashley Barnes from Brighton. But they wanted too much for him, so we would try to get him on loan. He did indeed arrive and it is fair to say that he eventually became a cult figure at the club, on account of his battling style, no-holds-barred attitude and the key goals he scored.

How handy it was to have little nuggets of knowledge I stored in my head or in my office. When it came time to actually get the stand roof repaired, the cricket club presented access problems. But hold on a minute, there was a 1925 agreement in the land sale that I knew meant they could not stop us from repairing the roof.

Burnley FC 1, Cricket Club 0.

Perusing all my old files and notes, what strikes me now, despite all the above, was that this was a relatively quiet season behind the scenes. But how some things cropped up over and again.

The UCFB was expanding, and who was supposed to pay for the gas and electricity? Next it was who was to pay for the hot water? Cash flow: ah, those two little words. The need for director loans. The inadequacy of the Gawthorpe training area. Converting Arthur Bellamy's former bungalow into rooms for the players. English Heritage were objecting to that. The thorny issue of bonuses for Sean and his staff. Two new directors arrived with a welcome influx of investment, Brian Nelson and Terry Crabb. And Brendan Flood wanted to return to the board.

Did I say that things were relatively quiet this season? I suppose they were until Brendan wanted to return to the board once his IVA had been completed. It has to be said that there was some unease about this in view of his previous statement that he had been forced out and would never work with Mike Garlick and myself again. Yes, I had perhaps been a thorn in his side but this was only because I continually questioned expenditure and costs and decisions that were made outside of the boardroom, no matter who was involved.

It led to the drawing up of a director code of conduct that we all had to agree to and sign. I felt he owed, certainly two of us, an apology. There were a number of reasons, certainly in my view, for not welcoming him back and I made these clear at a board meeting. However, in the interests of unity, I said nothing publicly, and return he did.

The new code of conduct, that had to be signed, covered a range of things, not the least of which was being aware of financial responsibilities, one of them being if you are subject to an IVA, you cannot be a director at any football club. Social media should not be used for disclosing matters that are confidential to the club. Expense claims should be presented within 30 days and be supported by clear paperwork. Directors should not sign off their own claims or those of their own company. No expenditures, be they cheques or bank transfers, should be signed by a director unless they had board approval for being a signatory. Directors should not negotiate for players or with agents unless authorised to do so. Quick and urgent decisions were at the sole discretion of the chairmen. Directors were entitled to four match tickets. Others should be paid for. Two for away games. All contracts entered into by a company belonging to a director should be honoured by that director. Communication with the team manager was the responsibility of the chairmen. The chief executive should report only to the chairmen.

On the field, things were going well. Sean had been Manager of the Month for September, there were fringe players that we all wanted to shift out on loan to trim the wage bill, certain pitches at Gawthorpe were unusable. In view of Lazio's possible partnership with the club and loaning us players, Mike Garlick and John B went over there on a fact-finding trip. I could only assume they didn't find many, because nothing came of this.

Sean at this point felt that we were reasonably placed to obtain promotion. The mere mention of the word sent shivers down us all. Promotion – really? In his opinion, both Danny Ings and Kieran Trippier would want to move on, whatever happened. Jason

Shackell would possibly want to leave. If Michael Duff retired as well, we would be thin on the ground to say the least. He was hugely concerned at this, wondering if he could build another team in the summer again, and a summer preceding a possible season in the Premier League. How lucky we had been to pick up those three free transfers, Heaton, Arfield and Jones, who had all fitted seamlessly into the team. Nor were there any young players ready to step up into the first team. He indicated he would like to sign a young lad from Oldham Athletic, James Tarkowski, for £250,000 and then loan him back to Oldham. It was agreed this would be investigated further but nothing transpired. Silly us. What a player he turned out to be and we later bought him from Brentford for a sizeable fee. He became a bedrock of our side for a number of years before electing to leave when his contract ran down. He was magnificent for us; the Mee/Tarkowski partnership at centre-back being one of the best, if not the best, in the Premier League.

Into March, promotion a real possibility, but in writing this book it is so easy to lose sight of what a football club actually exists for when you are company secretary dealing with the daily running of the club. Wages, bills, cash flow, politics, grievances, unusable pitches, legal matters, contracts, codes of conduct, the FA, the Football League, manager requirements, trying to get Gawthorpe to Category Three, retail, catering, lotteries, repairs and maintenance, accounts, bank balances, disciplinary actions, ticketing, sponsorships, a dispute with Hibernian FC, and, if we were to be promoted, should we let away fans have the whole of the Cricket Field Stand? It was also my job to handle share sales and purchases; Mike Garlick bought 4,250 shares from Barry Kilby and now he bought 12,500 from Brendan Flood.

All that plus how to celebrate the 100th anniversary of the 1914 FA Cup win? The great thing about Burnley Football Club is its history and all its achievements. I'll wager that no club of its size has achieved so much. The big event was an exhibition at Towneley Hall that ran through the summer and attracted hundreds of visitors.

On show were some wonderful exhibits. The game was the first time that a reigning monarch had ever attended an FA Cup Final. Burnley won 1-0.

Promotion was duly achieved, against the odds, against all expectations, against all predictions. When the season began it was the last thing on our minds other than that faint hope, of course, that all football fans feel whatever their club, that this might just be a decent season. Yet again there were decisions to be made; ticketing, prices, whether to upgrade the buildings along Harry Potts Way, getting rid of asbestos we had found in two stands. How to upgrade Gawthorpe to Category Three. What players to retain, which ones to release, which new ones to pursue?

Danny Ings would stay but run down his contract that ended at the end of the following season. A deal for Craig Bryson from Derby was fixed but fell through. He had a release clause in his contract but Derby were difficult with the paperwork. It was hugely messy. We agreed a deal for Craig Dawson from West Brom; the player asked for a transfer to enable it, but that fell through at the other end. We still pondered on approaching Spurs for Harry Kane, but Spurs needed to fill gaps in their team before agreeing. Fans might grumble when you fail to sign players, but the complications, hurdles and changes of mind by the selling club can be bewildering and so deals fall through. Fans then think that we are either incompetent or not trying hard enough.

Not just player deals fall through causing great frustration. Another deal we tried was to purchase or lease the pub across the road from the ground, The Park View, when it became vacant. It was for sale at £300,000 or for lease at £28,000 per year for three years with the right to buy at the end of that. What a splendid addition it would have been and could have provided a variety of uses as well as its basic pub function; a matchday fan zone, rooms and bedrooms upstairs that might have provided meeting rooms, community use, a museum/resource centre, extra office space, restaurant space. There was even a suggestion to call it The Barry Kilby.

And I have hardly mentioned the promotion. Yes, we were back in the Premier League with all the big games that went with it, the hullaballoo, the publicity, the extra marketing opportunities. We had played superb football in many of the games, the very best of which was the game that decided our promotion against Wigan when we won 2-0. Kightly and Barnes scored. What a glorious day this was. The boardroom afterwards was a very happy place. As for the evening, I can assure you, a fair amount of drink was taken. Wigan was a friendly club and Dave Whelan and his directors certainly joined our boardroom celebrations. The next morning with a clearer head, the realisation dawned. The hard work starts now.

Sean had created a team that was well drilled but at the same time a treat to watch. We had already experienced promotion once before with Owen Coyle but this one felt different. For a start we would not suffer the agonies of the play-offs. We achieved it on our own ground in front of our own fans who danced and sang and celebrated on the pitch with total delight. If you want the full details, then you need to read the Dave Thomas book *Who Says Football Doesn't Do Fairytales?*

As for me: I just felt a huge satisfaction at all the work I had undertaken behind the scenes. Much of it unseen and unappreciated, I have to add. I would never have said that Brendan Flood and I were the best of friends, but I will always say well done to him for the way he drove through the promotion of 2008/09. It would be equally nice for Brendan to say to me, just once, 'Well done, Clive, for all the work that you have done for this club.'

CHAPTER TWENTY-SIX

2014/15 Relegation but Only Just

BEHIND THE scenes, the work revolved around trying to get Gawthorpe and the youth set-up upgraded. Plus, planning for the remodelling, expanding and upgrading the buildings, offices and shop along Harry Potts Way. Oh, and cash flow, of course. I shouldn't really need to mention that. Or the £8m loss incurred during the previous season. Of course, there was the Premier League money to relish, but we had plans for that. In the first week of August, we were due to receive £24m from the Premier League.

But mention of the word Gawthorpe reminds me of one of the great characters that I met at Turf Moor, namely Flavio Briatore, who, when we met, was a co-owner of QPR. The connection between him and Gawthorpe was the large oil puddle that his helicopter left on one of the pitches at the training ground when he landed there. Our groundsman looked at it in horror when he found it.

His story would make a gripping TV drama series: convicted in Italy in the 80s on several fraud charges, received two prison sentences, although the convictions were later quashed by an amnesty. Once upon a time, a restaurant owner and insurance salesman, then time spent setting up Benetton franchises in the Virgin Islands and the USA. Next he was manager of the Benetton Formula One racing team. And then from 2007 to 2010/11 he was part owner, along with racing man Bernie Ecclestone, and chairman of QPR. Accused of motor-race fixing in Singapore, the Football League asked for details of the investigations. A chequered life you might say. Briatore then stepped down as QPR chairman.

He did say one very apt thing about football: 'I will never invest in a football club again, it's only ever a good idea if you are very rich and looking for ways to waste your money.'

My own meeting with him was when he had flown by private jet from Italy back to the UK, and then flew up to Burnley in his helicopter, landing at Gawthorpe. At Turf Moor he turned up in jeans. Our dress code insisted on collar and tie and jacket. He was denied entry by a steward who had no idea who he was. Briatore was baffled by the whole thing.

As ever, it was me that had to sort things out, so down I went to see what was going on and what all the row was about. What could I do? All I could do once I realised who he was was let him in and request that next time he came in a collar and tie. Crisis management at its best. I wish I could remember if we won this game or not.

I could bore you next with an account game by game of our relegation season, but perhaps far more interesting would be some examples of the hoops you have to jump through to raise the level of your academy. We had applied for Category Three membership, but an audit has to be carried out to see what facilities you have, and if they measure up to the standards required. An audit, by the way, cost £10,000. After the audit it was recommended that we should be awarded a Category Four status. We had failed miserably. Let me give you the 28 points that we had to improve on. You will find it either fascinating and eye-opening or deadly dull and leave you shaking your head. You have the option of heading straight to point 28. We had no such option.

1. Provide more detail in the Football Philosophy of the club. There needs to be more layers behind it and a DNA of the first team should be developed to allow the Academy to develop a coaching programme and a coaching philosophy closer in line with the first team.

2. There need to be multidisciplinary SMART performance targets for all departments with particular emphasis on time frames, and allocated to a person rather than a department.
3. Measurement of targets needs to provide outcomes for each phase to enable staff to assess current performance and plan for the future.
4. Provide formal statement in the Academy Performance Plan (APP) to identify how different departments work together.
5. APP needs to be reviewed and approved by the board.
6. APP needs to be communicated to wider audience within club and community.
7. Staffing chart needs to be re-designed to include individuals on Technical Board Academy Management Team.
8. Needs to be formal planning of CPD for AMT linked with appraisals, training need and outcome. Formal dates planned with documentation of how staff absences are to be covered during absences for CPD.
9. Further development of appraisal system.
10. Coaching programme needs to be age specific. More detail about learning objectives per age group to cover technical, physical and psycho/social learning objectives and periodisation. Learning objectives to be SMART.
11. Coaching objectives for goal keepers to be age specific. Link programme to outfield players. Document a code of conduct and fair play into the games programme.
12. Implement a bespoke Burnley session planner template for all coaches that lays down expected content including key coaching points for individual players.
13. Produce formal documents for match preparation to provide info on procedures expected on matchdays.
14. Coaching hours in PDP, U14s, U15s, and U16s must increase.
15. Contracts of employment are needed for ALL staff.

No more. I think 15 of these requirements is enough to show before you fall asleep. There are another 13 to wade through; and this was just to get to Category Three. Paperwork, reams of it, ticklists, checklists, vision statements, philosophy statements. SMART, CPD, AMT, PDP, FP, YDP and PMA. I still don't know what some of them are. An exercise in jumping through hoops. But it had to be done.

SMART, by the way, is 'Specific, Measurable, Attainable, Relevant and Time-bound'. I am sure you are thrilled to know that.

Today, as we write, the academy faces demotion from Cat One to Cat Two. My suspicion is that aspects of the paperwork have been neglected. Obviously, you need certain tangible, visible facilities, equipment, buildings, rooms, and a high level of staffing, but so much of it is paperwork and more paperwork. We had employed someone, an ex-official who knew this system and all the requirements inside out, especially the paperwork. He got us through it and eventually as far as Category One. This had even more requirements and hoops to jump through. His knowledge was invaluable. After the takeover, he left.

At the commencement of the new season, Sean Dyche in general was pleased. But he – we – still sought new players. Craig Dawson from West Brom, Henri Lansbury from Nottingham Forest, Troy Deeney from Watford. None of them happened. The clubs involved simply offered their players better terms than us. Sean was finding it difficult to work in the transfer market, money being the issue and wages. But George Boyd did sign and none of us will forget the winning goal he scored against Manchester City later in the season. McArthur from Wigan we valued at £3m. Wigan wanted £5m. We were all pretty much agreed; we'd not had the best of transfer windows although the addition of Michael Keane from Manchester United on loan was a huge success story.

Danny Ings was determined to run down his contract and seek a move to a bigger club. But with his knee problems, this was dangerous for him if he did not sign a new contract with us. With yet another attempt to persuade him to sign, we offered £22,000 a week rising to £27,000. We would have offered even more if his agent had been willing to sit down with us. But no. At this point we did wonder if he had been tapped up. If he then went on a free transfer, his signing-on fee would be substantial.

We had hoped to purchase or lease the Park View pub across the road from the ground to be our fan zone, amongst other uses. But Punch Taverns decided they were not going to sell or lease. Instead, they suggested a joint venture with us to turn it into a sports bar. It would set us back £80,000 and we decided no. We had conducted our enquiries through a third party so that Punch would not know of our interest, but somehow they must have found out. A new tenant moved in. Eventually he went bankrupt and Punch put the place back on the market asking for a rent of £35,000 a year. What we needed was an option to buy and, with the feeling that Punch was on the back foot, we decided to bide our time and see if we could lease it for less. Yes, we could, at £30,000 a year, and it was suggested it could be converted into the club shop as well as a fan zone.

Should we extend the Bob Lord Stand or not? We could add another 14 rows of seats at the back and build a new roof. Should we go ahead with Gawthorpe improvements at a cost of £3m? Yes, planning applications were put in. Should we erect new floodlights to comply with new requirements? Yes, but next season. Should we seek new sponsors? Did we market ourselves well enough in the Far East? Should we proceed with the refurbishment and extensions of the building along Harry Potts Way? Should we phase them or build in one go? Should we allow home supporters in the Cricket Field Stand or let it all to away supporters? Should we continue to try to move the cricket club to somewhere else? At one point they were indeed interested, but, as ever, the problem was where to move them. One thing we did all agree on was how nice it was to be able to work each month without having to worry about how to pay the wages.

An Italian player interested us, but Sean clearly preferred to work with homegrown UK players. He was familiar with them but unfamiliar with overseas players. Nor was he sure that they represented good value for money and he was always wary of them settling in and coping with the Premier League. It was almost a red-letter day when Steven Defour later arrived from Belgium.

A hugely significant moment arrived in January. The issue of having two chairmen was raised. It was joint chairman Mike Garlick that called for a special meeting to decide who should be the chairman going forward. He felt that having two chairmen was not working as well as it might and the chairmanship should now reflect that he owned 47 per cent of club shares, more than the rest of the directors put together. John B, on the other hand, felt that it had worked well and had no real wish to be reduced to the role of vice-chairman. Prior to this meeting they had both met privately to see if they could resolve the issue between them without involving the rest of the board. They had not been able to agree how to proceed. The other directors had meanwhile come up with the proposal that Mike Garlick would be chairman elect, and thus John B would become vice-chairman from May 2015. After a general discussion at which John B was not happy, he declined the new proposal but stayed as a director for the sake of unity. There's that word again, unity, a word I used when Brendan Flood rejoined the board and I accepted this. All this was kept very much quiet for the time being, and it was not until the end of the season that John B issued his own statement to say he was stepping down as joint chairman so that he could spend more time with his family as they grew up. Barry Kilby stepped into the breach as the vice-chairman, his health problems now well under control.

Mike Garlick was now, effectively, in the driving seat.

On the playing side, Danny Ings continued to stall on any new contract. Leicester City bid £7m for him. We offered him £35,000 a week. We looked at players from Norwich and Cardiff City without success. We looked at players from Hamburg, PSG and AZ as alternatives but it was back to the old problem of Sean not being keen on overseas players. The board were not 100 per cent happy about this but the manager must have the final say, we felt. Nor was Sean too happy with Danny Ings, now riding out his contract, and was particularly unhappy after a game against QPR. It is, I suppose, just possible that Danny was distracted a little by the disability project he was setting up in the community to which he had contributed £16,000. It was Sean who suggested that we should make him no more offers.

Meanwhile, down at Gawthorpe, we needed a new bridge across the river, so, yes, we agreed to go ahead with that. Barnfield would be the preferred contractor if they would reduce their bill in exchange for naming rights. Soon we would be able to look forward to the day when we deliberately did not show prospective signings the muddy pitches and basic changing rooms. But as with everything that involves building, two snags emerged, in this case bats and snipe. Snipe used Gawthorpe as a wintering area. Oh, and the National Trust, they had worries about the road in and out and their car park. Bit by bit all these things were sorted out.

By May, of course, relegation had been confirmed and it looked like Ings was going to Liverpool. We wanted £8m for him. Had he been distracted by this prospect during the season. Had it affected his performances? Only he knows.

As for the relegation itself: it was a tough one to take. We had never been thrashed or humiliated, had played extremely well, but with Ings and Vokes out for several spells with injuries, they had not had the same sparkling season that they had enjoyed before. That was our downfall, scoring goals. Defensively we were very good. It had taken us until our 11th game to get a win under our belts. I remember four games in a row that were all lost 1-0 – against Arsenal, Everton, Leicester and West Ham – when nothing went right in any of them. I know that this is the familiar cry from all relegated fans, managers and directors when we point to various hard-luck games and results. But regarding these four games, it was as if someone had planned the whole thing in advance. Arsenal: when the ball hit Duff on the head and bounced to Ramsey, who said 'ta very much' and scored. Everton: when we might have had two penalties with any other referee. Leicester: we missed a penalty at one end and less than a minute later Duff diverts the ball and Leicester score. And West

Ham: when Duff was mistakenly sent off early in the game. Poor Duffo, he unwittingly comes into all this three times.

Of course, those four games weren't the only reason. There was always the careful spending and controlled limit, but Dyche was adamant that nobody was going to spend millions and throw the club under a bus. There were actually two players lined up in January, one of them as far as at the medical stage, until their clubs pulled the plug. The board was never trying to hoard the money; it was simply that prices were too high. Don't forget we played against teams with players that were genuine superstars. Fabregas when he came with Chelsea was from another planet, Eto'o when he came with Everton was just unplayable, Sanchez at Arsenal was untouchable.

Images of several games come back. A two-goal lead over Crystal Palace at Turf Moor became a 3-2 defeat. The two-goal lead against West Brom was lost when they remembered all they had to do was crock Marney and to score from corners with holds and blocks and grappling that would have taken wrestling to new levels. Losing 1-0 to Swansea, Vokes burst through but Williams had him round the waist. Penalty if he'd gone down, but Vokes, made of stronger stuff, tried to stay on his feet. Liverpool were played off the park at Turf Moor, but then Sterling broke away and that was another 0-1.

Marney was a big miss whenever he was injured. Of 46 games so far won by Dyche, Marney had appeared in 40 of them. Matt Taylor too was a big loss. But what never disappeared was the spirit, the energy and the refusal to be cowed. Always stubbornly competitive and so damned hard to beat. They were a credit to Sean Dyche and the town. A Dyche mantra has always been that the margins are so fine. We were not despondent and the final game was a 1-0 win at Aston Villa. Down indeed, but parachute payments would help us out.

I got to point 15 in the list of 28 areas that we needed to improve to be awarded Category Three for the academy. I confess I got tired of churning them all out, but I did say I would let you see them all. So, here are the remaining items. Enjoy.

16. Education philosophy to include informal education principles for FP and YDP players and parents that is supported by a formal timetable for all phases.
17. Welfare philosophy to have more detail including sections on diet, racism, life skills etc.
18. Send 12-weekly reports to parents on educational progression of scholars.
19. Records of players' games consistently uploaded on Performance Management Application and monitored by head of coaching.
20. Record more detail on injury data to enable analysis of information. Input treatment time, rehab time etc to try and spot trends.
21. Maintain up to date records of achievement and players performance clocks to include type of game time, and more injury audit. Extend to games and coaching programme achievement of learning objectives. This must be assessed against objectives and not themes.
22. Develop performance reviews in line with coaching programme and available for all players. Review should show multidisciplinary targets.
23. Make annual reports available to players and parents and upload into PMA. Reports should reflect global picture of development and progression and identify critical success or development pointers.
24. Implement formal protocol for meetings with players and parents which should be held at least twice over the course of a season. Those staff expected to attend should be identified.
25. Scout protocols require highlighting arrangements for scouts attending games at other clubs and protocols for the approach of scouts to players.
26. Not enough pitches to support games programmes.
27. Insufficient grass/artificial facilities at training ground. Must also include a designated goal keeper area.
28. Insufficient changing rooms.

So, there you have it. The complete list of where we were failing. I read it and think back to people like Harry Potts, Jimmy McIlroy, and even Alan Brown, the man in the 50s who spotted the potential at Gawthorpe and that it was for sale, and then had chairman Bob Lord buy it. What would they have made of it all? The likes of Bill Shankly and Brian Clough would have looked at it and shook their heads, bewildered. I doubt they would have read even half of it before asking, 'What the hell is this?' I can remember when Burnley had the first team, the reserves and then the A, B and C teams. Just one man was responsible for each of them, with none of these Audit Recommendations for Entrance Conditions, demands and paperwork. Gather the first-team squad these days for a pre-season official photograph and the backroom staff will outnumber them.

So, are things any better? Are the players any better? Is the success rate higher? Does Burnley have a conveyor belt of talent like it once had, players that walked seamlessly into the first team? Perhaps it needs a whole book to answer those questions.

CHAPTER TWENTY-SEVEN

2015/16 A Wonderful Promotion

A NUMBER of things dominated this season: a fabulous promotion with a side in which no player was on more than £15,000 a week. Twenty three games unbeaten from late December to the end of the season. We actually at last reached a settlement with the law firm that had bodged the sale of Turf Moor and Gawthorpe to Peter Ashton. There was a bit of a spending spree on players. We saw the arrival of Joey Barton. I relinquished my role as unpaid company secretary. The club fell victim to a Lloyds Bank scam that took almost over £1m out of our bank account.

It was a marvellous season. Back to the Promised Land in some style and with a degree of swagger. At the beginning of the season, I'd chatted to some of our players and asked them how many games any side could afford to lose and still go up as champions. Five is the maximum was the consensus. So that was the target; do not lose more than five games. And how many games did we lose? Just five.

It was the season I most enjoyed as a director and by now I had been there nigh on 30 years, had been part of the two Mullen promotions, the Stan promotion, the Coyle promotion, and the first Dyche promotion. There was something that felt different about this season, but I can't exactly put my finger on it. Maybe it was the 23 games unbeaten. Maybe it was beating Blackburn twice. Maybe it was a fairly quiet time in the boardroom; nicely harmonious, although being company secretary had its moments. I'd taken it on as a temporary measure and here I was, still doing it.

The last game of the season, at Charlton, sticks in the minds of all who were there. Not because we won or were champions but because the Football League, in their wisdom, sent the trophy up to Middlesbrough, just in case they were champions. So, we had the ridiculous sight of the players celebrating and cavorting around the pitch brandishing a plastic blow-up thing, or cardboard cut-outs wrapped in silver, as if they were the real thing. My suspicion is that, because of the troubles there were at Charlton between fans and owners, the League decided that to present the trophy to Burnley after this game would cause a minor riot at the ground by their disgruntled supporters. In my home I have a framed picture of our very happy party on the pitch, a wonderful memory. But this triumph and promotion possibly marked the end of my meaningful and practically useful time as a director at the club, for reasons I will come to later.

I'm going to say right now that Joey Barton was a credit to the club and was one of the driving forces behind the promotion. His chequered past was a worry to many; initially to Sean as well, and it is well documented, so we will not dwell on it here. But in this season, he was a paragon of virtue and hugely popular. He had been to Burnley as a QPR player and received much ribald abuse; he was also hit on the head by a bottle that was thrown. What I remember clearly is that he made no fuss, just picked up the bottle, threw it to the side of the pitch and then carried on playing. I can think of other players who would have gone down, rolled around, feigned serious injury with an Oscar-winning performance, clutched their heads in agony and taken five minutes to pretend to recover. Joey impressed me that day. In the dressing room he was an inspiration and a motivator. Two games come to mind: away at MK Dons and then away at Charlton, when he gave the side a bit of a roasting. As we write this book, he has taken Bristol Rovers to a promotion as manager.

Joey wasn't the only signing that had a huge impact. Andre Gray was the other and his goals played a huge part in the success; £6m from Brentford. We made efforts to sign James Tarkowski but Brentford wanted £5m, which we decided was too much. Matt Lowton was signed for £1m from Aston Villa. Much credit for these signings went to Frank McParland, the new sporting director. Alas, he would not be with us for long, soon heading off to Glasgow Rangers. Several attempts were made to sign Henri Lansbury, so many in fact over the coming seasons that it became a standing joke with supporters. Richard Keogh from Derby was a deal that fell through when the player changed his mind. We looked at Chris Wood who was then at Leicester, but Leeds snapped him up for £2m. Dele Alli from Spurs was a possible loan but nothing happened. And then there was the curious case of striker Jelle Vossen who was bought and then sold in a matter of seven weeks.

Out went Danny Ings to Liverpool, Kieran Trippier to Spurs, moves that we expected, and then Jason Shackell to Derby. We wanted £10m for Ings but it would go to tribunal. With Barnes and Marney injured, the increased expectations, the pressure of again making decent players into good players all meant that Sean Dyche thought it would be a big ask to get back to the Premier League at the first attempt. In the 22 years of the Premier League, of 66 teams relegated, only eight had bounced back first time.

The Lloyds Bank scam cost us a lot of money. 'Conman stole £113m from bank clients in phone scam' was the newspaper headline when it all went public in 2016, with a full-page spread in at least one newspaper. The mastermind behind it had recruited Lloyds Bank staff as his assistants and then went on to spend his gains on a luxury lifestyle. Feezan Choudhary, a name we eventually became familiar with, nickname Fizzy, was making up to £2m a day at the peak of his scam. Victims were cold-called and duped into giving pass numbers to their accounts and their personal details. We were one of something like 750 victims. How many others were contacted but did not fall to it, we shall never know. To get into the Lloyds account you needed a user name, the individual password and then, to approve payments, a code number set.

Choudhary worked on a daily basis for two and a half years calling thousands of Lloyds customers and persuading them to hand over the details. Corrupt bank workers were paid £250 for every private bank statement that they provided that was then successfully plundered. No amount was over £100,000, to make it less obvious. The money was then siphoned into different accounts in other banks. Three Lloyds staff were eventually jailed along with Choudhary. He had been arrested in Paris whilst trying to board a plane with a false passport.

Once they had the club details there were 13 transactions that totalled £1,142,474.79.

'Oh,' somebody eventually remarked, 'why have we paid £98,999 and 99 pence to Khan Car Wash? Not once but twice. That's an awful lot of cars.'

'Oh, why have we paid Ruba Tailoring £100,000? Who are they?' None of us had new suits.

'Oh, why have we paid £99,999 to Ganny Cleaning? Who are they? What have they cleaned?'

'Oh, why have we paid £49,899 and 99 pence to San Mar Cosmetics? Who's had a facelift?'

When it came to light it, was me, as company secretary, who had the job of investigating all this, working with the fraud squad and grappling with Lloyds Bank, who basically said, 'Sorry, this is your own fault if you have been daft enough to have handed over your confidential pass details over the phone.'

The wrestling match with Lloyds continued through the season until at last we had managed to claw back £470,617.69. Can I say at this point it was not me that handed over the details and that if it was actually funny, all this would make a marvellous comedy film: *Carry on Scamming*, I suppose, along the same lines as the film about the gang of doddering pensioners who broke into the Hatton Garden vaults, except that Choudhary was just a 25-year-old whizz-kid. It was kept well quiet at the time because we knew how embarrassing this would appear. Negotiations with Lloyds were long and frustrating, involving our own solicitors, barristers and threats of court action. By 8 June it had still not been settled and at this point I stood down as company secretary. It was a big moment.

Let me say I was more than happy to relinquish this post when asked to do so by Mike Garlick as part of a restructuring of staff and their responsibilities. The work I had undertaken, the aggravation, the legal work, the negotiations with builders, the constant watching of finances, responsibility for the share register and 101 daily issues had been a mammoth task. Should I say that only an idiot would do it for nothing? But I loved this club and wanted to serve it to the best of my ability.

Being a workaholic had helped. Being the kind of person not afraid to ask questions and to point out problems, the kind of person, whilst not welcoming confrontations and argument but at the same time not being afraid of them, certainly helped. What it did do, stepping down, whilst not immediately obvious, was change my relationship with the chairman. From being the go-to person when there was something to investigate or a problem to solve or an action to take whilst still a director, I was now merely an onlooker, a bystander almost. I had huge knowledge of everything going on in every area of the club. I had so much information at my fingertips and they say that with knowledge comes power, but I was certainly never powerful. Influential perhaps, in a small way. But now, from being a key member of the board, I was a director of no real importance. It took a little while for that to occur to me.

But all that did not arise until the end of the season and, in the meantime, there was a promotion to enjoy. This is from *Champions* by Dave Thomas.

> Much of the summer had been spent discussing what might have been and missed chances that might have led to Premier League survival. But with the new season, it was time to

put all that to bed. It had been a tough relegation to take. In game after game, we had played so well but never got the rub of the green, those little slices of luck that make all the difference. It was a brave and defiant relegation.

On Boxing Day of that season, after a 3-0 defeat at Hull City and a lean period that had lasted several games, there were even calls for Dyche to be sacked. The majority stayed calm and so did the board, not that there had ever been any chance of reviewing his position. It would have been absurd. But by this time, few if any people, expected Burnley to do anything more than maybe ensure a play-off place in the top six. We were way behind the top position at this stage.

And yet, as the season reached the finale and with just two games to play and unbeaten in 21 games, Burnley were just about in the driving seat with three teams locked in an astonishing struggle for automatic promotion. This was surely the tensest and most unique end to a Championship season ever, with even the possibility that two of the three teams with identical records might have to have a play-off to decide who went into the actual play-offs and who went up as second. Our nerves could barely take any more as we settled to watch the penultimate game at Turf Moor against QPR.

'You can't be brilliant every day,' said Dyche after a game that was hardly one of the best. It was the day itself that was brilliant rather than the performance in the 1-0 win. But it's results that count. Away at Charlton, three more goals were slammed in and as soon as the second went in you knew that the title was Burnley's. The weekend was a blur for players and supporters alike. The pitch was a sea of Burnley fans, players and directors; there was the gala dinner on Sunday, and the then open-top bus tour on Monday. And all beneath cloudless blue skies.

So far this has not been a book with endless match reports, but this was such a special season that some games are worth mentioning. A 5-0 win away at MK Dons was an eye-opener. A win might not have raised our eyebrows, but to score five away from home was splendid. Andre Gray was back in the side after injury. Burnley's biggest away win since 1947 without conceding a goal. Result of the night said Sky. An unusual win with five different players scoring. Joey Barton got his first for the club. Full-back Matt Lowton got his first for the club. The win moved us up to fourth and the newspapers the following morning sang our praises. It was an almost-perfect performance.

It was immediately followed by Brentford 1, Burnley 3. It was a Friday-night game on Sky, although I was there at the ground. Supporters at home and at Brentford saw a superb display, with three fabulous goals all from distance. It was 3-0 at half-time and you wondered if Burnley would go on and get six. Alas, no, but there had been so many first-half chances it could have been six after just 45 minutes. Joey Barton got another goal with a 25-yard free kick. Arfield curled one in from the same distance. Boyd's goal was from just inside the box. Brentford player James Tarkowski, who knew we wanted to sign him, had refused to play. Not in the right frame of mind, he said. We wanted Alan Judge as well and he had a superb game. But a bad injury ended our interest in him. He was possibly the best player on the night, even though he was on the losing side.

Then a third consecutive win at home, against Derby County. Perhaps special is the wrong word but the fans' reaction to the return of Jason Shackell was truly memorable. He had helped the club gain promotion and then left when we were unable to match the money offered to him by Derby. Superb though he had been for us, and he had scored a memorable goal against Blackburn Rovers, fans give short shrift to anyone they deem disloyal. It meant that for 90 minutes he was barracked and jeered every time he touched the ball. It added to the sense of occasion when he gave away a penalty and then scored an own goal. In short, he had a nightmare of a game and a nightmare of an afternoon to the huge enjoyment of the crowd.

I'm not saying that those three games were pivotal because we were consistent for most of the season, but three wins on the trot is always special. Add to those the two wins against Blackburn Rovers, the games where football comes second to the result and bragging rights, a last-minute equaliser at home to Middlesbrough – significant because there was such bad blood between the two teams, mainly due to their manager Karanka – and then a 2-2 draw with another last-minute equaliser away at Brighton. The latter was especially memorable because just two minutes earlier, a goal that we scored from a powerful header was disallowed even though it was over the line. The same move, a corner if I remember rightly, resulted in another goal that blasted the back of the net. Such moments are not forgotten. Fans that had travelled were incensed one minute and wild with delight the next.

So, end of season, the gala dinner was packed and was a wonderful occasion, coming just a day after we were champions. Plus the relief that I was no longer company secretary, with all the exhausting work that this entailed. I could look back on what I and the club had done and achieved over the many previous years. I talked about this with Tim Quelch in his book *From Orient to the Emirates*. This particular weekend was a seminal moment in the story of the club.

> If we think about the club's recent history of success, I suppose we should start with Eddie Howe. For Eddie could certainly spot a player, Ings, Trippier, Mee and Shackell for example. They have all played important parts in Burnley's rise. But I didn't think that Eddie's heart was in the job, particularly after his mother suddenly died. He wanted to be in Bournemouth and throughout his time here, he kept going back and forth. It wasn't working for either party so a split was amicably agreed in autumn 2012.
>
> Once Sean Dyche replaced Eddie, he immediately tightened up the defence that had been shipping so many

goals. One thing that strikes me about Sean is that he appears very cautious as to who he brings in lest he upsets the team dynamic. However, I do think we should have stayed in the Premier League in 2014/15 had Danny Ings not signed a pre-contract agreement with Liverpool, which, I thought, turned his head.

Despite that setback, we developed so strongly and sustained a competitive Championship side without spending the earth, although if it were not for the parachute payments, it is doubtful that we could have competed as well as we did at this level. During the 30-year period that I have been involved in running the club, we have improved the ground enormously, providing covered seating for over 20,000 supporters. We have installed a superb, all-weather playing surface at Turf Moor that is fit for Premier League football.

We have covered the entrance to the Bob Lord Stand so that supporters are protected from adverse weather when buying food or drink before and during a game. We have introduced tighter access control arrangements with cameras installed in the turnstile booths to ensure that tickets are not being used fraudulently, for example by adults trying to gain admission with concessionary tickets.

And perhaps most significantly of all, we have upgraded the training facilities at Gawthorpe, restoring it to a state-of-the-art standard as it had been during the late fifties and early sixties. The £10million development taking place required some tough negotiations though. We have had robust exchanges with contractors in ensuring that flood defences were adequate. We discovered that foundations for the new buildings and the construction of the new pitches had not complied with the DEFRA flood report. Both the buildings and the pitches needed to be raised above the original height. At their previous levels both foundations and new pitches were overcome by the flood water during the deluges of 2015/16.

As was the case during the construction of the two new stands at Turf Moor, it was and is imperative that we kept tight oversight of the detailed building specifications, challenging any departure from these. My job was to hold the contractors to account ensuring that the development is fit for purpose and that we do not incur any unnecessary expense because of contractors not complying with the agreed specification. We have also had tough negotiations with the National Trust who own the land around Gawthorpe Hall. This has resulted in a re-siting of the gas pipe serving the training facilities so that it does not interfere with preserved trees. As with other historic sites, we must ensure that any new developments, including road access, does not damage any historic remains.

This has been some journey but one that I am proud to have helped the club to make. We know that without the resources that recent team successes have delivered, we would have had a major challenge in preserving our competitiveness at Championship level, let alone the Premier League. But we remain ambitious and it is right that we are, given the progress we have made since 1987, the Orient game, and my first year as a director.

All those words, even though so brief, do give a snapshot of all my involvement, from building new stands to arguing about road access to Gawthorpe. I haven't even mentioned the hours and hours spent negotiating with Burnley town council on various matters. But things were about to change for me within the boardroom and it would not be long before, despite every single bit of work I had tirelessly done for the club, I would be asked to step down as a director.

CHAPTER TWENTY-EIGHT

2016/17 Now Just an Onlooker

THIS WAS now a season of big change for me. From having a position of huge involvement and a central role, I was now simply a director. From this point on, it is fair to say that whilst I knew in broad terms what was going on, was party to all boardroom discussions, continued to vote for this and that, I was no longer involved in the nuts and bolts of the running of the club. As company secretary I had known just about everything that was going on and was fully abreast of finances and that all-important factor, cash flow.

On the field we did so well as we survived in the Premier League. We were not relegated, and all those pundits who predicted that we would be had to eat their words.

Off the field and in the boardroom, for me personally, it was a thoroughly unhappy year, and the events during it that involved me I found quite traumatic.

Back in the Premier League, we were now an attractive proposition to overseas buyers and the sale of the club was a topic that was being aired, albeit without anything really serious at this point.

I suppose, really, that a boardroom in which everyone got on like a house on fire, all united, all with one common purpose, nobody out of kilter, nobody with their own agenda, everybody the best of pals, would be very hard to find. Boardrooms consist of people who as a rule run businesses, exercise control on a daily basis, make decisions in those businesses, and therefore have firm opinions. It is inevitable that some will be more dominant than others and as soon as someone has a majority of the shares, then that person will perhaps feel that they should have the greater say in matters. Then there is the style of chairman. Some chairmen will delegate, some chairmen will seek consensus, some chairmen will want control. It is reasonable to say that at this point, the nature of our boardroom was shifting. The dynamics were changing.

Speaking of chairmen style, perhaps this would be a good point to mention the Darlington chairman, George Reynolds. He once used to sell ice cream from a van, but, on the side, he did a bit of burglary and safe-breaking in his early days. One day he was stopped by the police in his ice-cream van speeding along the local bypass. Since the van was where he hid his gelignite, under the ice-cream tubs, it was much to his relief that he only got a speeding ticket. Eventually he did do 'time' in prison and it was here that a priest advised him that he might be more successful in life if he became a businessman. This he did, with great success, so much so that he adopted Darlington FC and became their benefactor. Up in the north-east he became known as the chipboard king. He built Darlington a brand-new luxurious stadium, but it never housed more than two or three thousand fans. He told his life story in *Cracked It*. Sadly, I never actually met him and he must be the only football chairman to have appeared on *The Oprah Winfrey Show* in the USA.

By the end of the season, July actually, it was another director, not me, that brought up at a board meeting the lack of harmony and trust that was now evident in the boardroom, compounded by a lack of board meetings since the last one in January.

Things certainly began badly for me, in fact before the new season even started. As company secretary, one of my responsibilities had been keeping the share register, but this was now passed to a third party, contracted out, a service for which the club now paid, whereas I had done it unpaid. I held the register on my computer, with reliable backup, of course. To have lost it would have been a disaster and it was on a programme that required a special licence. Of course, until the new person responsible bought the programme and licence, I could not transfer the information. Yes, I could have transferred it, but at their end it would have been unreadable, computerised gobbledygook. Thus, I did not send it. I was accused of holding on to the information deliberately. I explained that until the correct programme and licence was held at their end, there was no point sending it. Let us just say that a shouting match took place on the telephone between myself and the chairman. Eventually the necessary programme and licence was purchased and the information was passed over.

At this point I also wrote to the chairman to explain my thoughts about any sale of the club. They were simple enough: that I would only be in favour if I felt that a new buyer could take the club to a place higher than where it was now, or could do a better job than the current board.

The real bombshell for me came on 8 February 2017, when I was invited to meet the chairman and he asked me to resign as a director. But, he asked, would I be the club president with its access to the chairman's lounge on matchdays? It did not take me long to turn this down and confirm that I wished to remain as a director, albeit with fewer, if any, responsibilities. The more I thought about it, the more upset I felt, after all I had done for the club over the years. I defy anyone to say that they worked harder than I did for the benefit and advancement of the club.

There were two further meetings with Mike, by now executive chairman, and I recorded them. After meetings with my solicitor, I suggested to Mike that if he wanted me off the board, he should call an emergency general meeting of shareholders. It might well have resulted in me stepping down, but the resultant poor publicity and my personal views becoming public would be something neither of us wanted. By the end of the month, it was agreed that I would be staying on the board. It crossed my mind to wonder whether or not all this would have happened if we had still had joint chairmen. There's this old expression 'when the dust settles …', but I'm not sure it ever did after this, in terms of the relationship between myself and the chairman.

So exactly why did Mike want me to step down? If I understood him correctly, it was mentioned that the board was too big. I had been here a long time. I had responsibilities and too much involvement in various areas of the club that were now being undertaken by others. On 18 February, I wrote to him.

> I must say on reflection I was just a little shocked to be asked to stand down from the board at the end of the company year, during our meeting on 8 February, for no real reason other than I have been on the board for a long time. You did also mention that you felt I got too involved on the facilities side of the business. As well as the football it is something that I am keenly interested in and have the expertise to help. If this is a problem with you, I will in the future not get involved, unless I am asked to do so by you, David or Doug, if of course I can continue as a director of the company.

As the letter continued, I explained my willingness to continue to help the club, explained that I had never been a freeloader and had put more into the club than I had ever taken out. I had saved the club a considerable amount of money over the years. As an addition to the letter, I listed some of the things I had done in just the last two years. I had worked on the buyback, planning permission for the upgrades at Gawthorpe and overcome all the objections. I had worked on all the legal agreements that were needed, worked with Burnley Council, worked with the National Trust and then worked with Barnfield once the go-ahead had been given. I had saved the club over £320,000 working on the business rates that applied to us. As company secretary I had been responsible for the share register and company returns. I had worked on the Lloyds Bank scam along with Forbes, the solicitors, and at this point it had still to be resolved. Thanks to me we now had an upgraded generator to power the new floodlights.

I pointed out to Mike that I had been supportive of him and suggested that it would be nice now to see that reciprocated. We were finding success at the club; I would like to be able to enjoy that. I had the time to devote to the club now that all my business matters had been settled. To resign as a director would now leave a huge hole in my life and on being asked to step down, I had suffered several sleepless nights. If remaining as a director meant stepping back from all my previous involvement, then I was willing to do this. My final paragraph was short and simple.

> I know sooner or later you/we will wish to sell the business as I expect a suitable offer will come in if we can get another year in the Premier League. Looking at prices on offer and the facilities that we do own, unlike some clubs, this could be north of £700 per share. For all involved, a good reward. So, I would like to see this through. I therefore look forward to receiving your ongoing support.

In the event, further down the line, the offer and share price that was settled on was more than double that.

We did indeed get another year in the Premier League, in fact six. This was a story that was, if you looked at it objectively, part fairy story, part romance, part bloody-mindedness and determination, and partly a stable boardroom and sensible running of the club. We were now being noticed and admired; other clubs lower down the leagues looked to us as a model of how to do things. Our football might not have been to everyone's taste, however.

Burnley's style of play is unique, said a Sky report. No Premier club plays quite like Burnley, it said. Dyche had long faced criticism and now accepts that. They are one of only a few teams to play long goal kicks. Teams that do this are generally seen as dinosaurs and after just five games into the season, goalkeeper Nick Pope had hit 100 long kicks. So far, 89 per cent of his kicking had been long. Twenty-four per cent of Burnley passes are long but Dyche is entitled to feel that it works for Burnley. Moves consisting of, for example, ten passes or more had happened on only 20 occasions so far. In this stat, Burnley were in the bottom three. They have the least width of any team in the division but progress upfield quicker than any other team bar one. Burnley have made the fewest errors leading to shots than any other team and the fewest errors leading to goals by the opposition. On top of all this, they rarely lose the ball in their own third. It's a bit like golf, says Dyche. The object is to get the ball in the hole with the fewest possible shots, and so it is with football. He plays the game that suits his players. If he was at a higher club with a higher skillset, he'd play a different game. In 134 out of 160 Premier games that they had played, they'd had less possession than opponents.

I loved seeing pieces like this and seeing what was correct and what was not. It was, in fact, pretty accurate but masked the times that we did play good football. Yes, what we played was practical and functional and it was effective. Other fans labelled us as anti-football; our own fans at this point revelled in it. It was fine by them; it had won us a promotion and would now see us stay in the Premier League.

The search for new players continued. This might give you an idea of how hard the club worked at this time. The chairman was speaking to Swansea City about international Neil Taylor. Flanagan from Liverpool was available on loan. There would be a loan fee of £1m. The manager had discounted options from France and Spain. A bid for Charlie Taylor from Leeds had been turned down. Hendrick of Derby was a target at £5.5m. Several bids were rejected for Dale Stephens of Brighton. A £5m bid for Steven Defour of Anderlecht was turned down. He was eventually signed for £7m. We discussed Charlie Adam, Joe Ledley, Henri Lansbury and Oliver Norwood, but the manager preferred any two of Hendrick, Stephens or Defour. Hakim Ziyech was another one and the chairman was meeting officials from FC Twente to discuss a possible deal. An offer was made for James Wilson of Manchester United.

The system in place was that potential players were all passed to Martin Hodge for analysis and then Martin would sit down with Sean and staff and a list of targets would be drawn up.

It was agreed that we would not pursue the idea of a Jimmy McIlroy statue. He was still alive. Danny Ings, now at Liverpool, donated a week's salary to the community section. I was sorry to see David Jones leave for Sheffield Wednesday for a longer contract than we could offer. He had been an integral part of the lovely side that won Sean Dyche's first promotion. With his wonderful left foot, he could thread a needle.

Come January and the new transfer window, Sean confirmed that he would like to re-sign Joey Barton until the end of the season. Charlie Taylor at Leeds would be out of contract in the summer. Hull City were looking for up to £10m for Andy Robertson. The manager was not keen on Yuto Nagatomo on loan from Inter Milan. The club had offered £10m for Robbie Brady from Norwich. Robert Snodgrass was under review and the chairman felt that personal terms could be agreed. In the event, he went to West Ham. Hull accepted a £10m offer from them and us, and he chose them. At a guess, for higher wages.

At right-back, Calum Chambers was an option but wanted £50,000 a week. Phil Bardsley of Stoke was an alternative and eventually signed. Swansea accepted an offer for Jack Cork, failing that we would look at Gareth Barry from Everton. Charlie Taylor of Leeds was signed, the manager preferring him to Andy Robertson. Jon Walters would sign for us. We met Jay Rodriguez's agent, but he signed for West Brom for a wage far more than we could offer.

Troy Deeney of Watford, admired by the manager, wanted up to £90,000 a week. Callum Wilson was unavailable. Max Kruse, German international, was available at £15m but wanted £400,000 a month. Patrick Bamford signed for a year on loan. We pulled out of a deal for a skilful Polish winger, Kamil Grosicki, when we were asked to pay his gambling debts. Immediate red flag. Mike Garlick explained that such a signing would have been detrimental to the team spirit of the squad.

Nobody could possibly say we were not doing our best to add to the squad but all this work goes unseen until you actually sign someone. In January we signed Joey Barton until the summer. We sold Michael Keane to Everton for £23m. We had James Tarkowski already at the club to fill the place. It's a funny old game. We sold Lukas Jutkiewicz, a proven goalscorer but who just couldn't score for us. He went to Birmingham and couldn't stop scoring.

Of huge concern was the poor showing of the youth set-up. In 2011/12 we'd had a superb young team that reached the FA Youth Cup semi-finals and actually knocked out Manchester United at Old Trafford. One by one they had faded into oblivion. Not one made it into the first team. The team of 2015/16 was one of the poorest ever with appalling results, including a defeat in the FA Youth Cup at Turf Moor to the London Met Police side. This was a new low. Questions were asked. Was it the standard of recruitment or poor coaching and youth management? A leading coach had said that it didn't matter if they lost, as long as they developed and progressed to the Development Squad. I felt that this was seriously wrong, if not totally misguided. It was deemed a success if a young player was loaned out to a lower-league club or even a non-league club. They frequently were and then disappeared without trace.

As for me, now relegated to the sidelines, I remained as a director, turned up for every game home and away, determined to enjoy the season. And why shouldn't I? It was there to be enjoyed and there was huge pride by the end when we were not relegated and lived to fight another season in the Premier League.

We finished the season in 16th place to confound the critics and to annoy supporters from some other clubs who thought we were unworthy intruders playing dinosaur football. Nevertheless, a handful of games stood out.

Burnley 2, Liverpool 0: a stunning result and performance in only the second game of the season. Packed house, swirling wind, intimidating atmosphere – all the ingredients for an unexpected but deserved result. Liverpool's tip-tap passing style broke down again and again, their shots kept to long distance. Vokes and Gray scored for us in front of the away supporters who were utterly stunned at the sheer cheek that this could be happening. Klopp was disbelieving.

Burnley 2, Everton 1 on a beautiful, warm October day bathed in sunshine before a 21,000 crowd. This was a Tom Heaton masterclass and Mee was superb keeping Lukaku quiet. The defending and covering were superb, with several passages of good passing football. Who says we couldn't play? Vokes pounced on a parry from the keeper and tucked it home. Much of the game was all Everton, slick and clever with bundles of pace all over the pitch, so maybe the equaliser was inevitable after waves of attacks. But into the 90th minute and Gudmundsson smacked a 20-yard shot against the bar and Arfield cracked the rebound home. We just had to hold on through added time and this we did, with hearts racing and nerves shredded. It was the third win of the season. The artisans had beaten the artists. We were never going to play like Barcelona, but we had heart, we had resolve, we had spirit and we had grit. 'Authentic Burnley,' said Dyche.

Before the Palace game we had a huge offer to buy the club. This was £300m. Unfortunately, it came in an email from Luanda, Angola. Could we take it seriously? Of course not. Now, had it been from a Nigerian prince …

The 3-2 win at Turf Moor over Crystal Palace was another of those last-minute thrillers. Those of a delicate, nervous disposition would need to stop going to games if they were all going to be like this. It was a game to remember as Barnes, who came on for the last five minutes, ended up scoring a superb winner deep into injury time. It was a goal to savour, the kind they score at Madrid or Barcelona, and it ended a riveting game in which Palace had pulled back a two-goal deficit and had us all thinking that they would go on to win the game.

I always loved fascinating statistics. Of 277 teams to have had 14 points after 11 games, only seven had gone on to be relegated. This meant there was only a two per cent chance of Burnley being relegated. If only it were so simple. A BBC survey showed that we provided value for money. Our cheapest season ticket was 33 per cent less than the Premier League average. The most expensive matchday ticket was 25 per cent less than the Premier League average. A junior football shirt was 19 per cent less than average. It was the same for pies.

Burnley 4, Sunderland 1 at the end of the year showed striker Andre Gray at his best with a hat-trick of poacher goals. It was a game in which it was hard to fault any Burnley player and was a fine way to end what had been a wonderful year.

Burnley 1, Leicester City 0: a winning goal in minute 87 is always euphoric. A night game under the lights always adds drama and this was on a night of teeming rain. Who said Burnley could not play football and were not a passing side? Burnley 419 passes and Leicester just 293. We even had the most of possession – very unusual for us. Ashley Barnes was the battering ram that softened them up, and then on came Sam Vokes and Leicester had just about had enough. Vokes duly scored. The January transfer window closed and, to the astonishment of the football world, Burnley actually spent £18m. In came Robbie Brady and Ashley Westwood. These were heady days.

It was interesting to see that Sunderland, recently beaten 4-1 and we had also knocked them out of the FA Cup, were holding us to be the model club to follow. They praised us for staying with Sean Dyche after relegation. They praised the players who as a group were proud to wear the shirt. Hopefully, said the fans, the Sunderland board could learn from us.

Crystal Palace 0, Burnley 2: so far, we had yet to win away from home and it was now the end of April. It could well be that we would end with the unusual statistic of not being relegated but not one single away win. But then down at Crystal Palace came that elusive win. Vokes and Barnes terrorised the Palace defence. Heaton pulled off three super saves. It was a near faultless display so that you wondered why it had taken so long to win away from home, although there had been a couple when we scratched our heads in the boardroom afterwards and wondered how we had not won.

After this game there were three left, nine points to play for and Burnley were seven points clear of the bottom three. It could still go wrong. It didn't. Sean challenged the team to win the last home game, but it was a 2-1 defeat to West Ham in a damp squib of a game that was a tame end to the season. It had, in fact, been a strange season, as we had banked most of the points before Christmas and then after that scraped along with only four wins. The win at Crystal Palace was crucial.

It was almost a full house for the West Ham game. In previous seasons it would have been a nothing game, but now in the Premier League there was even more money to aim for, for each position above the bottom three. The higher you were the more millions you got in prize money. For a change the sun was out and it was a shirt-sleeves kind of day for many supporters. The team had done us proud. The applause for Peter Noble, who had recently passed away, was long and heartfelt. He had been one of the great club servants.

I drove home well pleased with the season's work, at least on the field. There were the new fixtures to look forward to. Premier League cash would see us comfortably off. One of the new teams to be promoted was Huddersfield, like us so long in the doldrums. They were another of those clubs that said, 'If Burnley can do it, why can't we?' And they did.

So, another season in the Premier League. It was a summer when fans could relax. But perhaps not me. I now had a new relationship with the chairman. Strained might be the best way to put it.

CHAPTER TWENTY-NINE

2017/18 and 2018/19 The Peak Years?

I WAS in a situation now where the involvement and knowledge I once had had been severely curtailed. Two men were now key: the chairman Mike Garlick and the manager Sean Dyche, and I did begin to wonder if the increasing influence that Sean was developing throughout the club would eventually cause problems between him and the chairman. But for now, all seemed harmonious.

Then, when the season began with the most unlikely of wins, a 3-2 victory away at champions Chelsea, the mood was buoyant and quite joyful. In fact, it would be reasonable to use the word incredulous. Three-nil up at half-time seemed the stuff of dreams, maybe even fantasy. Steven Defour was having the kind of game that we all hoped he would demonstrate; he had such skilful and deft touches and a vision in his passing, all allied to superb ball control and instinctive passing, that on his day he could run any game. With Chelsea down to nine men, what could go wrong? Well, this is Burnley and even with depleted numbers they pulled the score back to 3-2 and we ended up hanging on. But when that final whistle went, we retired to the boardroom to meet disbelieving Chelsea faces. But the Burnley directors, to use that well-known football cliché, we were over the moon. How glad I was that I had not allowed myself to be eased off the board. Who on earth would want to miss experiences like this?

Sean was concerned about people being able to wander around the training area, particularly when the place was busy and, with all the players either arriving or leaving, members of the public could get in. On one occasion he told us he'd had to smuggle a prospective signing in for talks through the back door. To this day I have no idea who it was and wonder if his head was covered in a blanket.

It had been a good summer for recruitment, with the manager well pleased. In came left-back Charlie Taylor, who Sean felt was a real prospect. Indeed he was and became one of our best and most consistent players. For a big man he had more pace than you might think and his runs down the left and crosses were an integral part of the team. Jack Cork returned to the club older and better. What a signing this was, a very classy player, one of those lads that with a wiry physique can go on playing well into his mid-30s. Time was when a career was thought to be over once you turned 30. Playing well beyond that is now the norm if you look after yourself and avoid injury. Chris Wood arrived from Leeds United like Charlie Taylor. Another inspired signing and for four seasons he reached double figures in the goals chart. Burnley fans loved this, saying that Leeds, in the doldrums at the time, were now our feeder club and existed only to supply us with their better players. Leeds-Burnley rivalry and dislike is well documented going right back to the Don Revie days.

A mention too for Phil Bardsley, bought as cover really but played many games. Tough, uncompromising, hard as nails and had been at Burnley years earlier when Stan Ternent signed him on loan, only for him to be injured and return to Manchester United. And then there was Nahki Wells. A strange one this, since Sean really liked him and what he had done at Bradford, where he was a regular goalscorer with a lovely, deft, skilled touch. But he rarely got into the team and only for a few minutes at a time. Sean was always prone to making as few changes as possible and it was difficult for any other striker to shift Barnes and Wood. Wells was quite the opposite of these two in style and build. He joined a long list of strikers who came and went, some of whom must have wondered why on earth they had come. He had come to the club on the advice of our CEO, Dave Baldwin, whose last job had been at Bradford. His advice was that he was worth a punt. We joked that Dave was his agent.

Three key players left. Joey Barton was in trouble with the FA for gambling and perhaps had reached his sell-by date anyway. But what a player he had been for us. Centre-back Michael Keane departed for Everton for big money. This was always inevitable; he had grown and matured playing alongside Ben Mee and there had been big offers for him already the previous summer. We had a ready replacement in James Tarkowski. Andre Gray also left; his goals crucial for us in the promotion season. There was the feeling that he felt that he had outgrown us and wanted a better financial deal. You can't blame any player for that and, again, selling him to Watford, Burnley got a good deal. Perhaps the only surprise was that he went to Watford, hardly a glamour club or much bigger than Burnley.

Dare I say this was a season with little or no controversy, or was it just that now I was no longer company secretary I just wasn't aware of them? The team was doing well. With just nine games to go we had 40 points on the board and there had been a run of five consecutive wins. There was even the possibility of qualifying for Europe on the horizon. Perhaps it was the habit of being able to see or ask what might come round the next corner, but at the back of my mind already I wondered if it would be more trouble than it was worth.

But that worry apart, it really was a huge achievement and the press were fascinated by what we were doing. And what we were doing was without the benefit of penalties. The exact statistics escape me, but we seemed to have been on a run of games without any penalty to benefit us for what seemed years. It was becoming almost a joke and Sean contacted head of referees, Mike Riley, to confront him about this. They looked at eight possible penalty incidents from the previous season. Riley agreed with Sean: seven of them were clear penalties. Penalties would come back to haunt us in the season in which we were eventually relegated; both those controversially awarded against us and those denied to us.

We said goodbye to Scott Arfield and I mention this because of the wonderful service he had given us. He had been signed on a free from Huddersfield Town at the beginning of the first Dyche promotion season and made a place in the team his own immediately. He was consistent, reliable, the type of player that Sean liked, clean cut, clean living, always professional and 100 per cent committed. He joined the elite group of players to have scored a winning goal against Blackburn Rovers. He had the opportunity to join Glasgow Rangers on a four-year deal. How could he say no to that, his boyhood team?

The season ended with us in seventh place but a tame home defeat to Bournemouth. Next stop: Europe. Town and press were buzzing; this was an incredible achievement. The press asked whether Burnley could do even better next season and improve on seventh place. We thought not. That would mean breaking into the top six group of the super-clubs. The chairman said he was just happy to be best of the rest. Sean thought it unlikely, wondering if this would be as good as it could get for a club like Burnley. The aim was to grow just a little bit each season and, so far, we had done that. I do know that the number of extra games weighed on his mind. For now, what we wanted was to be a recognised Premier League team, an established Premier League team.

Well and truly in the spotlight, the press enjoyed digging out obscure Burnley bits of information, such as Turf Moor became the first senior football ground to be visited by a member of the royal family when Prince Albert Victor, son of Edward VII and grandson of Queen Victoria, watched Burnley lose 4-3 to Bolton on 13 October 1886, while in town to open a hospital. And Burnley have played at Turf Moor since 1883, making Turf Moor the longest continuously used ground of any of the 49 teams that have played in the Premier League. Burnley are one of only five teams to have won all four of the English professional leagues, along with Portsmouth, Preston, Sheffield United and Wolves.

Fans are amazing sometimes. Justine Lorriman renamed her pub from The Princess Royal to The Royal Dyche when we qualified for

Europe. It's a pub that's just a few hundred yards from Turf Moor and has become a Burnley institution now, with visitors and TV crews from all over the world. On offer is all the beer that Sean can drink, on the house, and even though we are now relegated, he took up the offer very recently. His birthday and that of Henry VIII are on the same day. Not a lot of people know that, as Michael Caine would say. A full-page spread in *The Times*, no less, featured the pub and our foray into Europe. Justine's comments about Sean were spot on: 'He seems to have a mould. If you don't fit that mould, you don't come. He's very particular on the players he brings in. That's why it works.'

That was true enough, and it did work. But then you could argue that eventually it was one of the reasons we stagnated and, come 2022, it was no longer working.

But that was to come and for now Euro fever filled the town. Burnley in Europe, staggering. I was one of those at the Orient game in 1987 when survival hung by a thread and now this. Who do you thank? Jimmy Mullen, Barry Kilby, Stan Ternent, Owen Coyle and Sean, plus all those directors who put their hands in their pockets over the years, and all those players who won the games that dragged us out of the doldrums and up the leagues? Now it was beat Aberdeen and we'd be on a plane to Istanbul. Club officials had the unenviable task of organising all this. At this point it was a relief not to be company secretary.

As the Aberdeen game approached, we had not signed one single new player and yet there was the prospect of playing games every Thursday the longer we stayed in the competition. Warning bells began to jingle, albeit softly. Statistics showed that when clubs were in the Europa League, their league form suffered. Nevertheless, let the adventure begin, we all agreed.

Sylvia and I went up in the motorhome and stayed at Stonehaven on the coast for a week, a few miles to the south of Aberdeen. Another holiday for the springer spaniel, Gemma, as faithful a dog as you could wish for. Only someone who loves dogs will understand the sadness when they go. She was with us for 14 years. The Aberdeen club took us all out for a meal, a UEFA requirement, accompanied by a UEFA official, of course. If I were not a director, perhaps I would elect to be a UEFA official, with all the perks and travel.

Aberdeen were disposed of in a routine kind of way, I suppose. The idiot who ran on to the pitch in the home leg against Aberdeen cost us a fine of €25,000. Then there were bonuses to pay the players for beating them. Success is costly.

And next came what the fans really wanted, a proper overseas trip, this one to Turkey to play Basaksehir. The origins of this new club were a bit obscure – was it owned by the government? Someone was putting a lot of money into them and their rise had been swift, and this was on gates of under 5,000. For our supporters, there were 4,503 in a 17,000-seater stadium. Under UEFA rules we had to take the tickets over there and distribute them in Turkey, at the city collection point at the Blue House Hotel in Sultan Ahmed Square. Passports and other identification was essential. Ashley Barnes versus the Turks. Shades of Andy Lochhead versus Naples in the 60s. Sean said he couldn't even pronounce their name. The last time Burnley were in Istanbul was in 1951, when a team managed by Frank Hill and including young Jimmy McIlroy played six games, with three wins and three draws, over three weeks. The journey home in old propellor planes took two days, with a stop in Rome. Bob Lord joked that this was how he joined the board when the team were in Turkey and the directors weren't looking.

The team and support staff went out two days before the game by private plane. The costs were high, as I knew they would be. 'We won't make any money out of any of this,' was my abiding thought. The directors and ticket staff went out later that day, but to my great surprise who should we meet but Joe Hart in the lounge. I looked at him in great surprise and asked him, nonplussed, 'Joe, what on earth are you doing here?' He'd brought the wrong passport for the team flight, an out-of-date one, if I remember rightly, had raced back home to retrieve the correct one and we had rebooked his flight. It was his first week with the club. Knowing footballers as I do, I dread to think of the merciless ribbing he would have been subjected to when he caught up with the team. With us he kept a very straight face.

Supporters who went out there put their thoughts on paper afterwards, one of them Nicholas Beckett. He arrived there at eight in the morning on the day of the game, figured out how to use the metro and the tram system and sought out liquid refreshment, aptly enough in a bar wonderfully named the Cozy Café. First item for them was to collect their tickets and decide to use the coach transport laid on by Burnley FC. They were subject to inevitable searches but were panic-stricken when their hotel room key was taken off them. It was decided it was not a weapon and returned to them. The return coach journey was notable for several of the coach drivers using it as an excuse to race the others and see who could get back first. There were quite a few ashen faces as they hung on to the back of the seat in front for dear life. Their return flight was on the Friday afternoon via a delay at Moldova Airport. No grumbles, it had its own brewery and award-winning ales.

The team were allowed to practise on the pitch, which was fine, but Sean was dismayed to find that the press would be there. Eventually the press guys were required to withdraw, but while they were there, Sean took the team as far away from them as possible on the pitch. Our hosts took us to a fine Turkish restaurant in the city for a lunch that lasted three hours. Memorable, but so was the heat. Neither the game in Turkey nor in Burnley was a great advert for the game. The television stations had the foresight not to televise them.

Before any home game is played, the stadium is inspected by UEFA officials to see that all is well. Ours certainly was but for one thing; well, 5,000 to be more accurate. They were very concerned with the wooden seats in the Cricket Field Stand; a fire hazard they announced. They had been there since the days of Bob Lord, solid, near-indestructible, almost works of art. But UEFA said no. Our local fire brigade stepped in and helped support our claim that they were actually safer than plastic. A compromise was reached: if we reached the group stages, they would be replaced, even though the logistics of this were mind-boggling – removal of wooden seats, sourcing 5,000 plastic seats and installation.

What did Tommy Cooper used to say? 'Just like that.'

They were due to be changed at the end of the season anyway and we did not reach the group stages. It might not have been said publicly, but more than one director breathed a sigh of relief. Behind the scenes, the workload is enormous, the costs exorbitant, and UEFA demands, rules and regulations draining. At one point a delegation of four UEFA officials arrived to look at everything except the kitchen sink.

In extra time we won the return game with a lovely goal from Cork. 'The parabolic curve of the ball a work of art,' wrote Igor Wowk. They had that old warrior Adebayor playing for them who received merciless taunting from the Burnley crowd. Yet again a manager of an opposing team probably left the ground wondering how his team had lost, wrote Igor.

Forgive me if I now dwell on the game in Greece at some length. Looking back, perhaps it represented everything that was wrong and unpleasant with these European games. Olympiacos had a marvellous record in terms of appearing in Europe and I suspect they thought, 'Ah, little Burnley, no problem.' Their owner is Evangelos Marinakis, who also owns Nottingham Forest, a Greek shipping owner also owns a TV station. Despite owning a TV station, we never did get the game shown on a live feed at Turf Moor, due to a large fee being involved. Over there, the riot police presence was huge, with a great deal of unease about possible trouble. To my knowledge there was none, save for the unpleasant habit of home thugs sneaking up on away fans with a Stanley knife and stabbing them in the back of the leg. I heard that one Burnley fan was stabbed and four were beaten.

It was the police that insisted all Burnley fans should be transported to the ground by official coach, ostensibly for their own safety, plus the aim was to get them to the ground in the Piraeus docks area before the home fans. Some of our fans did not adhere to this arrangement and were collected by the police and ended up in a police compound somewhere. Certainly draconian, but when abroad you do as you're told is the best advice I can think of, and Greek police do not mess about, to put it crudely. The approach seems to be if you dress in full riot gear, look menacing and threatening, strut about, then visiting fans will be cowed into submission. The directors, after a fine lunch at the stadium hosted by Olympiacos, returned to our hotel, from where we too were later taken by official bus – with darkened windows for our own safety, presumably – back to the stadium.

You might recall a 1-0 win against all the odds against Liverpool in the days of Steve Cotterill, when their defender scored a wonderful and hilarious own goal as he tried to execute some sort of drag-back and twirl on the goal line and the ball slowly trickled over the line. I have half a memory that Benitez was the manager and he had come along assuming that this game would be some sort of a stroll in the park. It was one of those special Turf Moor nights that stay in the memory. Anyway, the Greek directors of another club, some time earlier in a pre-season friendly, brought this game up and asked us how we had managed to win. Had we bribed them? How much had we paid them? The way it was asked made me wonder if bribery was a feature of the Greek game?

As for the game, it leaves a sour taste still. Level pegging at half-time, 1-1. How things changed after the break. Did the Greeks realise that we were no pushovers? But come the second half, every decision went their way, some of them blatantly questionable, and Ben Gibson was sent off for the most innocuous and contrived offence and, lo and behold, they were awarded a penalty. We, the directors, learned afterwards that at half-time in the tunnel the Greek players, and anybody else for that matter, had gone mad with the referee, harassed, harangued and jostled him, and had pursued him as far as his referee's room. Our players and Sean and his staff saw all this at first-hand, with Sean commenting that even the tea lady was at it. In the first half, the referee had the audacity to award us a penalty and maybe that was what incensed them.

Sean was adamant. 'They were just waiting for the referee,' he said, 'and you could see the game was different in the second half. The scenes I saw at half-time, you were left just scratching your head. I don't understand why he has booked Ben Gibson a second time. He has gone to block a shot and the ball hits his hip, then his hand. How can that be deemed deliberate handball? It's impossible. It was probably a world record for how fast he got the card out of his pocket.'

He questioned the distance the Burnley wall was asked to stand back for a free kick that was given. A strange distance, he observed. The Greeks scored from the free kick. At such moments players begin to wonder if the odds are stacked against them. UEFA changed the referee for the game at Burnley; perhaps telling you all you need to know after our protests about him. The UEFA official at the game in Greece didn't want to know.

We took our Greek guests to the Fence Gate, a fine establishment outside of Burnley where there is a choice of private rooms. Another expense, of course. The Greek owner did not attend, but he did come to the game and stood the whole way through in the entrance to the directors' box. I was angry about this but, in consultation with chairman Mike, let it pass by. He was rather a large man, so I can only imagine that he found it more comfortable than squashing into a seat.

There was also the pre-match meal at Turf Moor, but the directors' room only caters for 12, so the other guests were in the guest lounge with no meal. But with some skilful ticket swapping and handing over, these guests also managed to come to the directors' lounge for a meal. It was too complicated to explain that there was no meal for them, so we ended up with two sittings and some hastily organised extra cooking. Despite the confrontations in Greece, the atmosphere was cordial and pleasant. The game ended 1-1 and, had we taken good chances, we could so easily have won.

Supporter Andrew Firmin went to the Olympiacos game and wrote, 'Until you get into this competition you have no idea how ridiculously short notice it all is.'

He felt slightly queasy at the expense. My feelings exactly. He needed a drink, he wrote. Some of the directors did as well; we too are supporters. His description of Athens was spot on: grimy and gritty, a decade of full-on austerity, sprawling, hilly and twisty, graffiti, crammed with antiquities. He arrived at 10.30 in the evening, hungry, and remembered this was Greece. Sure enough, a taverna just down the road from the hotel was open until four in the morning. Lamb, feta and ouzo did the trick. Andrew was one of hundreds for whom the whole experience was new, exciting and vibrant. He is a member of the esteemed London Clarets, whose beer-soaked away days are legendary. He was one of several there.

His account of the experience is masterful as he wrote of the warmth and professionalism of the ticket staff. The ticket came with a helpful flyer that listed the items that could not be taken into the ground – animals, toilet rolls and propaganda. The flyer also listed approved bars, but London Clarets are made of sterner stuff and sought out their own. According to a barman he met, there are now 600 small breweries in Greece, where five years ago there had been none. They took the Metro into Piraeus and found more shady bars, including the only one in Greece that was shut. But mercifully there were others. At each one they received water and nibbles. 'Can't see it catching on in Burnley,' he wrote.

The evening of the game: taxis got them to the ground but deposited them on the wrong side, far away from the away supporters' entrances. He smuggled souvlaki into the ground – 'a warm parcel of food happiness'. No violence, no antagonistic home supporters, the locals they met were warm and friendly, 'admittedly most of them bar staff'. The away fan buses had arrived first, so the London Clarets were in the second pen, high in the corner behind the goal. Double mesh prevented them from throwing all the things that they were forbidden to bring anyway. The atmosphere was overwhelming, with home fans coordinating their chants perfectly, the two ends of the ground urging each other on. There was something fevered about the place.

In the first half, a sign of what was to come when a spurious penalty claim was turned down and the whole home bench rushed onto the pitch to berate the referee. All around them people were singing about Jimmy McIlroy, who had just passed away, to the great sadness of the town. Of the game itself Andrew wrote little, being more concerned with the whole experience of the thing. At the end they were kept back for some time.

'A blank row of police barred the way and we remembered that these guys are normally busy beating up protesting anarchists in Syntagma Square.' They therefore thought it wise not to antagonise them. So, they carried on singing as the ground emptied; 'Something very Burnley about this sustained chanting, a defiant assertion of the parochial amidst the exotic, a bloody-minded refusal to be intimidated.'

Andrew hit the nail on the head when he wrote that this was an authentic experience of European competition, and we had taken part. All of it: the intimidating atmosphere, the cheating, the shocking refereeing, being kept in the ground forever – it all seemed the real thing.

He wanted more. On one level perhaps we all did, having seen two great cities, Istanbul and Athens. This was the romance of football. Yes, the supporter in me wanted more. On that level it was marvellous. With my director hat on, and the thought of the workload, the invoices flooding in, the costs and injuries, the two games a week in prospect, it was with some relief that we were out.

So, that was that. Adventures over and we were not entirely unhappy about that. Unhappy at the manner of the exit, of course, but with league results suffering, the experts were right on that score. We could focus on staying in the Premier League. An away game on a Thursday night, a four-hour plane journey home, play the next game on a Sunday; the prospect of that for another month was not exactly appealing with our small squad that was already carrying a number of injuries. I was mindful of the old saying 'all that glistens is not gold'. The directors were agreed. So many games in such a short period was draining. The target was the Premier League, with its far superior financial rewards.

In traditional fashion we had signed new players, but at the last minute, as we tried to find bargains. They had all arrived in time for the Euro games – Joe Hart, for example, to cover for Tom Heaton and Nick Pope, both injured. Sean regarded Joe Hart as a bit of a steal and remained desperate to sign Craig Dawson and Jay Rodriguez from West Brom. Ben Gibson came for £15m, I think, but such details were now out of my area. He actually took a pay cut. Sean urged us to look for more players to invest in and Matej Vydra arrived from Derby for £9m. Bargains were hard to find. Agents were a problem, and their demands; signing Alfie Mawson from Swansea fell through because of that.

I heard this expression 'peak Burnley' in one newspaper article. Perhaps the seventh place and the games in Europe were that. It was the best we achieved in our Premier lifetime. We still had two more seasons in the top league but even accounting for several high spots, they were never as accomplished as this one. In this particular season after seven games, we had just two points. Would the predictions be correct? Were we due for a real struggle and a relegation? The fans had this mantra: 'in Dyche we trust'. They accorded him this sort of mythical ability to pull us out of the fire. Indeed, he would by the season's end. Few, if any, fans would hear a bad word said about him, and why would they? He had brought the best seasons for years to the club, had developed the training ground, had raised the bar in all areas and was hugely influential around the club. He had an aura and a real presence and for now his position was safe as houses. Newspaper features focused on him and his achievements but always asked the question – why was he not pursued by any of the top clubs? He was the perfect fit for Burnley, but did he lack glamour? The top clubs went for the continental guys, the ones deemed to have flair and real tactical nous. Rightly or wrongly, Sean did not fit this elite group. It was a shame for him, but good for us.

The impact of the European games was clear enough; it was late September before we won the first game. It took until Christmas to get three wins. A point at Chelsea clinched our place for the next season, with three games remaining after that. Yes, there were worries at Christmas, especially when Everton arrived and won 5-1 at Turf Moor. There were glum faces that day. Sean tweaked the team and brought Tom Heaton back in goal and Phil Bardsley at full-back. There was a frank team meeting at which it was agreed they simply had to get back to basics and what made them so hard to beat. There was no panic, and the next three league games were wins. A run of seven undefeated came later. And then the Chelsea game in London.

Sean was recovering from a back operation that he had intended to carry out at the end of the season. The agony became too much. He had been struggling for four months but was now in good shape; it was almost a metaphor for the season. We were now all but safe. Everybody had warned us of the dangers of the Europa League, the effects on planning, balance, training and logistics. Why not just use the Europa games as pre-season training some fans asked. But they are real games with money rewards. You have to take them seriously. But before we knew it, we had just one point from the first league games. Then it's Christmas and you have just 12 points from 19 games and after Everton there was little optimism. Weirdly, from that a bit of clear thinking followed: it was roll-up-sleeves time, get back to basics, dig in, wandering minds were straightened out. Play hard and defend properly. As well as Heaton and Bardsley, Sean also brought Dwight McNeil in as a regular starter. He was a revelation with wing play, crosses and an occasional goal. Suddenly we had a superkid on the block and a resolve to put things back to the way they were.

So, by the time of the Chelsea game, Burnley were the fifth-best team in the Premier, with a better record than Chelsea since Boxing Day. Sean has since said that this turnaround gave him more satisfaction than the seventh place the previous season. The last visit there had seen us win 3-2; this time it would be a stirring 2-2 draw.

It was a game with everything – four rapid goals inside 20 minutes, a wonder strike from Hendrick for Burnley, Heaton booked for time-wasting, fast football from Chelsea, a monumental defensive effort from Burnley, confrontations, manager Sarri sent off, Barnes at his provocative best, an end of game melee on the touchline, post-match peevishness from Chelsea, vile tweeting from Chelsea fans, accusations of abuse from the Burnley bench, smart interview quips from Dyche and, above all, a point for Burnley that made them safe.

After the game Sarri refused to be interviewed, apparently upset and frustrated by the loss of two points and what he claimed to have been called by the Burnley staff. As a result, Chelsea were considering filing a complaint. Then from David Luiz there came, 'They scored two goals and then didn't want to play football. It's anti-football.'

It left me thinking that they don't like us down there, do they? The boardroom was quite subdued after the game; not much mixing, but you could feel the undercurrents.

I was still so proud the day after, pride at the resolve, commitment, blocking, clearing, the miles covered, concentration, heroism, Mee's goal-line clearance, bodies on the line, bravery and spirit. The anti-football jibe stuck and was thrown at us from then onwards. Then a new word was coined and those with a dislike for poor language should look away now. It came in a Chelsea fan's tweet: 'It's generally horrible when you are the opposition facing them, but Burnley's level of shithousery is so admirable.'

Burnley fans adopted the word with glee. We were not a dirty, alehouse side by any means. We didn't cheat or go down screaming when tackled. In fact, the most recent fouls chart showed Manchester City topping the list, with an average of 24 per game. Burnley's foul count was a meagre average of 15 per game. If there was a league table for fouls per team, Burnley were in the bottom three, with not a red card to be seen for months. Sean responded by asking whether we were supposed to be easy to play against.

There was a moment when we thought the FA might have held an inquest into the touchline abuse between the two benches and the players squaring up to each other. But the anti-football accusation: only City and Liverpool had scored more goals since Christmas. In fact, it was Chelsea manager Sarri who was charged with misconduct for his behaviour throughout the game. But all ended well, with the clubs issuing a joint statement saying that matters had been resolved and a line had been drawn under the matter. Maybe that was down to Mike Garlick and the Chelsea chairman sorting it out quietly between them.

Prime Minister Theresa May was at the Leisure Box in Brierfield, the dilapidated mill that BFC in the Community had converted into a superb facility. She was there to open it. The joke going round was that she asked us how we had managed to get out of Europe so quickly.

The next season we had VAR to look forward to. I think there was genuine optimism that it would help the game. As I write, that is highly debatable. One of our first experiences was a good goal chalked off at Leicester because the VAR officials looked for an offence where there was none. The rule was supposed to be red cards, or penalties and offsides would be awarded when they were clear and obvious. Clear and obvious decisions became submerged in tiny fractional offsides, sometimes by a hand, a shoulder or a toe. Games were held up for minutes while the officials came to a decision. Supporter celebrations for goals were more often than not delayed while the officials checked that a goal was valid.

Just prior to the Chelsea game, Sean remembered the goal that Chesterfield scored against Middlesbrough in an FA Cup semi-final. VAR would have shown that it crossed the line, instead of which the goal was disallowed. It would have made the score 3-1 and probably seen them through to Wembley. Instead, Boro came back to level the game. Sean was sure that sharp-eyed officials with their TV screens would eradicate the cheats and conmen in the game. I think we can safely say that this has not happened; simulation is as bad as ever.

CHAPTER THIRTY

2019/20 Tensions at the Top

WE FINISHED tenth and it was another good season on the pitch. In fact, at one stage it looked as though we might well get into that seventh spot again during a good run. In November, when we went 1-0 up away at Watford, for a brief moment we were sixth. Another season in Europe? I can't recall any enthusiastic conversations about it after the traumas of the last involvement. Perhaps trauma is too strong a word; concerns might be better, but the effect it had on the early part of the previous season remained strong in our minds. I am guessing, but I could easily imagine Sean thinking we are best out of it. Yes, it was an achievement and our prestige soared, but it was taxing, costly, and any joy it brought bore no relationship to the complications it produced. To this day the scenes at Olympiacos at half-time and the acrimony afterwards are vividly remembered.

It was a season when we had some quite stunning results, one of them winning 2-0 away at Manchester United and a superb win at Southampton. Of course, there were some big defeats, as usual to Manchester City and a horrible 5-0 away to Spurs, but this is Burnley – such things always happen. But overall, this was another season to be proud of. And yet all was not well behind the scenes.

By the end of June, the season being prolonged because of all the Covid problems, the news was in the public domain of friction between the chairman and the manager. These things rarely stay secret, with football reporters, particularly from the bigger papers, able to ferret out any signs of trouble, be it trouble with players or with managers. James Ducker in *The Telegraph* was followed closely by Paul Wilson in *The Guardian* in exposing the fracture lines.

The *Daily Mail* suggested next that the breakdown was a serious one, 'The mood at Burnley is that we are witnessing the start of a divorce and both parties are at a crossroads. A split seems inevitable after Sean's not-so-subtle criticism of the directors.'

A later article had 'Burnley's parsimony has become a major source of tension between Garlick and Dyche, who has been frustrated at the club's failure to agree contract extensions for players for the duration of Project Restart.' In the event, Phil Bardsley was given an extension but midfielder Jeff Hendrick turned his down.

Of course, I knew what was going on. I was there to see it at board meetings, but to see it in the national press so openly, so publicly, was disconcerting to say the least. It was not something that could be shrugged off and denied. *The Telegraph* news came at a time when Sean named just seven substitutes for the game at Crystal Palace, which we actually won. I have to confess to some surprise myself; after all, why did we have an under-23 development squad? There were reports of senior players at the club being somewhat taken aback as well. The question was asked by the press and by supporters, was Sean making a point to the chairman? The manager insisted these were the only players at his disposal.

Three days later, we beat Watford and all seemed well on the outside, but this simply masked the struggles that were taking place between manager and chairman. 'Power struggle' was the phrase used by reporter James Ducker. It has to be said that these two men had done so much to keep Burnley in the Premier League, but now the cracks were appearing and widening. Sean was asking the board to stretch things, to renew contracts that were due to expire, to get bodies on the pitch rather than money in the bank. Mike Garlick argued that this is what he was doing, but by appointing a technical director, investing in the training centre and improving scouting.

Ducker continued his piece by saying that there was now a degree of inertia and asked whether that was because the chairman had plans to sell the club and suggested that he was, indeed, close to that. Burnley's success and established position made them a real target for buyers. Mike argued that he was running the club the right way; there had been a profit for the last three seasons. Furthermore, he had always said there was money for transfers. There was simply no agreement between them.

Paul Wilson in *The Guardian* was even asking, could this be Dyche's last season at Burnley? He even wondered if Covid and games behind closed doors had prevented fan protests. That is to say, protests at the way the club was being run. But this was speculation rather than substance.

In the Ducker report, there was little to argue with. I had seen at first-hand how Sean had expressed his concern that he was no longer a manager but simply the coach. He pointed to players that he had not wanted to sign, but nevertheless they had been signed. He stated that he felt his professional relationship with the chairman was now non-existent and that it was now the chairman having the final say on football decisions. Chairman Mike disagreed and said that not one player had ever been forced on him, nor would the club ever do so.

The debate/discussion, call it what you like, moved on to Sean saying he felt there was no financial strategy to take the club forward and nothing was being done to renew expiring contracts. He was assured that this was not the case and that talks were ongoing with several agents. And, yes, there was certainly a financial plan and that they were mapping out the next transfer windows. But it was all to no avail.

The relationship between manager and chairman was broken and it was clearly no secret to the outside world. It was with this as the background that the team continued to defy the odds and the critics and simply went on winning enough games to achieve tenth place by the end of the season.

At the point when we had just taken seven points out of nine, Sean was asked what he felt his budget should be. This was after Sean had pointed out that he had no fixed budget to work to.

'Eighty to 90 million,' he replied; enough to get three quality players to take us forward. In the event, we bought Josh Brownhill for £7m from Bristol City, who turned out to be a very good buy. We had also been keen on Sander Berge, but the agent wanted £50,000 a week and the transfer fee was £20m. He went to Sheffield United.

For the City game, Sean had named only seven substitutes. The comments rained down ... absolute shambles ... worst bench in the history of the club ... got a stronger bench next to my garden pond ... makes us look amateur. It was interpreted by supporters and media as a direct comment by Sean on the lack of support he felt he was getting. When a journalist asked him whether the rest of the squad had missed the bus, he replied, no, the chairman would only pay for a minibus. We lost 5-0.

The White Lives Matter furore descended on the club during and after the game against Manchester City. This was a banner towed behind a small Cessna plane that had taken off from Blackpool, flew over the ground, and the banner read quite simply, 'White Lives Matter Burnley.' I say simply, but the repercussions and the outcry that followed were anything but.

It was in May 2020, that George Floyd, an African-American, was apprehended by police in Minneapolis and was then held on the ground when an arresting officer knelt on his neck for several minutes to subdue him. Floyd died. Out of this, the Black Lives Matter movement grew and there were protests around the world. One result was the taking of the knee, and this became a regular beginning to football matches. The banner that was flown was a protest against the BLM movement and was paid for by a small group of Burnley fans. It provoked condemnation and widespread criticism. It did the club and town of Burnley huge harm.

The police said that no criminal offence had taken place, although they did acknowledge that it had caused huge offence. Of course, there was immediate condemnation of the stunt by Burnley Football Club, and captain Ben Mee received huge praise for his comments and reaction. The press was quick to drag up the old Burnley Suicide Squad, although it wasn't specifically them that had organised it. But they provided a good topic. Described now as ageing hooligans with families and in some cases even grandchildren and jobs; nevertheless, they had not gone away in spirit and could always be conveniently linked to racism. The last time they had made headlines was way back in 2014, when 21 of them were convicted following an attack on Sheffield Wednesday supporters at the Burnley Miners Social Club. How easy it was for newspapers to link football groups to racism when they were involved in 'protecting' statues and monuments from BLM groups and 'woke' factions. Football and racism, so easy to link them. Racism and Burnley, how easy to join the two together.

The press had a field day. It resulted in a double-page spread in *The Telegraph* and full pages in most other dailies. Martin Samuel in *The Mail* went to town in his article that painted Burnley as still being a place of racism. If it was absent at the football club, it was certainly present in the town, he argued, and at any general election, the BNP would poll between nine and 11 per cent. Samuel dug into statistics but used reports from as far back as 2001, 2002 and 2006.

Samuel went down the path of looking at Burnley's socio-economic background. 'There has been no boom in Burnley of late,' he wrote. 'Regeneration money has not visited Burnley.' He quoted it having higher rates of infant mortality and alcohol abuse, higher crime and lower educational attainment levels than the rest of Lancashire. When Burnley made the news, it was often for negative reasons. So, how easy it was to paint Burnley in a negative light and how flippant some reactions were. Former player and now pundit Darren Bent even pointed to Burnley having no black players. That must have come as a surprise to Dwight McNeil, Ali Koiki and Aaron Lennon.

It was the season of Covid and allegedly we were going to go bust. Or at least that was the newspaper headline. The pause in the football programme during lockdown is still fresh in our minds. Would the season be completed? Would fans be allowed back in? Would Premier League clubs continue to get the same level of Sky payments? The latter was a huge concern to us, with Sky money forming such a large percentage of our income.

'WE'LL GO BUST' was the headline in *The Sun* on Sunday the fifth. It reported that the club would go bust in August if the football lockdown was not ended by then. The club would stand to lose £50m if the current season was cancelled and other bigger clubs could lose as much as £100m. It warned that Burnley, one of the best-run clubs in the league, would be pot-less unless the pandemic had eased. The newspaper quoted the chairman – 'The fact of the matter is, if we don't finish the season and there isn't a clear start date for next season, we, as a club, will run out of money by August. That is a fact.'

A club statement said, 'The club is keen to be transparent with supporters, staff and stakeholders. It is therefore able to confirm that due to the continued suspension of Premier League games, this presents some significant challenges for the club. Burnley FC are set to lose around £5m in revenue from the remaining home games, which in the event the season finishes would be unlikely to be recouped owing to the likely prospect of these fixtures being played behind closed doors. In addition, the Clarets face missing out on cash payments from the Premier League of up to £45m in broadcasting revenue and other items if the season is not finished.'

It was quite true that the situation was bleak. The economy microsystems in the streets around every football club were suffering, from pubs to chip shops. There was simply no matchday revenue, no sale of season tickets, no retail outlets or even online retail trade. Everything non-essential was shut down. And at this point there was no clear date for any restart. We were all asking, under these circumstances and with players sent home, how could the football industry survive? Everyone was desperate to complete the season, and, in the end, it was completed. Behind the scenes the worry was whether an unfinished

Steve Cotterill and right, Wade Elliott signed by Cotterill and how it paid off at Wembley in 2009.

2009 and Owen Coyle Wembley triumph. Barry Kilby hugs Martin Paterson and Clarke Carlisle shows off the trophy. (All pictures Burnley Express)

After the promotion of 2015/16 riding high. (Gary Rocket Ron Jenkins)

The directors always enjoyed visits to Old Trafford. (Clive Holt personal collection)

A visit from the King, but back then the Prince of Wales. Behind him the heroes of Wembley 2009. Robbie Blake prominent. Note the boxed pen. Extravagant or not? Promotion to the Premier League might have brought millions but it was all soon swallowed up on wages, bonuses, loan repayments, ground improvements and 101 other things. I wonder how many people we gave a pen, today even know where they are?

Joey got no medal; we were two medals short. He took it well. (Andy Pritchard)

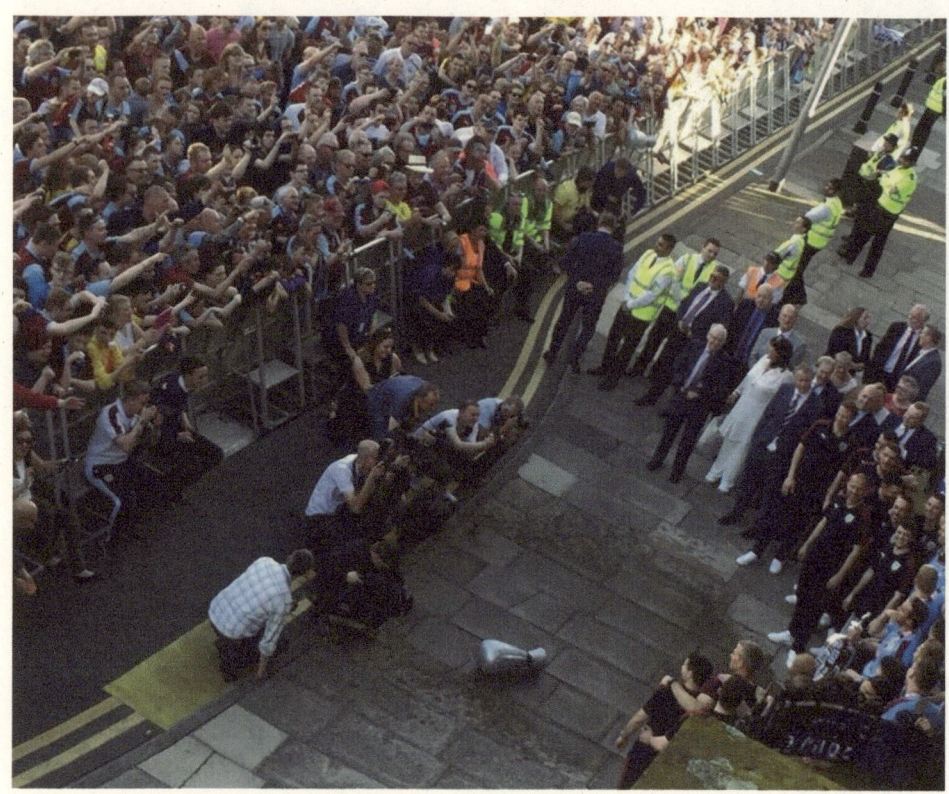

I'm in there somewhere, the plastic trophy no longer needed. (Amber Corns)

I worked with Barry Kilby for over 20 years in his role as Chairman and then when he became Vice-chairman. (Steve Lockyer)

Celebrating one of our promotions, Mike Garlick, Sean Dyche, Ian Woan and me. (Clive Holt personal collection)

Sean Dyche provided two promotions, years of success, the Europa League and lasting memories. John B had this little model made. (Chris Gibson)

In the middle, my two nieces, Jennifer and Megan, many years ago when they were mascots at the Maidstone versus Burnley game, played at the Dartford ground, wearing their Burnley shirts. (Clive Holt personal collection)

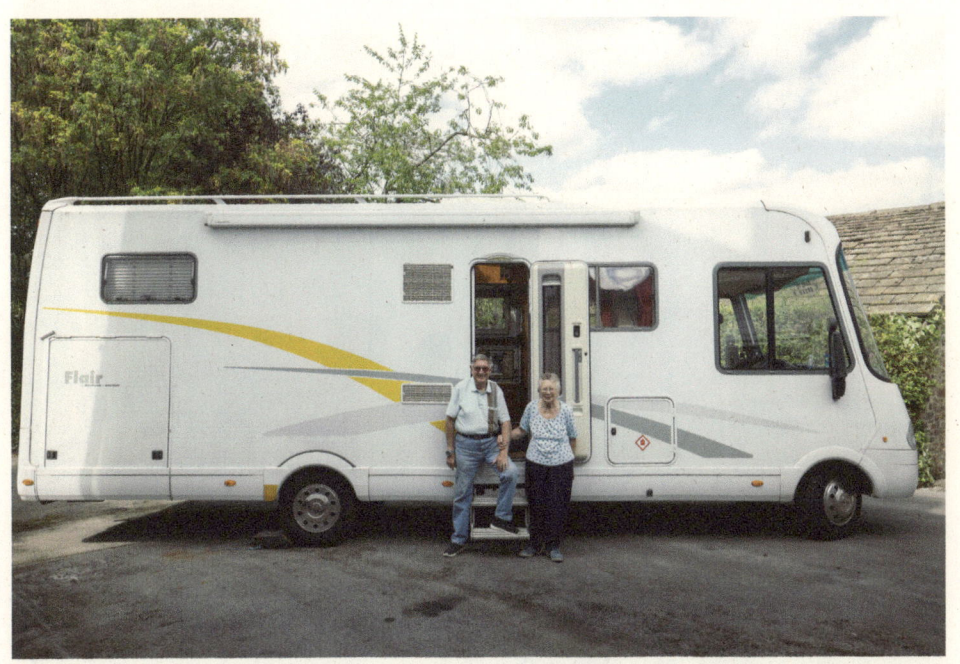

Our home on wheels and mobile kennel currently for Rosco. (Rebecca Bridges Photography)

Gemma on the left and new resident Rosco on the right. Rosco, a rescue dog, will be fine once he has calmed down. (Clive Holt personal collection)

Onwards to the next game, wherever it may be. Am I the only director who travels by motorhome to away games? (Rebecca Bridges Photography)

season would result in directors once again having to put money into the club?

Meanwhile, with everyone at home behind closed doors, although permitted to take a walk and do food shopping, Sean Dyche was learning a new skill; that is to say, the art of Zoom conferencing. Life was now upside down, revolving around washing the car, power washing the drive and a bit of cooking. So, 170 miles away from Turf Moor he was keeping in touch with staff, the management team and players on Zoom, a skill taught to him by his son Max.

The press lauded his management skills. Wins at Old Trafford and a draw at Anfield brought him even more into the public eye. One piece by Josh Butler was typical and I am grateful to Josh for his permission to reproduce extracts from his 2020 article.

> If the eighth wonder of the world was Stan Ternent's 19th place finish in 2003/04; then Burnley's ascension to, and sustained membership of the Premier League, is surely the ninth wonder of modern times. This town of fewer than 75,000 people, one of the smallest to ever host a top-flight club, can now boast one of the most financially secure, pragmatic and stalwart sides in the division.
>
> Sean Dyche has carved a niche for Burnley without the raiment of opulence, thanks to the long-term vision provided by a chairman and board who have the interests of the football club firmly at the forefront of their operations.
>
> With Dyche now the longest serving manager in the top flight, here is a dependability that many rivals cannot lay claim to, and there is a clear vision with which to take the club into the next decade. Yet, this vision is, understandably, somewhat risk-averse, given the huge financial implications a relegation can have on a club the size of Burnley.
>
> Criticism from armchair fans and the Twitter masses have grown in recent years towards Burnley thanks largely to Dyche's insistence on playing a rugged and pragmatic

brand of football not in keeping with the more glamorous trends propagated by the Man Cities and Liverpools of this world. But to dismiss Burnley as old-fashioned and worthy of constant lampooning would be a folly. Often accused of being a long ball side as if it were some sort of scathing insult, Dyche's men rank second only to Sheffield United in that regard; a team who have been lauded during the 2019/20 season for playing attractive football, but who curiously escaped the brunt of the criticism aimed at the Clarets. Not that Dyche has any quibbles about playing to his side's strengths.

With the exception of the 2018/19 campaign, which saw Burnley's small squad stretched almost to breaking point by their Europa League commitments, Dyche has ensured that his sides are defensively resolute. Twice now, Burnley have conceded the fewest goals out of any teams outside of the top six, a testament to a somewhat unorthodox defensive strategy that almost welcomes shots being taken at goal. Such is Burnley's defensive organisation, they rarely allow inroads into their box, instead forcing teams into making an inordinate number of ranged attacks. Since their promotion three years ago, Tarkowski and Mee both rank highest in the league for average number of blocks.

That is not to say that Burnley are an inherently negative side; Dyche often plays with two physical strikers in Wood or Barnes or Rodriguez, all of whom are players that either thrive off aerial duels, or running the channels, but who also possess the nous and clever movement required to find space in an opponent's penalty area, where Burnley score the vast majority of their goals.

Burnley's four-year stay is sprinkled sparingly with notable victories over the Premier League big boys; Chelsea, Liverpool, Tottenham and Leicester have all been vanquished, but not with any real regularity. Rather, Burnley have developed a reputation for being extremely efficient at beating teams around them; and when your goal is to remain in the division, that's an excellent starting point. Dyche's plucky side have dismantled the likes of Crystal Palace, Watford, Brighton, Bournemouth and Southampton, home and away over the previous campaigns.

As much as Turf Moor has become a proverbial fortress, especially for visiting teams from the lower reaches of the table, they have become equally ruthless away from home. To quote an oft-used phrase, Burnley are quite happy to turn up and spoil the party. As such, by deflecting some of the unjust criticism and sticking firmly to their beliefs, they have made the Premier League their home for four of the last five seasons, and it is their incongruity that has become the defining characteristic of this rugged, unorthodox side, that Sean Dyche has curated, nurtured and organised.

It's a pretty good summary of how Burnley did things, but I have to say there was also a certain Jekyll-and-Hyde aspect to our performances. Away at Sheffield United we were given a football lesson and the message boards and airwaves howled their derision. In the very next game at home to West Ham, it was Burnley that gave the football lesson and West Ham were dispatched 3-0. Fans were happy again; so was the boardroom. It brought a run of three defeats to an end. It was a display that dispelled the notion that Burnley were just a long-ball side and could not play football; at their best they could be quite exhilarating.

One fan certainly made his voice and displeasure felt at the negative messages coming out to the club at this time: 'The misery-guts announcements from the hierarchy about not expecting anything; the boardroom needs an injection of positivity, vitality and fresh thinking. It needs a repeat of the Brendan Bounce of ten years ago. The chairman and board members need to stop sending out these miserable, negative messages and so does Sean Dyche. It's basic PR. It wears people out. They need to stop saying it's hard, it's difficult, we are being priced out of the player market.'

Andrew Greaves wrote in the *Lancashire Telegraph*, 'Not strengthening would be nothing short of criminal. When the summer came, we signed goalkeeper Will Norris on a free, and a Brighton player, Dale Stephens, for something like £1million. Two years on and looking back, it's fair to ask, was this in any way adequate?'

And yet what may not be common knowledge is that we did ask after Kalvin Phillips from Leeds and offered £20m. It was turned down.

Chris Boden then wrote in the *Burnley Express* that sympathy was in short supply from some sections of supporters. He reminded us of something that Sean had said back in 2018, 'Eventually my rhetoric will get boring, what we go on about will get boring, and the model of the club will get boring.' How prophetic that was. But for now, Sean was secure in his job and the accolades continued. This one from the *Daily Telegraph*.

> There is much to admire about the way that Burnley have carved out a place for themselves in the Premier League. But they do not worry too much about whether they look good as they accumulate enough points to stay in the top flight for another year. They are a team of substance rather than style; Dyche is a man who knows what he wants and how to get it and the Lancashire town is very proud of its scufflers and scrappers. Direct, physical and uncompromising, they are excellent at what they do. They have nothing to apologise for, but there is no disguising the fact that they are a difficult team to watch. They are the guests at the party who outstay their welcome; the person shouting down their mobile phone in the quiet carriage of a train. They are annoying, and that should be taken as a compliment. Burnley do not need to change a thing.

As we all know, the season was completed behind closed doors and how strange that was. As officials of the club, we were allowed to attend all matches home and away and, in most cases, we did meet other clubs' officials, albeit at a distance. At one match we saw no one. Norwich away. We were on one side of the ground and the Norwich officials were on the other, Delia Smith included. They had already been relegated and we beat them 2-0. My wife was unable to attend, so she watched on TV in the motorhome. Director Brian Nelson's wife was nearly in the ground, in the hotel in the corner of the stadium. She was not allowed to watch from the bedroom window and she too watched on TV.

We did have one person who received special treatment via Mike Garlick and that was supporter Dave Burnley, who had seen every game for something like 40 years. Thanks to Mike he received permission to see some of the games, so that he could keep up his remarkable record. This did not go down well with our wives who looked at us furiously when we told them. Dave is such a nice fellow, but I believe he lost his record when ALK took over the club, as did I so had to settle for my large TV screen. I remember doing this for the first time after I had resigned as a director.

'What am I doing here?' I thought. For over 30 years I had been there at the games in the directors' box. Now I sat at home.

But that exit was to come later and, in the summer, we received the splendid news that the academy had been granted Category One status. It had passed the Elite Performance Plan audit to gain the highest status, just three years after moving to Category Three. It meant that our teams would play in higher-level leagues and games, and the club also had the option of playing the under-23s in the Football League Trophy against League One and Two sides. Criteria had included investment, facilities, infrastructure and staffing. In a previous chapter I went through the criteria we had to satisfy to gain Category Three. To get to Category One, it was double that.

The upgrading of the training area had been crucial. Surely this would entice young players, and parents would always be attracted by better conditions. It meant we could attract better-quality youngsters. The aim was to improve the flow of players to the first-team squad. It was far from cheap to run but it attracted grants and Premier League money.

Within two years, it had been demoted back to Category Two, but by then I was no longer part of the board.

The end-of-season run of results was splendid and only a defeat at Turf Moor against Brighton on the final day denied us eighth place and an extra £4m merit money.

Should we be worried?

CHAPTER THIRTY-ONE

2020/21 Takeover

AS THE early part of the season progressed and we got into the autumn, it was fairly clear that moves were afoot to sell the club. How advanced they were by this stage, indeed who was the favoured bidder, were not in my purview. I can shed no light on the negotiations. I had very little idea of what was going on.

On the football field, things got off to a poor start. The new season did not begin until 20 September, but there was no win until November. The critics sharpened their knives, but bit by bit, point by point, occasional wins every now and then, we hung on. Three of those wins were quite memorable. We won 1-0 away at Arsenal, we won 1-0 away at Liverpool and we put four goals past Wolves at Molineux. The final league position was 17th with 39 points, ten wins, and a comfortable 11 points clear of the bottom three. Another season then to look forward to in the Premier League. But in that, there was a problem. It was quite clear that fans were by now becoming more and more dismayed, more disgruntled and dissatisfied with the football that was on offer. There is a limit to the number of times you can watch your team losing 5-0 to Manchester City or being robbed by Arsenal. They had seen us spend just £1m on a Brighton player already in his 30s. And they were hearing and reading about the club being up for sale. On top of all that, they were well aware of the disconnect between manager and chairman. These were not happy times.

The five subs allowed in the restart period after Lockdown had been abandoned after the Premier League clubs voted to revert to three subs again. The joke in Burnley was that Burnley had proposed having just one sub because that was all they could manage. If there was a strong first-team group, there was nothing much to back it up. Meanwhile, Dyche continued to be the subject of more accolades; another one on the EPL website as set out below. Such things added to the value of a club that was seen to have a miracle worker at the helm who would always manage, somehow, to rescue any situation where the club seemed to be heading for relegation. And indeed, he would, yet again.

> Dyche is one of the best managers in the Premier League and deserves to be talked about as such. Nobody gets more out of his players and not many develop players as well as he does. Not many get so much out of so little. He is perfectly capable of managing any of the non-top-six sides and being successful. Perhaps if he looked more like a Mafia hitman along the same lines as Diego Simeone whose style of play is similar to Dyche's, he would be widely lauded as one of the best managers in the game.
>
> Burnley are often dismissed as an agricultural team. They are often written off as boring but that is simply not the truth. They are just an incredibly well-drilled team, focused and efficient. They rarely make mistakes and are hard to beat, but they have plenty to offer going forward as well. It is true that it is not always attractive football but beauty is in the eye of the beholder. It is also a necessity for Burnley to employ a certain style of play given the gulf in finances between them and the vast majority of the league. If Dyche had more backing he could potentially get Burnley pushing for another Europa League spot. He's that good; he takes players and gets the most out of them, and makes them better.

Much of the piece was true enough, but looking at the players we had now at the club in the first team, they were not going to get any better. Yes, he had developed them, but he had got them, at this point, as far as they were going to get. And a 30-plus player from Brighton, bought on the cheap, was not going to transform them.

Come September and James Ducker in *The Telegraph* was reporting on the club's drastic need for new signings and that two rival bidders were competing to take over the club. This in itself, he wrote, was wreaking havoc with the money available for team strengthening and he added that Dyche was now no longer in the loop that determined contracts and extensions. Senior sources at the club, he wrote – and don't ask me who they were because I have no idea – now said that Dyche and Garlick barely spoke.

The local press, the *Lancashire Telegraph*, reported that 'American sports investment company ALK Capital have emerged as the front runners to complete a takeover of Burnley Football Club. It is understood there are two rival US companies bidding for ownership. ALK Capital, fronted by Alan Pace, are the favourites to finalise the deal. Talks were said to be at an advanced stage, with the group that includes a number of private investors, not only taking ownership, but also a direct, hands-on role in the running of the club. This would be a huge off-field shift.'

I knew nothing of what was going on save for what appeared in the press. But how accurate was it? I had no idea on that score either. If memory serves, it was called something like Operation Wellington.

Sean was vocal on Sky, 'The board and chairman have been told by me that the club needs players. I've told them who I want and now it's down to them to get the transfers into action. But it's always difficult at this club to do that.'

The whole thing was now seen as a battle of wills between himself and the chairman. Mike, in private, continued to insist that money was available. Manchester City, meanwhile, had just paid £65m for another player. The transfer window was almost closed without a hint of another signing. The squad was the oldest in the Premier League, the run of injuries was now horrendous.

The famed one-club mentality promoted by Sean was now in pieces. A Covid complication was having to repay £13m to Sky and there were real worries regarding lost income. Sometimes lockdown produced really bizarre decisions. Wealdstone were playing Chesterfield – no spectators in the ground, of course – but the game was to be shown on a screen in the clubhouse with a few socially distanced spectators. The windows overlooking the pitch would be blacked out. On the pitch in the leagues, players were asked not to celebrate together, hug, kiss or spit. That seemed a good idea.

Newcastle United beat us 3-1, with our former player Jeff Hendrick in the side. 'It was a situation that could have been avoided,' said Dyche in the press. But could it? He had been offered a contract and turned it down. Burnley provided what can only be described as a horror show. Was it lack of regeneration? Was it players affected by the behind-the-scenes differences? It was a team running well and truly on empty. Relegation seemed a real possibility at this stage, whilst in the background negotiations regarding the sale of the club were ongoing. Were the players aware of that and unsettled? Although in reality they shouldn't have been. They were paid handsomely.

'Burnley take-over can't come soon enough,' said Jack Gaughan in *The Mail*. He was another reporter who seemed to have someone feeding him information, and still does. Gaughan suggested that the deal was taking longer than expected and there was a rival party from Dubai. The players were exasperated, he added. Maybe the new buyers were as well, since every defeat might make them think twice about any deal. And was Dyche vetoing possible player deals, he asked, namely Harry Wilson from Liverpool?

Mid-October and all was quiet on the takeover subject. But we did sign a player and for 15 seconds there was a frisson of excitement. Alas, he was only for the Development Squad. Mancini, his name, a name steeped in soccer history, from France. Brexit was upon us but we had a French import.

It was £14.95 to watch a game on Sky. There was outrage. Sky said it was a Premier League decision. The 0-0 game between West Brom and Burnley was the first 0-0 draw of the season and was an abysmal game with few people watching it. Who wants to pay to watch rubbish like this?, people asked. After just a few more games the charge was dropped. Perhaps we may thank Burnley and West Brom for that and the abject game they provided.

We lost 1-0 at home to Tottenham, but it led to one of the quotes of the decade from a Spurs website. 'Good old honest Burnley. They knock the fuck out of you, but at least they don't dive.' It was presumably inspired by Ashley Barnes laying out their centre-back with an accidental elbow that cut his eye.

We were relying on the press for news of the takeover. Now, *The Mirror* was saying that it was going to be an Egyptian bid. Egyptian businessman Mohamed El Kashashy was based in Dubai in the restaurant and food industry and was set to buy the club in a £200m deal. He and sports lawyer Chris Farnell had signed sale-and-purchase agreements after agreeing a deal with Mike Garlick. I think we all knew we could take this with a pinch of salt. Kashashy had one more obstacle and that was to pass the Premier League owner-and-director test. Local reporters were saying that this bid had leapfrogged the ALK bid, but that ALK were still talking. I scoured the newspapers and the Claret websites for news and rumour. Local man Chris Boden reported that ALK wanted to be in by Christmas. But Covid was causing hold-ups to meetings.

'ALK and CLARETS' was the headline in the *Daily Express* and allegedly the deal was done. Clearly it wasn't. As regards this particular deal, I did begin to wonder if there were similarities to the Peter Shackleton saga many years earlier, when Frank Teasdale pursued a deal that was based on thin air basically.

In September of 2020, I had been a director for 34 seasons and proud of what I had helped to achieve, but now I was uncomfortable and very concerned about the state of the club. Football is a team game and if everyone pulls in the same direction, so much more can be achieved. One tries to keep club politics away from the players and once upon a time that was easy enough, but in this day and age of agents and reporters and the media and WhatsApp groups, there are few secrets. News soon filters down into the dressing rooms and it is not rocket science to suppose that the players knew full well that all was not happy between manager and chairman, or that the club was being sold.

Much of this came to a head during October. It was traditional that the directors and wives took the senior staff out for dinner around this time. Chairman Mike and John B did not attend and, if memory serves, neither did Brendan Flood. We took a private room at the Fence Gate near Burnley and the four directors in attendance were soon being bombarded with questions from the senior staff about what was happening. They had seen interested parties being shown around Turf Moor and there was news of a data room having been set up in our solicitor's office. When there is a company up for sale, all the paper history is placed for inspection so that interested purchasers can get a full picture of the company's state of health. It was news to us that this data room had been set up. I had heard something vague about it, but senior staff confirmed its existence.

The last board meeting had been earlier in the year, as far back as February. And yet here we were on the verge of selling the club and we didn't know a great deal about it. Since then, I had requested, to no avail, further board meetings and to see management accounts and cash flows. I had no idea what the cash reserves were and relied on newspaper reports, which clearly were either decidedly inaccurate or unreliable. Support and pressure for a meeting grew and this took place on 31 October, socially distanced, before the game against Chelsea that we lost 3-0. There was very little time for questions and answers. Mike outlined where we were at; I took notes and then passed them round. Mike disagreed with some parts of my original notes, so I put my assumptions in italics in an amended version, so that they were recognisable as such.

Mike advised us that we had two offers to purchase the shares from himself, Brendan Flood and John B. The rest of us could join in the sale if we wished. The two offers were currently with the Premier League for their approval, which would take another three to four weeks to approve or reject. Apart from Mike and John B, it would be unlikely that any other directors would be allowed to continue as directors.

The ALK offer amounted to £190m for 84.5 per cent of the shares in the company. ALK were backed by a well-known billionaire in the USA, but he did not disclose the name, only that we would know of him. It left me wondering, if there was backing from a billionaire, why was money being borrowed? The offer to directors would be paid over a period of months. Hence John B and Mike would remain on the board. Director Brian Nelson was concerned about the £65m in the club account and what would happen to it.

The second offer was from Mohamed El Kashashy and Chris Farnell. This was £190m for 100 per cent of the shares.

Mike felt that there was no mileage in disclosing any further information until one or both of the offers had been approved by the Premier League. We asked to see their business plans, but this would not be possible until a decision had been made whether to go ahead or not. Kashashy withdrew his offer at a later date.

Staff at the club, reported the media, had given up hope that there could be a reconciliation between Dyche and the chairman. Dyche was pointing to lack of signings and said he was in the dark about any takeover; Mike Garlick was saying that money was available.

We lost 3-0 at home to Chelsea. We lost to Tottenham, it rained all week, we were rock bottom of the table, it was goodbye to Bobby Ball, Nobby Stiles and Sean Connery. Another national lockdown was announced, to last until 2 December. On the message boards and airwaves, fans were now asking, was it time for Sean to go? The rumours circulated that he had turned down the chance to sign Harry Wilson and Theo Walcott. Without board meetings to cast light on these things, I had no idea. What a rotten week.

Ian Herbert in the *Daily Mail* added his two penn'orth, 'The team I fear for are Burnley whose owners seem to be on a sort of Kamikaze mission. Chairman Garlick is so desperate to make the club financially attractive to buyers that he didn't even give Sean Dyche an idea of the overall transfer budget this summer. They spent £25,000 on a reserve keeper and £1million on a 31-year-old midfielder. It's an insult to Dyche who deserves more respect. Fail to sort it out and the club could descend into open civil war.'

We never did descend into open civil war. At this point, James Tarkowski said he would not sign a new contract, but he would give 100 per cent while he was at the club, which he most certainly did. He wanted to play for England, and at Burnley there was a slim chance of that. But was he also tired of the infighting, the stagnation and lack of any real prospect of getting the team to a higher level?

Into November and the club made a statement: 'Regarding various comments in the media, Burnley Football Club confirms that the club's ownership remains in discussion with interested parties regarding future investment in the club. In full respect of ongoing processes, the club will not be providing any further commentary on this matter until those discussions have reached a conclusion. The club wishes to assure supporters and the local community that the future of Burnley FC remains the primary concern in these issues, with any potential investment needing to support the long-term sustainability, and retain its position as a cornerstone of the local community.'

The sale of the club was no longer a secret. Here it was, out in the open. But as for the details, I was as much in the dark as anyone else. But something to cheer us up; that is to say, if you liked watching *I'm a Celebrity Get Me ... Out of Here*! I'd never heard of Jordan North until this moment, but by all accounts he was a Radio One deejay and a celebrity, plus a Burnley supporter. So, there he was, in a box, covered in slithery snakes earning points for his team, terrified, and suddenly he began to shout, 'Turf Moor, Turf Moor, happy place, happy place.' The nation loved it, and him. In that moment he did for Burnley what Captain Tom had done for the NHS. Everyone loved us.

Happy place indeed, with the first win of the season, a 1-0 win over Crystal Palace at Turf Moor. The ALK deal, according to the press, seemed to be progressing, with a firm of Leeds solicitors involved for ALK. Into December and ALK were closing in. As far as I could make out it was being driven by the two larger shareholders, Mike Garlick and John B, but in truth, I knew little about what was going on.

Lo and behold, we won at Arsenal with an Arsenal own goal. The press focused on how Arsenal had managed to lose, rather than how Burnley had managed to win with a marvellous display. Kashashy withdrew from the race to buy the club; ALK had the field to themselves. Another win against Wolves but then a controversial defeat at Leeds on 27 December. Some defeats leave a really sour taste and this was one of them. Leeds were at their peak at this point with manager Bielsa, but it is true to say we dominated the game. Patrick Bamford scored with a dubious penalty. That it was Bamford was certainly ironic. As a former player at Burnley, he'd had a poor time and rarely featured. A perfectly good equaliser was disallowed. A ball came into the Leeds box, the Leeds keeper clattered into the back of Mee as Mee rose to head the ball. The keeper collapsed to the floor. The ball broke free and Barnes lashed it home. Alas, the referee decided that Mee had fouled the keeper and disallowed the goal. Every pundit in the land condemned the decision. Former referee Keith Hackett said it was poor and any offence was by the Leeds keeper. Even Leeds fans were sympathetic; they knew they had been lucky.

Someone spotted and tracked a private executive jet, a Gulfstream 450, flying from a private airfield in New York to Manchester. Could it be Alan Pace asked fans on the message boards. Chris Boden tweeted that Alan Pace and co. had indeed landed in the north but would not be at the game as they had no access to the club until the deal could be completed.

On 2 December, I was asked to sign a non-disclosure agreement. The completion date was set for 11 December, but this was amended to the end of the month. Realising there was no longer any place for me at the club, I sold the majority of my shares and the NDA prevents me from giving any details, although by now much of it and the mechanics of the deal are in the public domain.

My last game as a director was on 29 December 2020, against Sheffield United and a 1-0 win. I had a hollow feeling that day. My time was done. It was over. Thirty-four years' service had been ended; I was losing part of my life. I exited the directors' box for the last time, went into the boardroom for the last time, and drove home after the game with Sylvia, feeling very emotional and dejected. Empty.

As for the deal, I only knew what was in the public domain. For example, David Conn in *The Guardian* had written a very perceptive piece. ALK had borrowed from Dell Holdings, had invested some money of their own, and would use the club's reserves to pay off some of the debt. Some of that debt was money to be paid to the former directors for their shares. The new owners would be hands-on, Alan Pace would live in the area and become chairman. New directors would join him. Mike Garlick and John B would remain on the board.

What was finished, however, was Burnley the little club being owned by local people. Now, we were a little club owned by ALK, an American company. Fans were not unduly depressed by this, although of course they were aware of the seismic change that had taken place. It was most definitely at a crossroads; stay as they were and slowly and inevitably decline, or look for new owners that could bring new money, raise commercial income, bring new ideas, broaden the horizon, inject some dynamism. There was certainly an acceptance that the club had plateaued, but at the same time fans realised that the club now carried debts, whereas it had just been debt-free.

One thing was for certain: this was an enormous change in the direction of the club's history. Something unique had come to an end. Previous chairmen had been born and lived in the streets of Burnley and been to Burnley schools. It needs a few words to sum up this change. I liked what London Claret Andrew Firmin had to say in the *London Clarets* magazine, some of which, from his much, much longer article, I quote:

> You never know, maybe this will work. Maybe the new guys are bringing to the club hitherto unseen marketing genius, brilliant new ideas that no-one had come up with, cutting edge technologies beyond our comprehension, and maybe these are going to grow the club, push us on to whatever the next level is, and assure a bright future at Burnley FC. After several years that have already been the greatest time to be a Claret in a couple of generations, perhaps even more exciting times lie ahead.
>
> Maybe it is OK to feel a little sad right now. Even if such vaguely articulated hopes transpire, something will have been lost and its passing should be marked. Watching Burnley play several successive top-flight seasons, besting all the big boys at one time or another, and winning a place in European competition, has been an astonishing ride and not something that seemed remotely possible to this fourth-division era Claret. I'll always be thankful that I experienced these times. But for many of us, hasn't there been a special sense of pride about doing things our own way? Hasn't part of it been about defying the standard owner/investor model, of not buying ourselves into the Premier League, but getting there through guile and hard work, while being carefully stewarded with an eye on the long-term viability of the club, debt free, sustainably run, locally owned.
>
> Well, that's gone now. Whatever we do from here, we're just like all the others now. We're just another club. We're now one of seven or eight top-flight clubs with US owners. We have 'owners' now. I never felt like we did before.
>
> It seems that the search for new owners was underway long before the Covid crisis. But I guess the events of the last year might have concentrated minds, and if Garlick and

the others felt they'd contributed everything they could and wanted to hand over the reins, who could blame them? A takeover might seem to offer the only way out of the picture of apparent stasis and presumed eventual decline.

It would be good if the new owners acknowledge that they understand all the hard graft that went into getting Burnley FC into the position that we are in, with several years of top-flight football to our name, a top-class manager, a first-rate training facility and a category one academy; all the work that made the club an attractive one to buy, the sets of sturdy shoulders they stand on. As for how the recruitment strategy may change, time will tell, but I hope they have a plan for avoiding relegation, but also a plan in the event of relegation. I hope they understand that for many of us, the most important thing, notwithstanding this current moment in the sun, is that there is still a Burnley FC for future generations to be a part of. I hope they understand the special importance of Burnley FC to the area and community, and of Turf Moor as the heartbeat of the town.

By now, earlier in the month, Sean had been in discussion with the chairman regarding his precise role at the club. It had involved lawyers. What it boiled down to in its simplest terms was that Sean was now responsible for coaching and little or nothing else. Transfers, budgets, recruitment and strategy were matters that ultimately lay with the chairman and the board. His response was to point out to us that with another transfer window on the horizon, there was no alignment regarding planning and recruitment. He pointed out to us that the club was not in good health, that there were problems with the lack of any relationship and communication between himself, the board and the chairman, and that player contracts needed sorting. By now he was aware, as indeed we all were, that the sale of the club was in the offing, but he assured us all that he would continue to get the last drops from his players. This he certainly did.

CHAPTER THIRTY-TWO

2021/22 No Longer on the Board, Shares Sold, Goodbye Sean and Relegation

I CANNOT say enough about how distressed I felt when I resigned as a director; and when that moment came, a vacuum descended. For nigh on 35 years, half of my life, through four decades, I had done this job; the club part of my life, my life inextricably geared to the needs of the club. And matchdays, of course, in the directors' box. That was finished. Nor were there any more seats in the directors' box at away games. Now, if I want to attend, I buy tickets, the same as anybody else. And I'm still as mad keen as any other supporter.

Yes, I have been paid for my shares. Actually, as I write, partly paid; October 2022 and we have just received another tranche, but that is no consolation for the huge space that now exists. On the outside I am now looking in. I pay for my season ticket and that of Sylvia, and we sit in the Bob Lord Stand. From here I watched the rest of the season unfold, with great relief after the Fulham game and a 2-0 win that guaranteed another season in the Premier League.

ALK were now in charge and in the summer of 2021 backed Sean with new players. Maxwel Cornet came in at a reported £13m and was an immediate hit with some spectacular goals. I think it reasonable to say this was a signing driven by the new chairman.

Connor Roberts came from Swansea, a Welsh international right-back with pace and flair. And then Nathan Collins from Stoke City, whom Sean had been eyeing for some time, for an alleged £12m. He was an outstanding prospect and was signed with a view to replacing the soon-to-depart James Tarkowski.

The new season did not start well, with not one win until 30 October. The writing was on the wall. But at this point Newcastle United seemed in an even worse position. The big surprise was the sale of Chris Wood to Newcastle in January of 2022, but unknown to most people, or had been forgotten about, was an automatic release clause if a certain size offer came along.

Newcastle had been taken over by a Saudi group, controversial in itself because of Saudi human-rights issues, but the fans made them welcome by wearing tea towels on their heads at the first game. Cultural appropriation at its finest. Eddie Howe was appointed manager and my immediate thought was, 'Is he going to be a fish out of water again this far north?' But no, he took to the place like a duck to water and set Newcastle on a new course, upwards. Signing Wood for a reported £25m gave them a proven goalscorer and took away ours. Having said that, he had stopped scoring for us and never really hit the ground running at Newcastle. The £25m for us was hugely beneficial.

Alan Pace acted again and signed Wout Weghorst for half of the Wood money. The initial performances looked good but when a striker begins to struggle, the knives are out and, at Burnley, initial fan approval turned to disdain as he struggled more and more. But the margins are so small – had he buried a wonderful chance in the away game at Aston Villa, which might well have won us the game, he would have been a hero.

When Maxwel Cornet, never quite the same player when he returned from the Africa Cup of Nations, missed another golden chance at Norwich as we battled for survival, that was the end for Sean, terminated a few days later, following a second-half display that was 45 minutes of inadequacy. With most of his staff, he was dismissed on 15 April 2022 and an amazing era was over. Quite simply, this was the best manager I had worked with, and I'd had a few in my time, nine or ten of them. Stan Ternent came close and he had worked with an even tighter budget than Sean.

The football world was quite simply stunned. Dyche and Burnley; did they not fit together like pie and peas? He was synonymous with the club. We lost on the Sunday, but it was Friday before the announcement came. Not much more than a year earlier he had been given a new four-year contract. The irony was that the display against Norwich came just days after a stirring win over relegation rivals Everton, 3-2 at Turf Moor. It was a blistering game in front of a febrile crowd that gave us all such hope. How could we be so poor at Norwich?

But Sean had been marvellous, giving us a football journey that no one could ever have predicted. Nobody can underestimate what he did for the club and the town. He left his mark in so many ways, raised our thinking and ambitions, brought us together, raised our profile, worked so hard on the infrastructure, not the least of which was the training ground that today rivals most others. Without those promotions and Premier League money, so many improvements to the ground would never have taken place.

As we know, it all ended badly with the disconnect between him and chairman. It was sad. Perhaps a problem was that we were small directors of a small club in a small town. There was a ceiling for us. We were cautious and prudent; overly so said many, especially some of the press. We had seen the hard times at the club and so found it difficult to think big. Sean once likened us to the old Burnley mill owners, looking after every penny.

I'd once questioned the bonus we were paying him. He replied, 'You should be paying me double.' Two promotions, six consecutive seasons in the world's richest league and then the Europa League. Perhaps he was right.

Since his departure, Sean has said nothing, but he did return to Burnley to claim his free pint, at last, at the pub renamed in his honour, The Royal Dyche. Fifty invited guests enjoyed a Q&A session, but nobody is saying what his answers were. Something else he said to us was that one day, when he writes his own book, the truth will out. A third of the players will still be happy with me, he commented, a third will be indifferent, and a third will be glad to see me go. It emerged from the dressing room that, yes, some players indeed thought things had gone stale.

If there was one disappointment, it was that there was no opportunity for supporters to say their thank yous. There was no final game, such as we had seen when Stan Ternent was leaving, at which our appreciation could be shown and heard. Yes, his time at the club might have ended with football that was merely functional, but earlier years had been simply magnificent. This was the manager that invented Proudsville.

All that aside, the Alan Pace decision to replace Sean so very nearly paid off. In his first four games, acting manager Michael Jackson drew one and won three. Then, alas, our luck changed so that a contentious VAR decision and penalty cost us the game at Spurs. An identical incident at Villa that would have earned us a penalty was ignored. Even so, everything was still in our own hands when rejuvenated Newcastle came to Burnley for the final game. Match whatever Leeds did and we were safe. When Nathan Collins gifted Newcastle a penalty with a handball, the game was lost at that moment. Leeds won at an indifferent Brentford. We were relegated.

Reactions were pretty much agreed. This was a relegation that had been coming with a grim inevitability, with a brand of football that now had many fans switching off. That is not to decry Sean Dyche. He played a style that was dictated by the players available and the money available for strengthening. He once told us that, come what may, he would wring the last ounces of effort from the players. But they had no more to give. And at this point I am not sure that Sean did either. Some fans said that in some ways it was a relief that this losing, one-way struggle was now over. The club could regroup, plan again, follow a new path; not to mention solve the inevitable financial problems that relegation would bring to a club once comfortably in the black but now in the red.

Would the new owners cut and run? To their credit, no they did not. With a vastly reduced wage bill, plus what we think was £70m from player sales, plus the £42m parachute payment to come, plus a substantial chunk of the Dell loan repaid, despite relegation the ship was in calm waters and there were grounds for optimism.

Perhaps this is where I can now ruminate a little and ponder on just where we go from here. I'd like to think that the knowledge I have at my fingertips might still be useful to the club, should the need ever arise. That knowledge ranges from covenants on the cricket-field ground, to flood problems at Gawthorpe, to the old coal tunnels under Turf Moor; from land that the club still owns straddling the M65, to property no longer owned in Norwich. I met with Alan Pace after the takeover with a list of 20 items that it would be to his benefit to know.

With Sean gone, 'What will happen next?' was the question asked by all supporters. The appointment of Vincent Kompany as manager was a real coup. 'What would Vincent Kompany bring?' was the next one. This was 'new-broom territory' we were in. Which players would be cleared out, which ones would be sold? Who would we sign?

It was goodbye to the wonderful defensive trio of Tarkowski, Mee and goalkeeper Pope. They had been the bedrock of the defence for what seemed forever. Nathan Collins went to Wolves for an alleged £21m. Pope went to Newcastle for £10m. Super-rich Newcastle arranged to pay in instalments. Dwight McNeil went to Everton for £20m. Huge sums were saved on wages when players on top money left, most of them in their 30s, by the way. Fans wanted Maxwel Cornet to stay, the bank manager preferred him sold. He went to West Ham for another £17m, it was reported.

Then with bewildering rapidity in came new players; young, inexpensive unknowns, sourced from abroad or the lower leagues.

What a shift in policy this was. It was unheard of. But who were they? Could they play? Would they be good enough? Could Kompany get them to gel in such a short space of time? A core of experience remained – Taylor, Roberts, Barnes, Rodriguez, Cork, Gudmundsson and the rehabilitating Westwood. Don't expect instant miracles was the message, this is a season of transition.

My only involvement with the club now is as a director of the Memorial Garden Trust. I would love to see the establishment of a dedicated Burnley FC museum and library. We need a building somewhere and funding. There are several Burnley writers desperate for somewhere to bequeath all their work and resources before their uninterested family members head for the nearest skip.

I say my only involvement, but there I was for the pre-season friendly at Shrewsbury on Friday, 15 July. It takes a special kind of supporter to head for such a game. Nice place, Shrewsbury, and we journeyed down there for a few days in the motorhome. I'd contacted Steve Cotterill a few days before the game, but he was in Spain on a pre-season with the team. But there were no problems with my request if he could help me and he arranged for tickets in the directors' area, the use of the Sovereign Lounge and a car-park space. We didn't get to meet because of his matchday duties but I had been in touch with him several times during his long Covid illness. It was good to see him back on the touchline.

The journey down there was fraught enough once we got nearer the campsite. It was Church Eaton, right in the middle of farming country, but only 11 miles from the motorway. I'd booked the site blind before checking any details and then only when I'd booked it and read the notes on how to approach it did I see the words 'single track lanes with passing places'. The motorhome itself is 8.5; with the car on the A frame, it is 14 metres. Backing up is a devil in this outfit. I could only hope we didn't meet anything along the four miles of narrow lanes. We made it without any mishaps.

What a lovely way to go down to a football match. We arrived on the Wednesday, lunch at local pubs near the River Severn, some sightseeing, a wander round Shrewsbury itself and then leave for home on the Saturday morning after the Friday game.

It was a team filled with new faces and even after all these years, I felt the same moment of anticipation when they ran out as I had done years earlier in the old Fourth Division when I first joined the board. Football fans will understand this feeling, no matter what club they follow. It never leaves you.

By the end of September, these new players were producing a new brand of football based on pace, possession and passing. Players like Zaroury, Tella, Benson, Harwood-Bellis, Vitinho, Bastien, Muric, Churlinov and Maatsen and more came in at a bewildering speed, mostly signed at low cost from the Continent. After 13 games there was just one defeat and we were in the top four. The signs were good.

Things change – owners, players and managers; directors too, for that matter – but whatever comes out in a claret-and-blue shirt is my team. It might only have been a friendly at Shrewsbury, but we won 3-1. It's good to smile and a win helps you do just that.

When I first joined the boardroom, we had seven years in the old Fourth Division, the wilderness. When I left the boardroom, we were out of the wilderness and in the Premier League.

Today, no longer on the board after all these years and back in the Championship. But still smiling. Still eagerly awaiting the next game.

Final Thoughts

MY THANKS go to Dave Thomas for assisting with this book. We could have written so much more, but in this day and age of high publishing costs we worked to a word limit. It meant that we had to take some sections out, but with the price of books going up and up, there was the realisation on our part that we would need to keep the price to a reasonable level.

It's 14 November 2022. I'm sitting at my desk, having completed the second reading of the book. Writing this book has been a labour of love and such a marvellous trip down Memory Lane. Since leaving the board of directors there has been such a huge space in my life. Much of that space has been occupied in the writing of these recollections.

A couple of weeks ago, ever the glutton for punishment, I watched the under-21s play Sheffield United at Leyland. The other night I watched us beat Norwich 1-0 at Turf Moor in a marvellous game to go top of the table. Prior to that there had been an incredible turnaround at Sunderland to win 4-2 after being 2-0 down. A big defeat at Sheffield United was a wake-up call.

So, the club at the moment. I am one of many not keen on leveraged buyouts and the club now carries debts. Amongst many supporters, however, there is the clear view that debt is now the way of the football world and that it is the 'new' Burnley. Those of us that criticise this are the ostriches and we are told that we are now no different to most other clubs. Whilst we sit at the top of the division, fans are accepting this. Success masks financial problems. But as an old-stager and one who has always lived by the creed of

'HOW MUCH?', debt carries worries and consequences. We have had plenty of those over the years and the memories of very close brushes with administration are still painful.

When the takeover by ALK was being constructed, we were advised by the then chairman, Mike Garlick, that there was a billionaire supporting the purchase. But it turned out to be the Dell Foundation, offering a loan at a high interest rate. There was no generous sugar daddy. Clearly the resultant debt is being managed and, bit by bit, the previous directors are being paid for their shares. However, there are clear limits at a club like Burnley as to how much income can be generated and how successfully debts can be repaid painlessly.

I am delighted to see the ladies football team going from strength to strength, but if this is seen as a source of income, it may well take a few years for this to happen. Perhaps it needs them to play at Turf Moor to raise their profile. Income comes from the men's team, TV and the commercial spinoffs. Current success might encourage new investment, as long as that is simply not more loans.

ALK, at the moment, are doing the right things on the football field and are playing a good hand in the terrific young players they are signing. Zaroury, I suspect, will go on to great things and at some stage be sold for big money if the need arises. One transfer fee was disappointing and that was the reported £10m for goalkeeper Nick Pope. Surely he was a £20m player? But then we could say that this was balanced out by the very generous £20m-plus received for striker Chris Wood earlier in the year.

As I write, at the beginning of the World Cup break, the appointment of Vincent Kompany as manager seems to have been a masterstroke. Every manager appointment is a gamble. You can do all the necessary homework, but a new man can still be a flop. The speed at which he has put a new team together and got them playing such dynamic football has been breathtaking. The football is exciting, a total contrast to the final couple of years of Sean Dyche when there was so little investment in new players. It is only mid-

November as we now take four weeks out, but the position is hugely promising.

From my new seat in the Bob Lord Stand I look across to the directors and other than Alan Pace I have no idea who they are. Do our supporters? A programme feature about them with a small picture would be useful. Mike Garlick and John B remain on the board, but I understand they will leave when the sale is finally completed. For years and years supporters knew the directors as local men, knew their place in the town, knew them by name, recognised them. It's all so very different now.

What a way to bring this book to a conclusion. Yesterday was the derby game against rivals Blackburn Rovers, both of us now in the same division. Second against third and the winner would top the league. When the fixtures came out, I looked for two things. When did we play Blackburn Rovers, and are we at home on Boxing Day? Blackburn Rovers: the memories came back of previous meetings, transport by compulsory bus, and consultations with the police about matchday operations.

I was told by one senior police officer that it was a day when even law-abiding grown men go mad and simply want to seek confrontations and hurl abuse at the opposition. It was their justification for insisting on ground-to-ground bus transport and a £30,000 bill for policing. Over the years we tried hard to ease these draconian measures but with no success. Some of the buses we had to use must have dated back to World War One.

The directors of both sides have always got on well; there has always been an edge but with good humour, and for ten years we have had the upper hand. The famous name at Ewood Park was Jack Walker and he had his private Walker Suite but always spent time with us. I got to know him well and, in my opinion, despite buying the title by paying the best wages to the best players like Alan Shearer, he was a friend to football. A few years ago, one of the Blackburn directors was complaining about the levels that wages had got to. I had to laugh as I told him that it was Blackburn that started it. On Jack Walker's death, his family did not have the same interest. So, enter the Venky family with their Indian business empire.

I remember the week they took over. The matriarch, Mrs Desai, said she knew very little about football, but that one of her sons watched a lot of Premier League football on TV. The first thing they did was sack Sam Allardyce and they were promptly relegated. How much they are losing is anyone's guess and could be at least £100m. But they are still there, and for that they deserve credit.

What a marvellous win it was against them on Sunday, 13 November. This was everything good about football, with a wonderful display from Burnley, who totally outplayed Blackburn. Ashley Barnes was the hero with two goals. Kompany's team selection was perfect, bringing in the old warrior to ruffle a few feathers. Someone said it was like seeing an old boxer brought out to teach the upstart a lesson. Ten years he has been at the club. His place in the Hall of Fame is assured. Amazing to score against the b*stards, he said in the post-match interview. A slip of the tongue, he said, but classic Ashley.

There were no compulsory buses for this game and behaviour was good; the Remembrance Day silence was observed impeccably. The stadium filled to the brim and, as each of the three goals went in, the noise erupting to a level that shook the stands. I may have asked the question before, but is there anything more wonderful than the spectacle of 20,000 people jumping to their feet as one, in an explosion of noise and celebration? At the end of the game, as players and management gathered on the pitch, it was hugely emotional; we could not have dreamed of such an emphatic win. Slowly they drifted off to enjoy, if that is the right word, the World Cup break. We all have our own thoughts on the rights and wrongs of this particular tournament.

In the Brian Miller Suite, once the old Directors' Lounge, now used as an overflow for the Chairman's Lounge, on our table we sat with two old Blackburn players, Derek Fazackerley and the ageless Bryan Douglas, now in his very late 80s. Bryan in his career goes right back to the days of Jimmy McIlroy and Jimmy Adamson. Before the game they were reasonably confident, with Bryan believing that if Blackburn scored first, they would win. After the game, ageing he might be but not without humour, he suggested that Burnley had been lucky. Both put on a brave face, obeying the unwritten rule that as guests of the opposing club, you remain polite.

From where we now sit in the Bob Lord Stand, just behind the visiting directors and their guests, you do have to be careful what you say out loud. At the Rotherham game I have never seen such time-wasting and well done the referee for adding the ten minutes of extra time. The win created a Burnley record. For the first time ever, Burnley scored two goals in added time to win the game, a good future pub-quiz question. The Rotherham people were incensed. I cheered like mad but said nothing at all to them.

The future: for the club, if this team continues to blossom and enjoys the luck that you need, a possible promotion. We cross our fingers. But money will always be in short supply at a little club like this, even with Premier League income. In between now and the end of the season so much can happen, injuries, loss of form, bad luck, decisions going the wrong way; so, we count no chickens.

And me personally: yes, two years on and I still badly miss the day-to-day involvement with the club, although there is a tenuous link via my work with the Memorial Garden. That plus the project to establish a Burnley FC resource centre, somewhere that several of us can lodge all the documents, files, folders, scrapbooks, videos, DVDs and programmes that we have accumulated over the years. Dave Thomas, for example, has a mountain of material that he has built up over all the 20 years that he has been writing Burnley books. Talks are ongoing with people that might help us find suitable accessible space where people can come and read and browse and undertake research if they are working on a project or a book.

But my big news, perhaps, is that we have a new dog. Only a dog owner and dog lover will understand the sentiment of that simple statement ... we have a new dog. Rosco joins the long line of spaniels that we have owned. He's a rescue dog, friendly, affectionate, six years old, and inseparable from his tennis ball. Dogs, wonderful companions to unwind with, trusting, loving and always there when you need them. Stressed? Just walk the dog for half an hour, whatever the weather. He will no doubt make the motorhome his own.

No longer a director but still plenty of games to go to and look forward to. Watching a televised Burnley game with Rosco's head resting on my knee. I'll be happy with that. And if you have enjoyed this book, I'll be happy with that as well.

Maybe just one more story. I didn't tell you, did I, about the time in the early 90s when we stopped at a motorway station so that some of the players could collect their cars? Unfortunately, we hadn't realised that the cars were on the other side of the motorway and there was no connecting bridge. When I saw the players legging it across, my mouth …

Maybe we need to do a volume two.